We Dare You!

2011

Enjoy & have fun ☺!

XOXO

Mema, POPPY

TA TA

Also by Vicki Cobb

Bangs and Twangs: Science Fun with Sound
Fireworks
I Face the Wind
Light Action! Amazing Experiments with Optics
On Stage
Science Experiments You Can Eat
Sources of Forces: Science Fun with Force Fields
Squirts and Spurts: Science Fun with Water
Whirlers and Twirlers: Science Fun with Spinning

Also by Kathy Darling

Arctic Babies
Desert Babies
Rainforest Babies
Seashore Babies
There's a Zoo on You

We Dare You!

Hundreds of Fun Science Bets, Challenges,
and Experiments You Can Do at Home

**Vicki Cobb
and
Kathy Darling**

Skyhorse Publishing

Skyhorse Publishing books may be purchased in bulk at special discounts for sales promotion, corporate gifts, fund-raising, or educational purposes. Special editions can also be created to specifications. For details, contact the Special Sales Department, Skyhorse Publishing, 307 West 36th Street, 11th Floor, New York, NY 10018 or info@skyhorsepublishing.com.

Skyhorse® and Skyhorse Publishing® are registered trademarks of Skyhorse Publishing, Inc.®, a Delaware corporation.

www.skyhorsepublishing.com

10 9 8 7 6 5 4 3 2 1

Paperback ISBN: 978-1-60239-775-0

Cobb, Vicki.
    We dare you! : hundreds of science bets, challenges, and experiments you can do at home / Vicki Cobb and Kathy Darling.
        p. cm.
    Includes bibliographical references and index.
    ISBN 978-1-60239-225-0 (alk. paper)
    1. Science—Experiments—Juvenile literature. 2. Scientific recreations—Juvenile literature. I. Darling, Kathy. II. Title.

Q164.C534 2007
507.8—dc22

Manufactured in China, March 2011
This product conforms to CPSIA 2008

To our fifth- and sixth-grade grandsons
who know how to play with science:
Jonny Cobb, Ben Trachtenberg, and Hunter Lyon

CONTENTS

3. Going Public   91

4. Fluid Feats   121

7. Forces of Deception   255

INTRODUCTION: A WINNING STREAK

Bet you can get hooked on this book after trying only one trick. Pick any page. Try any trick. It looks like you will have to go against all odds. Your first reaction, which is only normal, is that these challenges are s-o-o-o ridiculously crazy or impossible only a fool would even try. But we bet you *can* do them … and we're no fools.

You can't lose because these are all fixed bets. In each one the odds are stacked … and they are all in your favor. We guarantee you're going to win. We're betting on a sure thing when we say you'll be hooked on these challenges. That's the best part of these tricks. No question about it, winning is fun.

Creating this book was fun, too. Kathy went over to Vicki's house to play. We played with TV remotes. We blew bubbles, sent each other secret messages, stabbed balloons, made nutty putty, tied bones in knots, ripped apart disposable diapers, cut up rubber balls, munched Life Savers, and set nuts on fire. We had some amazing experiences. Would you believe that you can make your lips lie to you? That you can set a speed record for unrolling toilet paper? Or that it's possible to give artificial respiration to a fly? And how about making fireworks from a grape or a saw from kitchen cleanser? These things sound outrageous and they are. They are also true.

How do we know? We did each trick. (We also tried a lot more that didn't work. Flops and bombs didn't make the cut.) Nothing beats doing it yourself—except maybe sharing it. While we were researching this book, friends, family, even the mail carrier, looked forward to hearing us yell, "You gotta try this!" We laughed a lot. No doubt other grown-ups would think we were weird. Too bad for them. We know fun when we're having it. We figure you do, too.

What you might not know is that the winning formulas in this book are all fixed by science. The odds were stacked at the beginning of time by Mother Nature. It took some of the greatest minds in the history of the world to figure out what was really happening. Galileo, Newton and a number of others saw beyond the limits of human senses and experiences. They reasoned and experimented and figured out why some obviously easy things just won't work and why some seemingly impossible things will. Now you can cash in on their discoveries.

Science is a way of knowing by trying. So don't take our word for it. It's not in the spirit of science to believe what you read or to believe what someone tells you. This book is the key.

Surprise yourself. Fool your friends. Amaze your parents. Outsmart your teachers. With Mother Nature as your secret ally, you can overcome some of the most amazing challenges you've ever heard of. You're bound to have a good time. We'll bet on it!

—Vicki Cobb & Kathy Darling

1. THE HUMAN WONDER

Who is the Human Wonder? It's not Superman, Wonder Woman, or even the Incredible Hulk. It's someone with the power of science. Surprise! It's you.

You can perform "superhero" acts you didn't know were possible. We're going to reveal some of your unbelievable powers in this chapter. The Incredible Hulk may well envy your ability to hold down someone with a single thread, and you can "outsuper" Superman with secret messages sent by your blood.

You're better connected in some ways than you thought you were. Would you believe your upper lip has a direct link to your temperature sensors? So does your heart. Brainless connections also exist between your nose and your ears. Some messages aren't sent through the brain. Muscles can act as if they have minds of their own, making moves that are out of your control. And in a real brain bypass, the spinal cord can be tricked to give you a fake fright.

On the other hand, don't believe what you see or trust what you hear, smell, or feel as you do some of the tricks in this chapter. Your senses can fool you. So can your body. The way you perceive the world is not always the way it really is. This allows us to include a crazy bunch of specialized con games—a trip into the world of inner space—for your own mind and body. You'll think you have taken leave of your senses as we trick your eyes with an optical illusion, prove that the hand is not always quicker than the eye, fix it so one hand doesn't know what the other is doing, and set it up so that your body will disobey your mind. You can be tricked into seeing spots that aren't really there, and in our version of a truly tasteless joke, an apple seems to be a potato.

The most surprising thing of all is that these talents have been there all along. But most people can't use these quirks of taste, touch, and sight without the kind of help we're going to give you. The capacity of the human mind and body has long fascinated scientists. Their testing, stressing, and pushing of the limits of the human being have led to many useful discoveries. This chapter probably will not introduce things that will make medical history. The Human Wonders were selected for the highest possible "fun and stun" factors … but this is just the beginning …

Welcome to science—up close and personal.

KEEPING THE LIDS ON

Bet you can roll your eyeballs so that you can't open your eyes!

THE SETUP

Roll your eyeballs so that you are looking up as high as you can. Do not tilt your head backward. Now close your eyes. Keep your eyeballs in the raised position and try to open your eyes.

INSIDER INFORMATION

This is impossible. The muscles that are required to raise the eyelids are already hard at work in the opposite direction keeping the eyeballs looking upward. In fact, there are many people who can't even shut their eyes with their eyeballs rolled back. So if you are one of these, shut your eyelids and roll back your eyeballs under your closed eyelids. Now try to open your eyelids.

HOT STUFF

Bet you can taste hot peppers with your wrist!

THE SETUP

Place a few drops of Tabasco sauce on the inside of your wrist. Wait a few minutes.

INSIDER INFORMATION

In a few minutes you will definitely feel a burning sensation on your wrist. The burning sensation is not as great as the burning sensation you would feel on your tongue, which has the most receptors for the "hot" chemicals. These are not taste receptors but pain receptors.

In Tabasco sauce and other "hot" spices there is a chemical that triggers nerves that respond to "hotness." Be sure to wash the Tabasco sauce off your wrist with soap and water when you have finished the experiment. Hot peppers can cause irritation over a prolonged period.

OUT OF TOUCH WITH REALITY

Bet you can't tell hot from cold!

THE SETUP

You will need three bowls of water: One cold, one very warm, and one room temperature. Soak your left hand in the cold water and your right hand in the hot water for about three minutes. Then, plunge both hands into the bowl of room temperature water. Is the water hot or cold?

INSIDER INFORMATION

You will not be able to answer because the water feels both hot *and* cold. The brain is getting conflicting signals from your hands. One says the water is cold; the other says it's hot. You will be thoroughly confused.

Hot and cold are relative terms and depend on what you use as a reference. Here you use two different references. The hand that has been in the cold water now feels hot. The hand that's been in the hot water now feels cold.

MISSING THE POINT

Bet you can't make two pencil points meet on one try!

THE SETUP

Take a sharp pencil in each hand. Hold your hands about two feet apart and with the pencil points facing each other. Close one eye. Keep it closed! Now try to get the points to meet.

INSIDER INFORMATION

This trick proves that you can't always believe your eyes. You can't bring the points together because you eliminate binocular vision (vision from two separate vantage points) when you close one eye. Binocular vision helps your brain calculate the distance of an object. When one eye is covered, the familiar depth cues are missing. Depth perception is most difficult on objects as close together as the pencils. And the margin for error with targets as small as the pencil points is enormous.

Practice will make you perfect in this stunt. The body learns other ways to judge depth when given practice. See if you can get the pencil points to meet after a few more tries. Bet you can!

ONLY BY A THREAD ...

Bet you can hold a friend on the ground with a thread!

THE SETUP

Get a friend to lie face up on the ground. Hold the ends of a piece of thread about two feet long in your hands. Place the middle of the thread under your friend's nose. Now let your friend attempt to stand up.

INSIDER INFORMATION

The "thread victim" will have to lie helplessly on the floor. The reason? The upper lip is an extremely sensitive spot. It hurts too much to try to break a thread held there. It won't take much force, on your part, to keep a good friend down.

Your friend is not the only one with a touchy upper lip. You can lead a bull around with a ring in his sensitive nose area. And cowboys subdue a wild horse with a nose string called a "twitch."

TIGHTWAD'S DILEMMA

Bet you can't crumple a sheet of newspaper into a wad with one hand!

THE SETUP

Take a double-page sheet of newspaper and crumple it into a tightly compressed ball. Use both hands. Set this ball aside. With one hand, grasp the edge of another double-page sheet of newspaper and try to crumple it into the same tightly packed ball. This time you must use only one hand for the task. The newspaper may not be pushed against anything and you must get the same-sized ball you got with the two-hand crush.

INSIDER INFORMATION

Most people underestimate the size of a sheet of newspaper. It soon fills the normal-sized hand, leaving only the tops of

> **NOTE**
> Choose a subject with fairly small hands for this trick. A man with gigantic hands might come close enough to claim he is a winner.

a few fingers free to deliver power to crumple the remainder. Even if you are big-handed enough to wrinkle up the entire sheet, you will not be able to compress it. The fully extended hand cannot cover enough of the surface of the sphere-shaped wad. To compress a sphere, pressure must be exerted over most of the surface.

TIME TO GET CRACKING

Bet you can't crack a knuckle twice in five minutes!

THE SETUP

Cracking your knuckles is easy, but we bet you can't crack any particular joint twice in five minutes. So take out your watch and get cracking. First, crack the joint until no more popping noises are heard. Then begin the timing. Another pop in the same knuckle within the five-minute limit wins.

INSIDER INFORMATION

The minor medical mystery of knuckle cracking has been investigated by a number of scientists. This is how far they've gotten. Joints have fluid in them containing dissolved carbon dioxide. When the joint is stretched, the pressure is reduced (because you've made the joint larger) and gas bubbles pop out of solution. (You've seen this phenomenon when a bottle of soda is opened.) Scientists believe that these gas bubbles are involved in the knuckle-cracking sound but they are not quite sure how the bubbles produce the sound. X-rays of stretched knuckles show bubbles of gas. The gas in the knuckles can't escape from the joint. But it takes about fifteen minutes for them to be reabsorbed. So that's how long you must wait before you can crack again!

SHAKY ODDS

Bet you can't hold your hand still!

THE SETUP

Unfold a paper clip. Smooth out all the bumps and bend it into a "V" shape. Put the "V" upside down on the back edge of a table knife. Hold the knife over a table with the ends of the wire resting lightly on the table. Try to hold the wire still.

NOTE

You may **not** rest your hand on the table or any other object.

INSIDER INFORMATION

The strangest part about this "walking wire" is that the harder you try to hold your hand still, the faster the wire walks down the back of the knife. Muscles are made up of cells that exist in alternating states of contraction and relaxation. When you contract your muscles to hold a position, only some muscle cells are in a state of contraction. Others are relaxing and recovering, getting ready to take their turn. This constant changeover creates a very slight motion or tremor that can't be seen easily. The walking wire magnifies this motion. The harder you try to hold your hand steady, the harder you muscles are working and the greater the difference between the tensed and relaxed parts of the muscle.

TIGHTFISTED ABOUT MONEY

Bet you can't drop a penny held between two fingers!

THE SETUP

Place the tips of your ring fingers together. Fold the other fingers down so the knuckles touch. Have an assistant put a penny between the tips of your ring fingers. Now try to open your fingers and drop the penny. You may not slide your fingers apart.

INSIDER INFORMATION

The ring fingers cannot move independently of the other fingers. Ligaments connect them to the other digits, especially the middle finger. When the middle finger is immobilized, so is the ring finger. The penny is trapped.

Some people, especially pianists, have stretched the ligaments that control the free motion of the ring fingers. When just the middle fingers are restricted, the ring fingers can still move. However, if the knuckles of all three other fingers are made to touch, even musicians can't make the penny drop.

QUICK BUCK

Bet you can't catch a dollar bill!

THE SETUP

Put a lengthwise crease in a new dollar bill. Hold it at one end with your thumb and index finger. Have someone place their thumb and index finger around the bill. They must now try to catch the bill when you drop it.

INSIDER INFORMATION

Here is one case where the hand is not quicker than the eye. Don't worry. Nobody is going to get their hands on your money, because their reflexes will be too slow. The catching mechanism works like this: the sight of the bill dropping must register in the brain, which then sends a message to the fingers. Although this relay takes less than a second, it's too long.

It is possible to catch a dollar on the drop, but only if you are the one doing both the dropping and the catching. Your *proprioceptive* sense (sense of your own body movements) coordinates the movement of your hands. The hand that catches the dollar reacts to the message activating the release, not the sight of the dropping bill. Sight is not involved when you are both dropper and catcher. Prove it by doing the drop/catch with your eyes closed.

FOOT FEAT

Bet you can tell shoe sizes without looking at feet!

THE SETUP

Measure the distance from your elbow to your wrist. Then measure the length of your foot.

INSIDER INFORMATION

Nobody would guess it, but the two measurements are the same. Your body has some very surprising proportions. It's hard to believe that the distance around a closed fist is also the length of your foot. Still another fooler is that the distance from fingertip to fingertip of your outstretched arms is the same as your height.

The convenience of such "portable" measuring devices led to the use of the parts of the body as linear measurements: the first knuckle of the thumb (inch), the foot, the distance from fingertip to nose (yard), and the hand (four inches), which is used to measure horses.

A TONGUE LASHING

Bet you can suffer excruciating pain from a can of soda!

THE SETUP

Open a can of soda and pour it into a glass. See how long you can keep your tongue stuck in it.

INSIDER INFORMATION

Bet you don't last a minute. Most people can't stand the pain and you can use this to stage a pain endurance contest with your friends to see who is the toughest. You feel pain because there is a chemical in your mouth that changes the carbon dioxide in the soda bubbles into carbonic acid—a weak acid that your tongue finds irritating. When you drink soda, you swish it around in your mouth and no one place gets too stung. Holding your tongue in place makes sure it gets such a strong dose of the irritant that you eventually have to remove it.

Scientists did two experiments to discover the source of the pain from carbonated beverages. In one experiment they gave the drinkers a drug that blocked the ability of the mouth to change the carbon dioxide bubbles into acid. They felt no sting. In another experiment people drank soda in a high-pressure chamber used by deep sea divers. Here the bubbles stayed in solution. Nevertheless, the people felt the sting as their mouths changed the dissolved carbon dioxide into the acid.

WRITE WRONG

Bet you can write backwards!

THE SETUP

Hold an index card against your forehead. Write a word on the card going from your left to your right (using cursive script if you can). Imagine you are writing normally. Don't stop to think about it.

INSIDER INFORMATION

When you look at what you've written it will be

stranger than a hieroglyphic and just as hard to read. But hold it up to a mirror or turn the paper over and hold it up to the light and lo and behold it's legible! Amazingly, you have perfected mirror writing. Ordinarily you would not be able to do this, but when you hold the paper against your forehead, the right and left sides of your brain get confused and a mirror or backward image of normal writing occurs. Some people can do mirror writing with a paper in front of them. Leonardo da Vinci was one, the famous scientist and artist from the fifteenth century. He wrote backwards to keep others from reading his ideas.

A NOSE JOB

Bet you can hang a spoon on the end of your nose!

THE SETUP

For this trick, use any nose and any metal teaspoon. Heat the bowl of a spoon either by

rubbing it with your hand or placing it in a cup of hot liquid. When the spoon is warm, tilt back your head just slightly and let the bowl of the spoon run down the top of your nose, with the handle hanging down. As you return your head to its normal position, the spoon will stick to the end of your nose and hang there. Some people have been known to "hang spoon" for several hours. Good "spoon hangers" can talk and even laugh during the experience.

INSIDER INFORMATION

We honestly don't know why this trick works. We think the spoon sticks because the heat from the metal causes the tissues of the nose to swell slightly and conform to the shape of the spoon. But we are only guessing.

.... AND I'LL HAVE THE SPOON BREAD...

This is a stunt that some people can do the first time they try it. Others have to practice a few times before they get the "hang" of it. If you aren't one of the lucky first-timers, continue rubbing the bowl to heat it and stroking the spoon down the top of your nose. The effort is well worth it, for this is a mysterious and amusing stunt that is guaranteed to get you noticed in any restaurant.

DISJOINTED DIGIT

Bet you can make your finger hang loose!

THE SETUP

Hold your hand with the fingers extended straight out. Bend the ring finger down at the second joint but keep the other fingers fully extended. Flick the tip of the ring finger repeatedly with the index finger of the other hand.

INSIDER INFORMATION

Weirdness reigns! The fingertip appears to be disjointed and wobbles up and down with each flick.

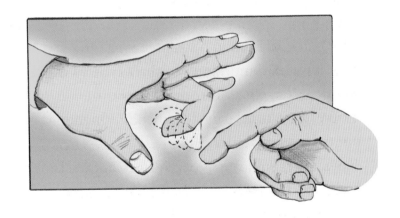

The bones are held together with strong ropelike connections called ligaments, and the muscles are attached to the bones by ropelike connectors called tendons. When you bend your ring finger the ligaments and tendons holding the tip of your finger are completely relaxed. Your finger joint wobbles freely at a mere touch but you can't move it without outside help. The same phenomenon occurs with your other fingers but not to the same extent as with your ring finger. The "disjointed" fingertip doesn't work if you bend all your fingers or if you extend all your fingers straight out. Try it. Strangeness itself!

NEW MOON?

Bet you can make a full moon shrink!

THE SETUP

This illusion has two parts:

1. Look at a full moon after it has risen. The moon should be near the horizon.
2. Next, view the moon through a little window you make from the space between the thumb and forefingers of each hand with the fingertips touching each other. Hold the tiny window close to one eye. View only the moon. Don't let any of the objects on the ground enter your little viewing window.

INSIDER INFORMATION

The "shrinking moon" illusion has been known for hundreds of years. Although the ancients realized the moon seems much smaller when it is high in the sky, the reason behind this illusion is still not completely understood.

Scientists have measured our perceptions, and we see the moon as two and a half to three and a half times larger near the horizon than high in the sky. The best theory to explain this phenomenon is that the moon appears larger when it is near identifiable objects. When you remove these visual cues by blocking them out with your fingertip window or by waiting until the moon is high in the sky, the moon appears to shrink. In the case of your tiny window the shrinkage is instant.

BLOOD TELLS!

Bet you can write a secret message without using any ink!

THE SETUP

Use your fingernail to scratch a message on the inside part of your forearm. Do not break the skin. The words will appear lighter than your skin color for a moment and then disappear. Later, when you wish to reveal the message, rub your arm briskly and the word will appear in blood-red letters.

INSIDER INFORMATION

When you scratch your arm you are scraping away dead skin cells. Brisk rubbing of the arm increases heat at that spot and stimulates the blood flow. The letters of the message appear red because the skin over them is thinner and more transparent than the skin that has not been scraped. The blood shows through. Your secret message still will be readable ten or fifteen minutes after you have written it.

A TASTELESS TRICK

Bet you can fool your taste buds!

THE SETUP

Hold your nose and put a pinch of dry coffee in your mouth. Can you identify the coffee taste? Chew it. Let it dissolve on your tongue. Roll it around your mouth. Do anything … but don't let go of your nose.

INSIDER INFORMATION

You'll be fooled, all right. Taste buds aren't what identify coffee flavor. Out sense of smell is the coffee detective. Prove it by letting go of your nose. Coffee is instantly recognizable in the nose and surprisingly in the mouth, too.

Only a few flavors—sweet, salt, sour, and bitter—are detected by the taste buds alone. Without smell, some things like coffee are not recognizable and other tastes are confusing.

WIDE EYED

Wanna bet you can make your pupils bigger by squeezing your neck?

THE SETUP

This trick requires three people: a pincher, a watcher, and a subject. Have the subject face a bright light so that the pupils are small. The watcher looks into the subject's eyes. The pincher lightly squeezes the back of the subject's neck.

INSIDER INFORMATION

If you pinch the right spot, the pupils open wide. The right spot is over the place where your hair stands up when you're frightened.

When you are afraid your body changes to prepare you to fight or to run away. You feel a rush as a chemical made by your body, called *adrenalin*, stimulates your nervous system. One response is your pupils get bigger to let in more light so you can see better. The nerve that controls this is close to the skin at the back of your neck. Pinching this area is another way of firing this nerve.

The effect is more dramatic when the pupils start out as small as possible. That's why you begin by looking into a light because the pupils start out smaller

than in dim light. If you don't have two friends to do this with, try it on yourself in front of a mirror.

COLD-HEARTED

Wanna bet ice makes your heart beat faster?

THE SETUP

For this trick you need a bowl of ice-water and a watch with a second hand. Take your own pulse. To do this, put two fingers on the inside of your wrist just below the thumb. You should be able to feel your heart beating in the artery that passes close to the surface of your skin. Count the number of beats that occur in fifteen seconds. Multiply that number by four to determine your heart rate per minute. This is your pulse.

Place your hand in the bowl of ice water for no more than one minute. Take your pulse again.

INSIDER INFORMATION

The ice-water treatment should raise your pulse about ten beats per minute. Here's why. A cold hand tricks you into reacting as if the entire body is cold.

BEE STRONG

Wanna bet a fistful of honey makes your arm more powerful?

THE SETUP

This is a honey of a two-person trick. Put about two tablespoons of sugar in a large square of plastic wrap. Twist the wrap securely around the sugar. Do the same thing with two tablespoons of honey.

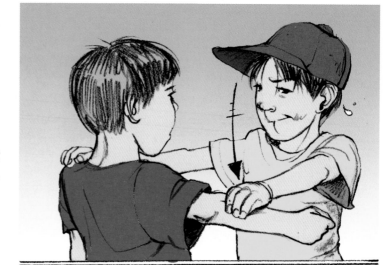

Make a fist around the bag of sugar and extend your arm to the side, at shoulder height. Have your partner face you and place one palm on top of your outstretched arm, near you elbow, with his or her other hand resting on the shoulder of your sugar-free arm. Squeeze the sugar and try to keep your arm horizontal while your partner tries to push it down. Repeat the big squeeze with the honey packet.

INSIDER INFORMATION

It is much easier to push down the arm loaded with sugar. Sugar grains can be compressed, or packed closer together. So some of the squeezer's force is diverted into compressing the sugar. Honey, like most liquids, is not compressible. More strength is available to keep your arm up. Sweetness has nothing to do with success.

BLOODSUCKING EARS

Wanna bet you can use your ears to get rid of a red nose?

THE SETUP

To do this, you need a red nose, the kind cold weather gives you in winter. To get the red out, just rub your ears briskly with your hands.

INSIDER INFORMATION

Your nose becomes colder than the rest of your face because it sticks out. Blood rushes in to warm it up, making it red. Rubbing makes blood rush to your ears. They steal the nearest extra blood, which, when you're cold, happens to be in your nose. Someone should have told Rudolph.

OFF THE WALL?

Wanna bet you can't stand up?

THE SETUP

Stand with your toes against a wall. Then step back four foot-lengths. With your feet together, lean as far as you can toward the wall, catching yourself with your hands. Rest your forehead against the wall and place your hands at your sides. Now try to stand up. If you don't move your hands or your feet, you will never be upright again.

INSIDER INFORMATION

This trick puts your muscle power against the force of gravity. The places where you are supported are called your *bases*. (When you are standing, your feet are your bases.) Instead of pulling on all of your body parts equally, gravity acts as if all the matter of your body is focused in one spot called your *center of gravity*. When you are standing, your center of gravity is directly over your feet. That's why you don't topple.

When you are leaning against the wall, your center of gravity is between two bases, your head and your feet. In order to stand up straight, you must bring your center of gravity over your feet. When you can't use your hands and feet, only your back muscles are available to pull you erect. They're simply not strong enough. Sorry, but we're going to have to leave you up against it this time.

TOTALLY TASTELESS

Wanna bet you can't taste the difference between an apple, an onion, and a potato?

THE SETUP

Put on a blindfold and hold your nose. Have a friend put a small piece of apple, potato, or onion in the center of your tongue. Try to identify it just by taste. No chewing allowed. Now do the same thing with small pieces of the other two things. You will discover a mystery in your mouth.

INSIDER INFORMATION

Learning how tasteless you are may be hard to swallow. Your tongue is able to identify only four tastes: salt, sweet, sour, and bitter. The identifying organs, called *taste buds*, are not spread evenly over the tongue. The center, where you placed the test materials, has fewer taste buds than other parts of the tongue.

What we think of as taste is really a combination of taste, smell, and texture or "mouth feel" of foods. This trick eliminates the smell and feel clues, and it leaves only the bitter taste of defeat.

Another taste tricker to try: Eat an apple while you hold a cut pear under your nose.

LIP SERVICE

Wanna bet you can use your upper lip as a temperature detector?

THE SETUP

You need three coins in a plastic container and a friend. While your back is turned, have your friend take a coin out of the container, hold it for thirty seconds, and return it. You cannot tell which coin was handled by looking at them. But the answer is right under your nose. Hold each coin in turn against the skin above your upper lip. Your built-in heat sensors will detect the handled coin every time.

INSIDER INFORMATION

There are many nerves in the skin under your nose that are sensitive to temperature. This part of your body is even more sensitive than your fingers. A plastic container is essential to this trick because it is an insulator. The heat of the coin doesn't escape as quickly in a plastic container as it would in a metal one.

EVENHANDEDNESS

Bet you can't make your fingers meet under a yardstick at any place but the center!

THE SETUP

Rest the ends of a yardstick on your index fingers. Slowly bring your fingers toward each other. They will meet at the exact center (the eighteen-inch mark) every time. Try to make them meet at some other place.

INSIDER INFORMATION

You prevent yourself from winning this trick. First of all, there is only one place under the yardstick where it will balance on a single support: the center of gravity. If your fingers meet anywhere else, the yardstick will be off balance and fall. Consciously, you are trying to make your hands meet at some other point. But these efforts are overridden by an unconscious sense called *proprioception.* This complicated feedback system coordinates your body movements to maintain the balance of the ruler. The hundreds of amazing adjustments in hand position always result in the same thing—a balanced ruler supported at its center of gravity.

Once you've got the hang of this balancing act, try your hand at the next trick.

A HANDOUT

Wanna bet only one hand will move from the center of a yardstick when you try to part your hands?

THE SETUP

We've recently discovered there's more to the yardstick balancing act than we originally thought. The second part is even more mysterious.

Balance a yardstick with the center resting on both of your outstretched index fingers. Slowly move your fingers apart. Surprisingly, only one hand moves.

INSIDER INFORMATION

In the first trick, the meeting place of your hands was determined by the stick's center of gravity. The same forces are operating when you move your hands apart.

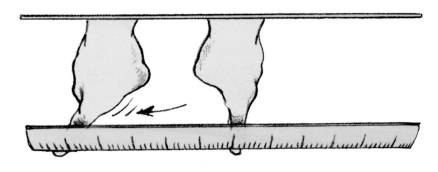

Proprioception is at work here too, automatically coordinating your body movements to keep the stick in balance. Notice only one hand moves at a time. This happens because the moving hand requires something to pull against in order to move. The friction between the stationary hand and the ruler is the force the moving hand pulls against.

When you move your hands apart quickly, things change. Speed reduces friction. Now both hands can be moving at the same time. However, the hand with the least amount of friction moves farther.

FALSE MOVES

Wanna bet you can move cardboard just by staring at it?

THE SETUP

You can't really move paper by staring at it, but this illusion is so powerful that it really seems to move. In this case, seeing is not believing. Fold an unlined 3 in. x 5 in. index card in half lengthwise. Place the folded card on a table so that one end of the card faces you and the fold is at the top, like a pup tent. Your eyes should be slightly above the level of the card. Close one eye and stare at a spot in the center of the fold. Stare hard. For a while, you will see the card as you positioned it. Then, suddenly, the card will appear to be standing on end. Keep on staring the same way at the standing card illusion. Move your head slowly from side to side. The card will appear to sway back and forth.

INSIDER INFORMATION

The illusion of the dancing cardboard tricks you in two ways. Closing one eye removes some of your ability to judge depth, so the folded cardboard doesn't appear to be

three-dimensional. The brain doesn't have enough information to judge whether the fold is bent toward you or away from you. The brain switches back and forth between the two possibilities. When the card appears to be standing up, the depth cues are reversed. The fold, which is really closer to you, now seems to be the farthest point from your eye. Now the motion illusion can occur.

Normally, when you move your head, you change your point of view, and the foreground appears to move faster than the background. As you move your head in front of the reversed-form illusion, the edges (which appear to be close) seem to be moving faster than the fold (which appears farther away) and the whole illusion seems to sway.

GRAY GHOSTS

Wanna bet you can see gray where there is no gray?

THE SETUP

Stare at one of the black boxes in Figure 1. Ghostly gray spots will appear at the intersections of the white lines. To be a ghostbuster, stare at one of the white intersections. That gray ghost will disappear, although ghosts will continue to haunt the other intersections.

Now stare at one of the white boxes in Figure 2. They're haunted, too. Very faint gray spots will appear in the black intersections.

INSIDER INFORMATION

These are brightness illusions. White appears whiter when it is next to black, and black appears blacker when it is next to white. At the intersections of the white lines, white appears to be meeting white, producing the illusion of something less than white—in other words, gray. The same is true when black lines meet black and produce something less than black—gray, again.

When you stare directly at an intersection, the image falls on the center of your eye. The nerve cells there are better at detecting the difference between black and white than are the cells of your peripheral vision. So, no ghost appears.

UPLIFTING EXPERIENCE

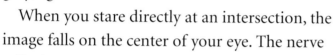

Wanna bet your arms can rise by themselves?

THE SETUP

Stand in a doorway and place the backs of your hands against the door frame. Press as hard as you can for thirty seconds. Step out of the doorway and relax your arms. Within a few seconds, they will rise automatically. If it doesn't work, do it again longer and harder.

INSIDER INFORMATION

As you press your hands against the door frame, your nerves tell your muscles to contract and lift your arms. The door frame prevents your arms from moving. When you step away and free your arms, the muscles continue to contract after you have stopped pushing. The only way you'll get this effect is if you keep your brain out of it. If you consciously try to keep your arms from rising, they won't.

IT ALL ADDS UP

Wanna bet you can read a message through a slit that only lets you see a slice?

THE SETUP

In a large piece of cardboard, cut a two-inch-long slit, as narrow as you can possibly make it. Place the cardboard over some writing. Size doesn't matter. Move the slit rapidly back and forth across the page. You'll get the message.

INSIDER INFORMATION

Your amazing brain puts the pieces together like a jigsaw puzzle. What you are really seeing is a series of slices. When the series appears rapidly enough (fifteen to sixty flashes

per second, depending on the brightness of the light), the images fuse, creating a single picture.

NO SWEET TOOTH

Wanna bet an artichoke can make water taste sweet?

THE SETUP

Pour a glass of water. Taste it. Eat a freshly cooked artichoke (with salt and butter, if you wish.) Taste the water again. If you're one of the lucky ones, it will taste sweet.

INSIDER INFORMATION

Artichokes, which are not sweet, contain a chemical called *cynarin*, which stimulates the same taste buds that sugars stimulate. You need to eat about half an artichoke before these

taste buds start firing. They stay fooled even after you've finished eating the artichoke. All food, not only water, tastes sweeter as a result. The effect lasts for a few minutes. Scientific studies have shown that six out of ten people have this sweet experience. In our experience, Vicki got it but all Kathy got was an overdose of artichoke, not her favorite food.

STRETCHING THE TRUTH

Make your lips lie to you.

THE SETUP

This experiment is not for people who care about keeping up appearances. You're going to have to stretch your face out of shape.

You will need:

- a piece of stiff cardboard (a business card is about the right size)
- a friend

Lips are very touch sensitive. Test this out and see for yourself. Close your eyes and mouth. Have a friend gently press the corner of a card between your lips. The card should be held vertically so that the corner of the card touches where your lips meet and the edges of the card press against the upper and lower lip at the same time. Try to determine whether the card is straight up and down or tilted right or left at an angle. Chances are you'll get it right every time.

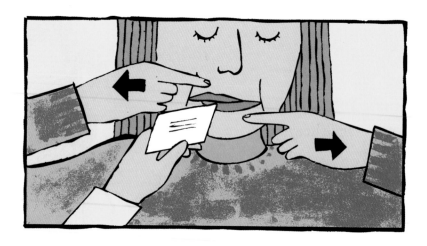

Now fix it so your lips will lie. Put your right index finger over your upper lip and pull right. Put your left index finger under your lower lip and pull left. Again, close your eyes. Now have your friend insert the corner of the card between your lips as before. This time even when the card is straight up and down, it will feel as if it's slanted.

INSIDER INFORMATION

When the card touches your lips, the pressure triggers nerves. The brain knows where those nerves are located. You have a lifetime of receiving messages from lined-up lips, but pull them out of alignment and the brain is fooled. In the absence of sight, the message from your twisted lips is interpreted by your brain to mean that the card isn't straight.

Can the brain learn to adjust to twisted lips and interpret things correctly again? Yes, but it takes time. Scientists had a man wear prism eyeglasses all the time so that everything he saw was upside down. After three weeks of living like this, he woke up one day and everything was right side up again. His brain had adjusted. When they took off the glasses, everything was upside down again. Fortunately, the effect wasn't permanent.

WEIGH COOL

Make money heavier by chilling it.

THE SETUP

Cold cash is heavier than you think. You can increase the weight of a coin by chilling it in the freezer … but there's a catch. You must use your fingertips as a scale.

You will need:

- a blindfolded friend
- 2 quarters
- a freezer or ice cubes
- a towel

Ordinarily, the pressure receptors in the fingertips are pretty accurate at measuring weight. Use a blindfolded friend as your human scale. Have the "weigher" face you with hands palm up and the middle and index fingers extended. Place a quarter on the fingertips of each hand. Ask your "scale" to compare the weights. The hands may be moved up and down to help make the evaluation.

Put one of the coins against an ice cube or in the freezer for several minutes. Dry it off with a towel and repeat the test. Surprisingly, the cold coin will feel substantially heavier.

INSIDER INFORMATION

Why a cold object feels heavier than one at room temperature is a mystery. One possible explanation is that the nerves responsible for pressure (weight) are also triggered by cold. Does a hot coin feel lighter than one at room temperature? We experimented and couldn't detect any difference. But check it out for yourself. Maybe your nerves aren't as frayed as ours.

FEELING THE HEAT

Discover how cool + warm = hot.

THE SETUP

You are going to find out what happens when you feel very warm and cool temperatures next to each other in a decidedly not normal way.

You will need:

- 2 1-foot long pipe cleaners (known as chenille stems in craft stores)
- 2 small bowls
- hot and cold water

Lay the pipe cleaners flat and bend them back and forth to make a zigzag shape. They should nest neatly together. Put one pipe cleaner in each bowl, and then fill one bowl with cold tap water and the other with very warm, but not overly hot tap water. Now, working quickly, remove the pipe cleaners and fit them together on the counter. Put your forearm gently on top of the pipe cleaners. Ouch! That's hot! You'll remove your arm in a hurry!

INSIDER INFORMATION

This is one hot illusion! Instead of feeling warm, or warm and cool, the combined stimulation produces a feeling of intense heat. The temperatures of the pipe cleaners stimulate both cold and warm receptors in the same area of the arm. In this case, the brain interprets this as a single, very hot sensation. You might say your brain is fried!

AN ANTISTRETCHING WORKOUT

Painlessly shorten your arm.

THE SETUP

Most workouts are designed to lengthen and stretch the muscles and tendons of your body. This is an exercise that does just the opposite. Or so it appears.

You will need:

- a wall

Face a wall and position yourself so that the fingertips of an extended arm just touch it. Keep your arm straight, and in a single motion swing it down and behind you, then back up to its original position. Your fingers are now unable to make contact with the wall. Honey, I shrunk your arm!

INSIDER INFORMATION

Relax. Your arm has not really shrunk. When you swing it behind you, you unconsciously lean backward. For some unknown reason, your body does not return to its original position when you swing your arm forward.

Now try the exercise again. Even though you know what happened before and why, it doesn't matter. You'll get the same "short arm." You can't override your unconscious sense of balance.

A SENSATIONAL RACE

Discover how winning a race to the brain changes how you feel things.

THE SETUP

You know that your fingertips are very sensitive. But how do they compare to other parts of your body? Tap your two index fingers together. Do you feel the pressure more in one fingertip than the other or do they feel about the same? Now tap your finger to your lip. Do you feel the pressure more in your lip or your fingertip? Tap your finger to your bare big toe. The sensation is much stronger in your fingertip than on your toe. And for the ultimate difference—this is only for flexible people—tap your toe on your lip.

INSIDER INFORMATION

You don't feel a thing until the stimulus—tapping your fingertip—reaches your brain. Fortunately, the message travels quite quickly through your nerves at about eighty miles per hour. Since we're dealing with very short distances, that's less than the blink of an eye. But still, the message from your toe travels a longer distance than the message from your lip.

In this sensational race to the brain, the shortest distance traveled wins the race. So the lip beats the fingertip. The message that wins becomes the dominant sensation. You feel it more on your lip than your finger. Another factor that determines sensitivity is the number of receptors where the stimulus is. Fingertips and lips are pretty equal in this department so it is a fair comparison. Since your arms are the same length, tapping fingertips together results in a tie—you feel the sensation equally when you tap fingertips together. The toe doesn't have the same number of receptors as the finger and it's in the Siberia of the body, compared to the brain—so the finger clearly beats the toe. And you can guess which wins between the toe and the lip without bending yourself out of shape.

UNWANTED ADVANCES

Bet you can't jog in place!

THE SETUP

Normally, you would have no difficulty jogging in place. However, you can fix it so that you can't. No matter how you try to restrain yourself, you will move forward.

You will need:

- a treadmill
- a blindfold
- a friend

Begin by jogging on a level treadmill. Hold on as a friend blindfolds you. Continue jogging for several minutes while still holding on. Have your friend turn off the machine. Then have him or her help you off the treadmill and face you toward a clear pathway. Do not remove the blindfold.

Try jogging in place. You will move forward although you will feel as if you are a super-stationary jogger.

INSIDER INFORMATION

Although it may seem like it, jogging on a treadmill is not jogging in place. You are moving forward. You don't go anywhere because the floor of the treadmill is moving backward at the same rate.

Nerves tell your muscles how to move. A repetitive movement such as jogging causes nerves in use to become fatigued. They continue to fire in the same pattern when the repetitive action is suddenly stopped. So, when you're on solid ground, you continue to move forward as you did on the treadmill. When you remove your blindfold, vision takes over, and you can make the adjustments that allow you to jog in place.

Now try hopping up and down while you are on a moving treadmill. After you get off, try to hop in place with the same leg you used on the treadmill. Once again, you will move forward. However, if you use the other leg, you will be able to hop in place.

BAD TASTE GENES

Use orange juice to see if you've inherited a sensitivity to bitter taste.

THE SETUP

You may be able to change the way orange juice tastes just by brushing your teeth.

You will need:

- a toothpaste containing sodium lauryl sulfate
- a toothbrush
- a small glass of orange juice

First take a sip of orange juice and notice its flavor. Rinse your mouth with water. Brush your teeth for at least sixty seconds with toothpaste that contains sodium lauryl sulfate. Rinse with water and taste the orange juice again. Does it taste different?

One out of three people do not detect any difference. The others do. And it's mouth puckering. Yuck!

INSIDER INFORMATION

The tongue is equipped with taste buds that can detect four basic tastes: sweet, salty, sour, and bitter. Sodium lauryl sulfate is a detergent

often found in toothpaste, mouthwash, and laundry products. This harmless chemical can alter the taste of the citric acid in orange juice. The sourness is almost unchanged but the bitterness is almost ten times stronger.

Your ability to taste bitterness in other substances is inherited as well. If both of your parents gave you the bitterness-detecting gene, then caffeine, the food preservative sodium benzoate, tonic water, and certain artificial sweeteners will taste especially bitter. If only one parent gave you the gene, you can detect a bitter taste but it won't be unpleasant. If you didn't get the gene, you might not be able to identify bitterness at all.

SPOOKY SURVEILLANCE

Try and escape the watching eyes of a mask.

THE SETUP

A stationary mask can appear to follow your every movement. No matter what direction you move, the face of the mask seems to turn with you.

You will need:

- a molded mask (we used a Halloween hockey mask)
- tape
- a sunlit window

This illusion depends on using a mask that is molded so that the inside surface is the exact opposite of the outside. (The inside surfaces of some masks are smooth. These won't work.) The mask must also be translucent. (Some light must pass able to pass through it.) It doesn't matter if the mask is painted on the outside.

To experience this illusion, tape the mask onto a sunlit window so that the outside of the mask is against the window and the hollow inside faces the room. The sun must be shining directly into the window because the mask has to be lit from behind.

Stand ten or more feet away from the mask. Position yourself so that you are facing the window and the mask is on your left side. Stand still and focus on the mask. It will no longer appear hollow, it will look as if you are viewing the outside of the mask.

If you have trouble seeing the illusion, try closing one eye. Watch the mask as you walk past it, moving parallel to the window. The effect is startling. You can't get away from the mask's spooky surveillance.

Mask taped to a sunny window

10 feet

INSIDER INFORMATION

The mask seems to be tracking you for two reasons, neither of which is supernatural. First, the backlighting removes some of your ability to judge depth. Your brain doesn't have enough information to tell whether you are viewing the hollow inside of the mask or the convex outer side. Since

you're more familiar with a bulging face, your brain goes with the more "normal" perception.

Not only can you be tricked by backlighting as to the shape of the mask, but you can be fooled by motion as well. If you tape a mask to a window with the normal side facing the room, the eyes and face appear to turn away from you as you walk past. When you walk past a mask with the hollow side facing the room, everything is reversed including the direction the face appears to turn.

The Haunted Mansion in Disney World makes good use of this chilling illusion. Instead of masks, hollow statues with lights inside them stare at you as you ride by.

CENTS OF HEARING

Sort pennies by sound.

THE SETUP

There's no challenge to sorting pennies by the year they were made if you look at the date stamped on them. It's harder, but still possible, to sort old pennies from new pennies by listening to the sound they make when dropped onto a tile floor.

You will need:

- an assortment of pennies—old and new
- a bathroom or kitchen with a tile floor
- a friend

Divide the pennies into two piles—one consisting of coins minted in 1982 and earlier and the other of coins made in 1983 or later. So far your sorting has been done by sight. Now you're ready to test your ability to sort by sound!

Close your eyes so that you can concentrate all your attention on listening. Have your friend hold the new pennies in one hand and the old pennies in the other. Your assistant should drop them one by one in a random pattern from each group onto a tile floor. Your assistant should identify which pile each coin came from after you've heard the sound. Soon you will be able to hear the difference in the sounds and tell the new pennies from the old by sound alone.

Practice by calling out "old" or "new" with confirmation from your assistant.

INSIDER INFORMATION

One-cent coins were once called "coppers" because they were made of copper metal. But the price of copper rose faster than the value of a penny. To cut costs the U. S. government decided to make pennies out of zinc, which is a cheaper metal, and plate them with copper. Zinc pennies were first mass produced in 1983. They look the same as the old copper pennies but they don't sound the same. Newer pennies make a dull, tinny sound when dropped. Older pennies make a sharper, ringing sound.

A BIG YAWN

Prove yawns are contagious.

THE SETUP

People usually yawn when they're sleepy or bored. But you can make a normal well-rested person yawn just by looking at you. In fact you can start a yawn epidemic.

You will need:

- people or animals

Make eye contact with someone as you noisily open your mouth in a gigantic yawn. You don't have to show your tonsils—a covered-mouth yawn is just as contagious. Don't worry if you're a bad actor, a faked yawn usually turns into the real thing. In fact, you're probably yawning right now.

The odds are very high that your victim will not be able to resist. In a room full of people, the yawn will spread rapidly, even to those who don't see yawners. Sound alone can spread a yawn.

INSIDER INFORMATION

Yawning is not just for the tired or bored. People will yawn when they are trying to pay attention in a difficult situation or when they are nervous. But, in spite of scientific research, we still do not know exactly why we yawn. The most popular theory is that there is a lack of oxygen in the brain. Yawning is a fast way of taking in a lot of oxygen in one breath. After all, the mouth is bigger than the nose.

While we don't know why we yawn, we do know exactly what happens during a yawn. Look closely at a yawning person. The pupils expand, the muscles in the forehead tighten, and the lips push against the teeth.

Yawns can be spread from one species to another. Watching your dog or cat yawn can make you yawn. Interestingly, cats seem to be immune to human yawning. Yawn in front of your dog and sooner or later, it will yawn back.

Research has shown that yawning is most infectious among strangers. Kathy doesn't know if this is entirely true. Vicki certainly makes her yawn.

Yawning isn't the only contagious activity. Scratching is also transmitted by the "power of suggestion."

2. DON'T TRY THIS AT HOME!

This chapter will make you want to leave home. It's not that your home isn't a perfectly nice place, but there are some discoveries that you just can't make there. This chapter and the next one are a field guide for the explorer on the go. Only when you walk out the door can you see secret messages on license plates or find meteorites at the beach. Some people may think you're a bit strange if they see you balancing on soda cans or making garbage bags fly. Don't let anyone discourage you. You're just being curious, a natural human trait. After all, Benjamin Franklin flew a kite in a thunderstorm and look what he discovered—electricity!

There are some seasonal activities here as well. Print photos on an apple or make snow in winter. Flirt with fireflies or fiddle with worms. See how far you can launch and fling an apple.

So leave your TV, your computer, and your video games behind. There's a real world outside just waiting for you and your incredible brain.

SPY LICENSE

See the secret markings on license plates.

THE SETUP

Counterfeit license plates are used by car thieves. The counterfeits may look authentic to ordinary people but police know how to detect the fakes. You can too, but you need to look at license plates from a whole new angle. Many license plates have secret images, but it's the viewing angle that reveals them. Although different states have different identifying symbols they are almost always placed in a vertical row down the center of the plate.

The secret symbols are invisible unless you view the plate from an angle of 30 degrees. So stand facing the license plate at a distance of four to eight feet. The correct distance for you depends your height. The taller you are the farther away you'll have to stand.

We easily saw the outline of New York State on our license plates in the daytime. But it was even more dramatic at night

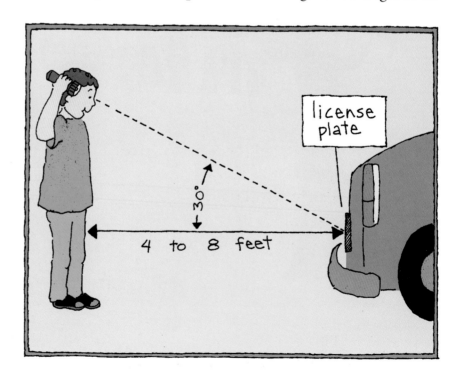

when the image was illuminated by a flashlight held over one ear pointed toward the plate at the level of the eyes.

INSIDER INFORMATION

The secret symbols are hidden in the reflective sheeting that covers the plate. The sheeting has a layer of tiny glass beads embedded in clear plastic. Behind the beads is a mirror-like coating. When viewed from most angles, the beads reflect back just about all the light that strikes them.

secret pattern!

However, the beads in the pattern of the secret image are treated so that they don't reflect any light when viewed from an angle of 30 degrees. The non-reflecting beads make up the dark areas of the secret pattern.

The reflective sheeting is provided to the states by the 3M Corporation, the only company that makes it. The manufacturing process is so sophisticated that it is unlikely that crooks will be able to duplicate it. Holograms on credit cards serve the same purpose as the secret images on license plates.

THE GLUE CLUE

Reveal hidden fingerprints with Krazy Glue.

THE SETUP

This is state-of-the-art forensic science. Detectives use Krazy Glue to uncover hidden fingerprints. So can you. Fingerprints will show up best on a dark-colored object.

You will need:

- a box with a lid
- a small square of aluminum foil or the lid of a jar

CAUTION!

Do this activity outdoors with an adult assistant. The fumes from Krazy Glue are toxic. The package warning reads "Avoid prolonged breathing of vapors. Use with adequate ventilation." Also, be very careful when handling Krazy Glue. If you accidentally get some on your skin, you can remove it with nail polish remover.

- Krazy Glue
- an object with fingerprints on it
- clear tape
- dark paper

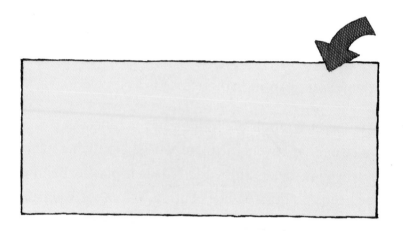

Find a box that comes with a lid. A fish tank with a glass cover would be ideal because you can see the fingerprints "developing." However, a cardboard box will also work. Make a shallow dish out of a piece of aluminum foil or use a disposable jar cover. Put the suspicious object at one end of the box. Pour a puddle of Krazy Glue in the foil or jar cover and place it at the other end of the box. Cover the box so the fumes don't escape. Let it sit in a warm place for several hours. Any fingerprints will show up as white images against the dark background.

INSIDER INFORMATION

The active ingredient in Krazy Glue is cyanoacrylate. Fumes from this compound contain a chemical that bonds with the oil in fingerprints to produce a white material. The fingerprint can be transferred to a piece of paper. Use a strip of clear cellophane tape to lift it and stick it onto a piece of dark-colored paper.

Each person in the world has his or her own set of fingerprint patterns—even identical twins. Fingerprints are so unique that they can be used to identify individuals. The FBI divides fingerprints into three basic patterns: loops, whorls, and arches.

aluminum foil

glue

box cover

cookie jar lid to be investigated

To make sure that the glue clue isn't you, fingerprint yourself. To get a clear print, press a finger on an ink pad (the kind you use with rubber stamps). Then gently roll your inked finger once on a white piece of paper. Don't roll your finger back and forth, or you'll smudge the fingerprint. If you don't have an ink pad, you can also rub a pencil on a piece of paper to make a large patch of graphite, then rub your finger on the graphite. Lift off the fingerprint off your graphite-coated finger with some clear cellophane tape and stick it on a piece of white paper. Inspect your fingerprint with a magnifying glass to see if you're a loop, whorl, or arch. Compare it the pattern of your print to the print you lifted from the suspicious object. If it doesn't match, fingerprint other likely suspects.

STINK BOMB

Turn an ordinary balloon into a secret source of stink.

THE SETUP

Don't do this inside your own home because it creates a big stink. It belongs outside or at someone else's party. Stink bombs can be made in the stench of your choice, or they can be an unexpected, pleasant smell.

Our favorite offensive odor is garlic. Crush a clove of garlic and roll a cotton swab in the juice. Rub the swab on the inside of a balloon. Don't rub it too close to the opening of the balloon, though. Remember, you have to blow up the balloon.

After you inflate the secret stinker, tie it off and put a string on it. Place it where lots of people walk by. Soon you will see them wrinkle their noses and try to figure out where the smell is coming from.

To make an equally mysterious, but this time pleasant smell, rub some vanilla extract or perfume inside a balloon.

Given a choice, we prefer garlic.

1. Roll swab in garlic juice.

2. Rub juice inside the balloon.

3. Blow it up... and tie it.

INSIDER INFORMATION

Believe it or not, a balloon is full of tiny holes called pores. The pores are smaller than air molecules but larger than those mighty, little garlic molecules. The garlic molecules seep through the balloon in a process called osmosis—the movement of molecules through a membrane. Then they spread rapidly through the air in another process called diffusion. Heat speeds up both processes—put the balloon near a light bulb and gross everyone out more quickly.

RECIPE FOR A MUMMY

Immortalize a piece of potato for future viewing (not eating).

THE SETUP

Traditionally, a mummy is a dead body, human or animal, that has been preserved. Breaking with tradition, you can make a vegetable mummy. This recipe for creating a potato mummy is almost exactly like the one used to mummify bodies by the ancient Egyptians. It will keep bacteria from rotting the vegetable remains.

You will need:

- ½ cup baking soda
- ½ cup washing soda (found in the detergent section of the supermarket)
- ¼ cup salt
- a plastic cup
- a spoon
- a slice of potato
- plastic wrap

TATER TUT

Mix the baking soda, washing soda, and salt together in the plastic cup with the spoon. Then lay the slice of potato to rest in the plastic cup "tomb." Cover the cup securely with the plastic wrap. Bury the future mummy in the ground.

To make this more scientific, cut two more slices of potato. Bury one beside your embalmed specimen. Place the other on the surface of the ground.

Wait ten days. Then examine all your potato slices for signs of rot and decay.

Mix sodas and salt.

plastic wrap

potato slice

sodas and salt

INSIDER INFORMATION

Mummification is an amazing method of preservation that has been used by humans for four or five thousand years. It also occurs naturally, through freezing, drying, or preservation in peat bogs or oil seeps. Some natural mummies are more than

WARNING!
Raccoons are known to be hazardous to the survival of potato mummies. Our neighborhood raccoons are notorious grave robbers.

25,000 years old. The Egyptians practiced artificial mummification. They removed the body fluids with a kind of washing soda called natron. Then they put herbs and spices into the body before it was wrapped in linen. The process took seventy days.

Water is contained in every cell of every living thing, and removing it without damaging the body is not easy. But, it can be drawn out chemically with salts. Washing soda, baking soda, and table salt are all part of the group of chemicals known as salts. Why remove water from the body? Bacteria which cause decay cannot grow where there is no water.

So Tater Tut is now officially a mummy.

A CLEAN GETAWAY

Walk on top of a liquid without getting your feet wet.

THE SETUP

Cornstarch and water—treat this mixture gently and it's a liquid; beat on it and it's a solid. Use this knowledge to do a phenomenal feat with your feet. But do this outside because it can be messy.

You will need:

- 1 box cornstarch
- 2 or more large baking pans (about 15 in. x 10 in.)—1 for each step you take
- newspapers
- measuring cup
- water

Spread newspapers on the ground, because you might not get this right the first time. You'll have to clean up the mess when you're finished. Pour about two cups of water into the baking pan. Sprinkle in a package of cornstarch a little at a time, mixing with your hands. This mixture has been called ooblick or gobbledygook. Ooblick is the proper consistency when it is about as thick as mayonnaise. It should be about one inch deep. Repeat the mixing process in each pan you are using.

Set the pans about one footstep apart on the newspaper. Make sure your shoes are clean. Wipe the soles with wet rags or paper towels, if necessary. Prepare mentally. You must be bold. Success comes only to those who stomp hard and fast. With forceful energy, step into the first pan and move quickly to the next. Don't stop until you're finished. Now check your shoes. If you walked on top of

the ooblick, your shoes will be perfectly clean and dry. Pussyfooters are exposed by the ooblick on their soles.

INSIDER INFORMATION

By now, you've probably noticed that cornstarch and water is not an ordinary mixture. The cornstarch doesn't dissolve in water. Why not? Each grain of cornstarch contains two kinds of structures—one is shaped like a crystal and it the other is non-crystalline. The non-crystalline structures absorb more water than the crystalline. When the mixture is handled—in this case when you step on it—the crystalline structures break down and become non-crystalline. More water is then absorbed and the ooblick becomes solid. When the pressure is off, the crystals reform, releasing the water, and the ooblick oozes once again.

WARNING!
Do not dispose of your ooblick down any drain. Do not empty it into the toilet or the sink. It can form a solid plug and clog the pipes. Seal it in a plastic bag and throw it in the garbage.

Treading softly doesn't put enough pressure on the cornstarch to break the crystals. As with a normal liquid, you'll get wet feet. Stomping makes ooblick solid. If you stomp hard enough, you may actually crack it.

Ooblick is fun to play with. Roll it between your hands and it becomes a ball. But don't try to throw an ooblick ball. As soon as you stop rolling it, ooblick drips through your fingers.

SUN RISER

Use the sun to launch a hot-air balloon.

THE SETUP

Flying garbage bags? That's a funny thought. But it's possible. A garbage bag can become a hot-air balloon. You, as ground crew, will need to wait for a sunny day with no wind. Shake open a large, dark, plastic garbage bag in a cool shady place. Hold it open and pull it through the air until it is almost fully inflated. Close it with a string or twist tie. Attach a short leash of string.

Tie the bag down in a sunny place and wait. The bag will struggle to get off the ground as the sun's rays heat it. It will expand and become lighter than air. You'll eventually get a rise out of your sun-warmed garbage bag.

INSIDER INFORMATION

Hot air balloons rise because hot air weighs less than an equal volume of cool air. The key

1. Fill with cool air.
2. Tie shut. Attach string.
3.
4. TA-DA!

to heating your balloon is the black surface of the garbage bag. Dark colors absorb heat rays from the sun. The air inside the balloon gets warmer and expands. Because the same amount of material takes up more space, the air inside the garbage bag is less dense than the outside air. So the garbage bag is now light enough to float.

Consider having a collection of garbage bag balloons for your next birthday party.

SUNBURNED BALLOONS

The ultimate in overkill! Use thermonuclear energy to burst a balloon.

THE SETUP

An innocent balloon is your target. A magnifying glass or Fresnel lens is your ray gun. And the blazing sun is your firepower in this blast of science fun.

You will need:

- balloon
- tape
- magnifying glass or Fresnel lens

Tape an inflated balloon down in a sunny spot. Position your lens between the balloon and the sun. Focus the rays of the sun into a bright spot on the balloon. This incredible heat will burn through the rubber in a split second, popping the balloon. A sunburned balloon pops so quickly you might want to challenge your friends to a balloon bursting race.

INSIDER INFORMATION

The sun's energy comes from an unbelievably enormous thermonuclear explosion that has been going on for billions of years. The distance of 93 million miles between earth and the sun protects us from its destructive forces. Lenses bend light and magnifying lenses are

CAUTION!

Do this with an adult assistant. This bright spot is concentrated heat and light energy! Do not stare directly at it and do not focus it on any part of your body or on anything flammable. The temperature in this focused spot of sunlight can reach thousands of degrees.

designed to bend light rays so that they come together at a single point. This concentrates the energy into a hot spot that can burn through rubber. Magnifying lenses can also be used to start fires. For this reason, they were once called burning glasses.

The shape of the magnifying lens determines how it will focus light. A simple glass magnifier is thicker in the center than it is at the edges. A Fresnel lens does the same thing as a magnifying lens. But instead of being a continuous curved surface, a Fresnel lens is flat, with a series of concentric circles or ridges cut into it. Each ridge has a tiny bit of curvature. If you could put all the ridges next to each other and eliminate the grooves, you would have the same shaped lens as a glass magnifier, but it would be much fatter.

Fresnel lenses are found in the scanners at supermarket checkout counters, in overhead projectors, and on the fronts of traffic lights.

While you're burning things up here's another question to puzzle over: Can you use a burning glass to melt an ice cube or clear plastic? The answer is not as simple as you might think. The heat in the sun's rays come from infra-red radiation, which is absorbed by colored objects. When an object is transparent, those rays are not absorbed. So check it out and see what happens.

WITCH WAY TO THE WATER?

Discover if you have dowsing talent.

THE SETUP

Dowsing is an ancient way of finding hidden water. Water witches, as they are sometimes called, search for underground sources of water with a variety of objects. The most common are a pendulum on a string, a forked stick, or two swiveling L-shaped rods. There are almost as many ways of dowsing as there are dowsers. A tried-and-true method is to hold a Y-shaped stick by the short ends with the long part parallel to the

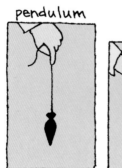
pendulum

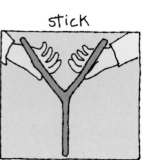
stick

bottles + coat-hanger wire

ground,
and then walk over the
ground until the stick points
downward. Dowsers claim that
the stick moves by itself when
it is over water. Dowsers also
say that not everyone is equal
when it comes to dowsing
ability.

See if you have a gift for
water witching. Hold a dowsing rod towards water and walk toward water. Even a puddle
will do, if you're talented. If you're successful at puddle dowsing, move on and see if you can
find the pipes buried in your yard.

INSIDER INFORMATION

Some people think that dowsing is a hoax. But there is some evidence that it works. In
Southeast Asia, a dowser pointed out 691 well-sites of which 664 yielded water—that's
ninety-six percent accurate. A German water witch has been one hundred percent successful
since 1980. In California, well-drillers who used a dowser were twice as successful as those
who didn't.

Dowsing has been defined as searching for anything in a way that does not use the five
senses. Just how or if it works, no one knows. But water is not the only hidden treasure that
dowsers have found. Many of them have located valuable minerals, buried pipelines, lost
keys and even hidden tumors.

LAWN GRAFFITI

Express yourself in non-living color by writing on your lawn with a garden hose.

THE SETUP

A green lawn becomes a writing surface and your garden hose becomes your writing tool. Arrange the hose to form a word in big, looping script letters or make a pattern or design. The message is limited only by the length of the hose. After twenty-four hours, peek under the hose. If the grass is pale green or yellow, remove the entire hose to expose your message in the grass. If the grass is still green, let the hose sit another day. Your message appears in yellow letters against the green background of the lawn.

INSIDER INFORMATION

You have just given your lawn a mild case of chlorosis. This disease is not fatal if you remove the hose in one or two days. Grass is green because of the green pigment chlorophyll. Without sunlight, the

chlorophyll breaks down, leaving behind yellow blades of grass. But when the sunlight returns, the grass quickly recovers and makes new chlorophyll, and your message disappears. This is earth-friendly graffiti—it's self-erasing.

EVERGREEN TOMATO

Prevent a tomato from ripening and fool the gardener.

THE SETUP

You are going to create a "stubborn" tomato. It will not turn red and it will not ripen along with the other tomatoes on the plant. Although it still looks normal, our secret treatment will keep it evergreen.

1. Select a green tomato.

Select a full-grown green tomato on a tomato plant. Being careful not to knock it off the plant, submerge the tomato in a container of very hot, but not boiling water. Keep it covered with the water for three or four minutes. That's all there is to it. The tomato is not cooked but the heat has stopped the ripening process cold.

INSIDER INFORMATION

Like many fruits, tomatoes produce ethylene gas, which causes them to ripen. The hot water treatment damages the enzyme that produces the ethylene gas. But it doesn't kill the tomato. You can prove this by planting some of the seeds from your treated tomato. They'll grow. The seeds from a cooked tomato won't grow.

2. Submerge it for 3 or 4 minutes.

Tomatoes don't have to produce their own ethylene gas in order to ripen. Ethylene gas from an outside source will work just as well. Commercial tomato growers often pick green tomatoes and pipe ethylene gas into the storage area.

Will the heat-treated tomato ripen if it receives a shot of ethylene gas? Test this by putting the evergreen tomato in a plastic bag with a ripe banana, an excellent source of ethylene gas. A "gassed" tomato normally takes three to four days to ripen. A tomato expert told us that the

3. Evergreen!

science of ripening is not completely understood. But clearly, this experiment proves that the ripening process has been blocked. Not only can't the tomato produce ethylene gas but it can't respond to it either.

FRUITOGRAPHY

Develop a picture of yourself on an apple.

THE SETUP

Find a film negative of a picture that you can sacrifice in the name of science. (If you don't have one you can use a cut-out stencil.) It can be either black and white or color. Both will come out red and green in apple fruitography.

Select a full-sized green apple on a tree. Enclose it in a light-proof bag such as the foil-lined bag used for take-out chicken. Leave the apple in the dark for a week. This will make the apple particularly light-sensitive. At the end of a week, remove the bag and glue your negative on to the apple with beaten egg white or tape it on with plastic tape. Cut a hole in the bag the size and shape of the negative. Put the bag back on the apple positioning the hole so it is over the negative and tape it in place. Give it another week to develop. Your image will appear in red on a pale green background.

1. Don't pick it!

2. Put a bag on the apple for a week.

3. Glue a negative to the apple with egg white.

4. Cut a hole in the bag the size and shape of the negative.

5. Rebag the apple, taping so the negative shows through the hole. Develop for one week.

6. A fruitograph!

INSIDER INFORMATION

During the ripening process, fruit becomes softer, sweeter, and tastier, and it changes color to advertise its deliciousness. Light plays a role in the development of the red pigment, called an anthocyanin, in an apple. The transparent parts of the negative let light through and the color develops. The dark parts of the negative keep the apple skin from receiving light and developing. Fruitography doesn't work on Granny Smith or Golden Delicious apples. There's not enough color change in these varieties to make a print.

We've heard that some fruitographers use tomatoes, eggplants, pumpkins and squash for their portraits. Maybe you have someone in mind for next year's Halloween pumpkin!

SNOW JOB

Create a snowy tempest from a teacup.

THE SETUP

Have your adult assistant carry a cup of very hot water outside on an extremely cold, dry day— near 0° F (-18° C) or below. Tell him or her to throw the water, not the cup, up into the air. Aim it away from the two of you, other people, and pets. Watch carefully. The water will turn into snow and fall to the ground.

CAUTION!
This activity requires boiling water so get an adult assistant to help you.

INSIDER INFORMATION

Snow forms when tiny drops of water freeze in the air. In order for water to change from a liquid drop into a solid crystal, it must lose heat energy.
There are several factors that affect snow formation:

- *Droplet Size*—the smaller the droplet, the faster the freezing.
- *Air Temperature*—the colder the air, the faster the freezing

- *Humidity*—the drier the air, the faster water evaporates. Because evaporation has a cooling effect, it speeds up freezing.

- *Droplet Temperature*—the hotter the water, the faster the water molecules at the surface of a droplet evaporate. This creates an enhanced cooling effect on the surface of the droplet making it freeze more quickly.

- *Water Purity*—since ice crystals form around foreign particles, the more impurities there are in the water, the more ice crystals there will be. If there are no impurities, water can be cooled to -40° F (-40° C) without ice crystals forming.

When the water is thrown into the air, it has to freeze before it hits the ground in order to make snow. It doesn't have a lot of time. To increase its chances, choose a very cold, dry day. Have your adult assistant throw the water as high as possible; this gives the droplets more time to form an ice shell. Use hot water to enhance the cooling effect of evaporation; this makes the ice shell form more quickly. Don't use distilled water; tap water has the necessary impurities to form centers around which ice can form. (You can also experiment with water in a spray bottle.)

Man-made snow is big business. Ski resorts rely on it when nature fails. Snow making was discovered in Florida in the 1950s when some farmers were spraying crops with water to keep them from freezing. They sprayed too fine a mist and got snow. This surprise gave birth to a new industry. Today, snow guns spraying water under pressure can create enough snow to cover a mountain of ski trails.

FAST FROZEN BUBBLES

Soap bubbles take on a few new wrinkles when you blow them in frigid weather.

THE SETUP

You might think that blowing bubbles is a summer activity. It is—but it can be a whole new experience in the dead of winter. Wait for an exceptionally cold day—10° F (-12° C) or below. Create bubbles in the normal manner with ordinary bubble solution and a wand. You should see some pretty amazing results.

First try drawing the wand through the air. Then try blowing on it.

At first, all you've got are normal bubbles and some of them break right away. But some live long enough to freeze. Their perfect surfaces develop wrinkles, and then they break. Fragments of frozen bubbles don't disappear into the air. Pieces of the frozen soap film, which look like broken egg shells, fall to earth.

INSIDER INFORMATION

A bubble's skin is like a sandwich—there is a layer of water molecules between two layers of soap molecules. Temperatures of 10° F (-12° C) and lower are well below the freezing point of water. This is cold enough to ensure that the thin layer of water that makes up a bubble will freeze quickly, before the bubble has the chance to burst.

The bubbles formed by drawing a wand through the air freeze almost instantly. Bubbles blown by your mouth contain warm air. When they hit the cold outside air, the air inside the bubble contracts as it cools causing the skin to crinkle like plastic wrap. The soap film adds strength to the frozen wall of the bubble.

When an unfrozen bubble bursts, the liquid soap film forms tiny drops as soon as the air escapes. The soap film is solid, in a frozen bubble, and stays that way even if it's broken into pieces.

SNOW FAKE

Create the illusion of snow on a summer night.

THE SETUP

Sometimes you can see trees glistening in the moonlight as if they were covered with snow—in August! The summer "snow" has been seen mostly by night drivers whose headlights strike dew-coated branches of certain trees. The dew appears white. Since dew lands on the top of branches where snow also falls, the sight is similar to a snow laden tree. It is only possible to see this illusion under special conditions. Although the right circumstances do not occur very often in nature, don't worry—they're easy to set up.

Do this well after sundown when it is very dark outside. Armed with a flashlight and a spray bottle filled with water, search for a plant with a waxy coating on its leaves. Shrubs and trees that make good snow fakes include blue spruce, juniper, cedar, hemlock, and rhododendron. (Pine trees do not work well.)

Spray water from your bottle on the waxy leaves. Then step back and shine your light on the wet area. Ta da. Summer snow!

INSIDER INFORMATION

This is an optical effect very similar in principle to the light-reflecting license plates that you investigated in Spy License on page 44. You may recall that the coating on the license plates is made of tiny glass beads with a mirror backing. In Snow Fakes your lenses are not glass beads but water droplets and instead of a mirror backing, there is a thin layer of air between the water bead and the leaf that creates a reflecting surface. Scientists call this reflection sylvanshine.

Leaves with a thick coating of microscopic waxy rods called a bloom make water bead up into almost perfect spheres. These spheres act as tiny lenses and channel light directly back at the observer.

If you find a hedge with good sylvanshine, you can spray an environmentally friendly graffiti message that can be read by drivers whose headlights strike the hedge.

SPRING FLOWERS

Discover the built-in springs of a dandelion.

THE SETUP

You probably don't think of plants as being especially quick moving. But dandelion stems can spring into action with amazing speed.

One of the first flowers you spot in the springtime are dandelions. Find a yellow dandelion blossom and pick it. With your fingernail slit the stem lengthwise into four strips.

Put the dandelion into a glass of water. Watch the stem. In a matter of seconds, it begins to move. Each section of the stem rolls into a tight curl.

INSIDER INFORMATION

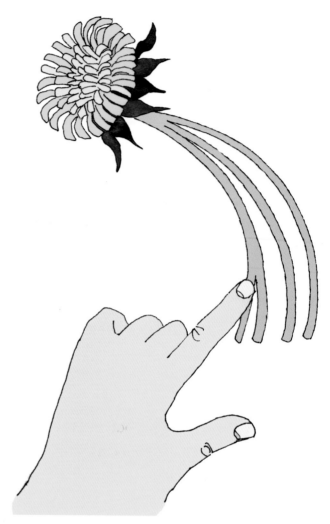

Dandelions are members of a group of plants called stem succulents. They store water in cells located on the inside of the stem and the water filled cells become a column strong enough to support the flower. This property has survival value for plants. Succulent cells can store water for a long period of time, enabling the plant to survive droughts. When rain comes, the inside cells suck up water rapidly. This is what is happening when you put your slit stem dandelion into water. Those interior cells swell up with as much water as they can hold, expanding in size. But now the cells on the inside of the stems are longer than the outer stem cells. And when one side of something is longer than the other, you get curls.

This phenomenon puts new meaning into the phrase "spring flowers."

PLANT THERMOMETER

Use a rhododendron bush to tell the temperature.

THE SETUP

The American rhododendron, one of the most common yard plants, has such a curious response to cold that you can use it as a thermometer.

In mild weather (40-50° F or 4-10° C) the leaves of the rhododendron are bright green and perfectly flat. Around freezing (32° F or 0° C), the leaves darken in color and start to droop, and the edges begin to curl under. When the mercury drops to 0° F (-18° C), the leaves turn almost black, hang down and roll up tightly.

So to see what kind of coat you will need on a winter morning, check a rhododendron.

50° F   32° F   0° F

INSIDER INFORMATION

The strange behavior of rhododendron leaves has been the subject of intense scientific study, and there have been many theories about why the leaf darkening and curling of these broadleaf evergreens occurs. The most current explanation of the phenomenon is that bright sunlight and very cold temperatures permanently damage the cells of rhododendron leaves. By curling up and drooping its leaves, the plant reduces the amount of leaf surface exposed to the elements. Support for this explanation comes from the observation that when the leaves are covered with snow, they don't curl up.

Brrr...

Scientists have also found that frozen leaves are damaged as well if they thaw too rapidly. Curled leaves thaw more slowly.

The rhododendron has clearly mastered some cold-weather survival strategies.

APPLE FLINGSHOT

Throw a green apple the length of a football field.

THE SETUP

A flingshot is sort of like a slingshot. With it, you can throw an apple a lot farther than you can with your arm alone. Where can you get such a powerful missile launcher? No problem. A flingshot is just a thin flexible stick about three feet long that will spring back when you whip it through the air.

WARNING!

Before you launch any green missiles, make sure that you are in an open field and don't aim at people, animals, or property that could be damaged.

There are always green apples under an apple tree in the summer. Ask permission to use the "drops." If it's okay, impale one on the end of your flingshot. But be careful! You are now in the possession of a potentially dangerous plaything.

When you've cleared your apple for

takeoff, grasp the end of the stick. Hold the flingshot so the apple is touching the ground in front of you. In one motion, bend your elbow and swing the apple back over your shoulder and then quickly bring your arm forward in a whipping motion. At the fullest extension of your arm, flick your wrist as your arm comes to an abrupt stop. The apple will rocket off in the direction your arm is pointing. As in other sports, flingshot skills improve with practice.

INSIDER INFORMATION

The ideal quarterback would have arms that hung to the ground. Extra length multiplies the speed and the distance of a thrown object. The flingshot is an arm extender, a kind of lever that increases the speed of the apple. The faster the apple moves, the greater the distance it will travel before it hits the ground. The little flick of the wrist that you give when you stop your arm is to shake the apple loose.

The texture of a green apple is absolutely perfect for this sport. Other fruits and vegetables can be launched but we haven't found any that rivals an apple for distance. Maybe you'll discover a record-setting veggie or flying fruit.

BEWITCHING FROGS

Become an expert in amphibian hypnosis with our four-minute course.

THE SETUP

You can be the master of a wild creature and put it in a trance. If you are new to casting spells, begin with a frog. In no way does this trick harm a frog so a pet store may let you try it on one of their animals.

Pick up a frog in one hand. Turn it upside down. Gently stroke your finger up and down its belly. It may struggle for a few moments but it will be unable to resist your magic touch. Continue stroking for a few more seconds to put it into a very deep trance. At this point you can set it down and it will simply lie there, motionless, completely unaware of its surroundings. Frog trances last anywhere from a few minutes to an hour. **Be careful not to let the frog dry out since it needs moist skin in order to breathe. If you turn out to be an especially gifted mesmerizer and your frog is entranced for more than fifteen minutes, sprinkle it with water.** The frog will come out of its trance

naturally or you can make it "come to" quickly by clapping your hands or gently prodding it with your finger. This is not a one-shot performance. You can repeat it over and over again on the same frog.

INSIDER INFORMATION

Scientists don't know exactly why belly-stroking hypnotizes some animals. But they believe that trances may be a form of protection. A lifeless-appearing prey is not as likely to trigger aggressive behavior from predators.

Just about every frog we've laid our hands on has fallen under our spell. We have not been as successful with toads. Some are hypnotizable, some are not.

Advanced charmers have also beguiled lizards, crocodiles, turkeys, chickens, ducks, rabbits, guinea pigs, mice, and snakes.

BEE CALCULATING

Honeybees can pass a test in higher mathematics with flying colors.

THE SETUP

Honeybees fly miles every day gathering nectar, the raw material of honey. When they find a good source they fly back to the hive and communicate to other bees the location of the sweet stuff.

With a brain the size of the ball in a ballpoint pen, a honeybee figures how long a round trip from hive to flower will take, factoring in distance, wind resistance, and the weight of the nectar. You have to learn math but bees are born with higher math skills. Here's an amazing test you can give the bees.

Dissolve as much sugar as you can in a half cup of water. Put some of it in a dish and place it about 20 feet from a bee hive. The bees will soon find the bait. The next day, move the dish 25% farther from the hive. (It will now be 20 + 5 or 25 feet from the hive. Refill the dish when the sugar water is gone.) On the third day move the dish 25% farther than it was on the second day. (That is, 25 feet + 25% of 25, which is 6.25 feet, feet for a total of 31.25

feet.) Each day place the plate 25% farther from the hive than it was on the previous day. Do this at approximately the same time every day for at least a week. After a few days, the bees will be waiting for you at the new location.

INSIDER INFORMATION

The bees are doing a set of calculations known to mathematicians as a *geometric progression*. Figuring out a geometric progression requires more than simple addition or subtraction. A geometric progression is a sequence of numbers where each number changes by the same percentage from the one before it. If you don't know how to do fractions or calculate percentages, you won't know where to position the plate.

No one has discovered how bees know what they know. Maybe you'll be the one to find out.

A SWEET CHOICE

See if ants can tell a diet drink from the real thing.

THE SETUP

Manufacturers of diet soft drinks depend on fooling people. They are counting on the fact that drinks containing artificial sweeteners taste pretty much the same as those flavored with sugar. Ants don't seem to be as easily deceived as humans. Set up a taste test for ants and see for yourself.

You'll need two cans of the same kind of soda pop, a diet one with aspartame (NutraSweet) and a sugar-sweetened one. Find an anthill. This shouldn't be too hard—ants are everywhere. Put a few drops of each soft drink on a hard surface such as a concrete walkway, a rock, or a patio stone near the anthill. There should be at least six inches between

your two samples. Now wait. It won't be long before the first ant scouts discover your sweet temptations.

Ants definitely prefer the real thing. Within a few minutes, the word on the hill is that the sugared drink is the one to visit. Talk about effective advertising!

INSIDER INFORMATION

The molecules of natural sugars fit into an ant's taste receptors, which are located on its antennae and in its mouth. Ants don't have receptors that fit aspartame molecules so the artificial sweetener doesn't taste sweet to them. Since ants are not trying to lose weight, they correctly pass up the diet drink in favor of the one that will nourish them.

Ants, however, are not foolproof. They can be tricked by drinks sweetened with saccharine.

ALARMING BREATH

Your breath can frighten an entire community of ants.

THE SETUP

You don't have to huff and puff on an ant hill to get the ant's attention. Breathe gently on a single ant and the smell will terrorize her. In a short period of time she will communicate her extreme panic to the rest of the colony. They will charge to the rescue, searching frantically for the intruder with the unforgettable breath.

INSIDER INFORMATION

The carbon dioxide in human breath is detected by receptors in an ant's antennae. She perceives this as a threat and responds with a typical ant alarm reaction. This consists of erratic movements and an odor that she makes to alert the rest of the colony. Soldiers come to the strange breath scene and fan out in search of the intruder while other ants run around in panic. The soldiers are fully prepared to give up their lives in defense of their home. However, if no more bad breath attacks are launched in a minute or two, they will sound an "all clear" and everyone will return to normal activities.

HOT MUSIC

Calculate the air temperature with a cricket.

THE SETUP

On a warm summer night, you can use the sounds of crickets to figure out how hot it is. A digital watch or one with a second hand is the only tool you will need.

Count the number of cricket chirps you hear in fifteen seconds. Add thirty-seven to the number you get. This is the temperature in degrees Fahrenheit. The frequency of cricket chirping varies a little from species to species, but your calculation will be surprisingly accurate.

An assistant is helpful. Let one person concentrate on the counting while the other watches the watch.

INSIDER INFORMATION

Crickets are living thermometers because, like most insects, they are more active when it is hot. Very few bugs have "voices." Most make sounds by scratching or rubbing their legs or wings. Crickets create their chirps by scraping the cover of the left wing across the rough edges of their right wing cover. The warmer it is, the more often they rub and the higher the pitch of the sound.

It's only the male crickets that fiddle away the night. Their song is a mating call designed to attract the silent females, who listen with ears located near their knees.

The music played at yard parties is not restricted to crickets' songs. Their relatives, grasshoppers and katydids, serenade, too. Katydids make music the same way as crickets. Grasshoppers, however, fiddle by rubbing their hind legs against their front wings. These songs can also be used to tell the temperature, but the math is complicated. (Use crickets. It's a lot easier.)

FLIRTING WITH FIREFLIES

Trick a firefly into seeking a flashlight as a mate.

THE SETUP

A firefly's flashing light is its language of love. Fireflies mate on summer nights. The female, who prefers not to fly, attracts a mate by flashing her light. A cruising male recognizes the signal from a female of his species and answers it. Seeing his response, the female

flashes again. The male flies closer and closer, repeating his flirtatious flashes. The two-way conversation continues until the male lands near the female.

You, too, can flirt with a male firefly. (In fact, it's a good way to catch one.) Here's how to speak "firefly" with a penlight, a very small flashlight. Look for the light of a flying male. One of the most common species has a J-shaped flight path and flashes about every six seconds. The female of this species waits two seconds before flashing back.

When you see a flying male's light, count off two seconds (one chimpanzee, two chimpanzee) and then hold your flashlight near the ground and flash it for one second. Once you have attracted his attention, keep flashing like this and he will come right to you—maybe even land on your hand.

There are thousands of species of fireflies, more than 200 in North America alone. Each one has a unique pattern of flashing and flying for each sex.

INSIDER INFORMATION

First of all, fireflies are not really flies, they are beetles. Most of their life is spent as immature grubs (larva). They only live two weeks as flashing adults, during which time their only mission is to find a mate. They produce a chemical reaction in their abdomens that releases energy in the form of a cold light. In fact, fire is another chemical reaction that produces light, but eighty percent or more of the energy released is heat, which would cook the creator if critters tried making light with fire. In contrast, ninety-eight percent of the energy released by fireflies is light! And that's cool! While many other animals produce light, the firefly is the only one that blinks.

On very hot nights a firefly Romeo is in a little more of a hurry. Like other insects, fireflies are more active when the temperature increases. This is easy to see with a

warm water

Flashes every 8 seconds   Flashes every 4 seconds

captured firefly. Catch one and put it in a glass jar with holes punched in the top. Time the seconds between flashes. Then place the jar in a bowl. Pour water that is warmer than the air around the jar until it is covered halfway. Don't use water any hotter than you can put your hand into. If you do, you will get no flashes—just dead bugs.

When the air in the jar has had time to heat up, time the flashes again. A firefly flashes about every eight seconds on cool summer evenings and every four seconds on hot nights.

When you have finished studying your captive firefly, be sure to release it.

FIDDLING FOR WORMS

A technique for attracting real creeps.

THE SETUP

Worms spend their days underground. At night they come out to munch on grass, which is why some people call them night crawlers. That's also why we say, "The early bird catches the worm." If you want to catch worms you have to get up early—before they go back into their burrows.

There is, however, a way to get worms to come out during the day. It's called fiddling. A worm fiddle is made of two sticks each about a foot and a half long.

To make your worm fiddle, ask an adult to carve a point at the end of one stick. Then have him or her cut notches every few inches along the length of the other stick.

point   FIDDLESTICKS

notches

about 18 inches

Drive the pointed end of the first stick into the ground.

Begin your worm serenade by drawing the notched stick, like a violin bow, across the stake in the ground. The bumping of the notches creates a rhythmic vibration below the ground. Continue your fiddling for five or six minutes. If you don't get results in ten minutes, move to another spot. The best places for a worm concert are lawns that are moist from a recent rain or watering.

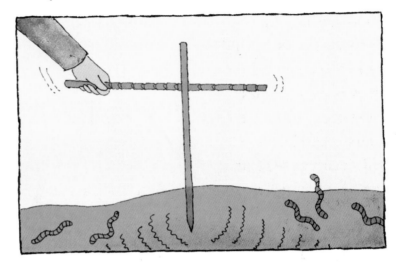

INSIDER INFORMATION

Worms don't have ears but they sense danger when they feel vibrations. Most of the danger for a worm comes from above (remember the early bird), so surface vibrations cause them to seek the safety of their burrow. However some dangers, such as moles, lurk in the soil. Worm fiddling sets up underground vibrations, tricking the worms into surfacing.

Charles Darwin, the noted nineteenth-century naturalist, had his own version of worm fiddling. He put a flowerpot with worms and soil on his piano. When he wanted to amuse guests, he played rhythmic bass notes on the piano. It was an odd tune but the worms danced to it. Modernizing

his parlor trick for the twentieth century, we used a rock-and-roll bass pattern on an electronic keyboard and got the same results from our wrigglers as Darwin got from his.

THE THOUSAND FOOT WORM

Listen to the sound of an earthworm walking.

THE SETUP

When you think about worms, you think wiggle, not walk. But they have hundreds of little foot-like bristles called setae that propel them through the dirt.

You can hear an ordinary earthworm marching along if you place it on a piece of construction paper. You will have to listen closely, of course, because these "feet" are very little. If you have trouble hearing the worm walking, roll a piece of paper into a cone and use is as a hearing aid. Put the small end near your ear and the wide end directly above the worm.

ANOTHER TIP

If your worm is not very active, place the paper in a well-lit spot and the worm will start searching for shade.

INSIDER INFORMATION

Not only can you hear the setae moving, you can feel them. Worms may be round but they have a definite underside. Run your finger gently back and forth on a worm. The side that has the most resistance is the underside. Each segment has four pairs of setae. With a hand lens, you can see them. A full grown earthworm has between 100 and 150 segments. That means almost a thousand marching "feet."

The worm uses the setae for traction as it pushes through the soil. When it is attacked, it digs them into the tunnel walls and hangs on for dear life. You must be careful not to yank on a worm to get it out of the ground. It will break in half before it will let go.

An earthworm has no eyes, eats dirt, and breathes through its skin. That doesn't sound like an important critter. But think again. Without earthworms, the soil would be so compact that plants would die. It takes a whole lot of worms to be gardeners to the world. An acre of soil may contain more than a million of them. If all the worms were gathered up, they would weigh ten times the total weight of the entire human population. Or, put another way, that's sixty percent of the weight of all living animals on earth!

When you are finished listening to worms, remember to return them to the place you found them. Don't just dump them on the lawn. They may have trouble finding their way back to burrows.

STRUGGLING MUSICIAN

Play music for a spider and see it come running.

THE SETUP

The original web surfer had to have been a spider. For millions of years spiders have been zooming around their wheel-like webs. You can get one of these eight-legged hunters to come scampering to you if you play music that sounds sweet to an arachnid.

To make the good vibrations, you need a tuning fork. (You can probably borrow one from your music teacher or your science teacher.) A tuning fork that vibrates about two hundred times a second is the perfect lure, although a fork that vibrates between ninety and five hundred times a second will also work.

Grasp the fork by the handle and strike it against something solid, such as a piece of wood. Then hold one of the prongs of the humming fork against the web and watch. The spider will rush to the fork.

INSIDER INFORMATION

A spider's web is a trap designed to catch flies and other insects. It's made of two types of silk. The circular strands are coated with an arachnid "glue"—which holds insects that fly into it. The strands that form the spokes of the wheel are not sticky. They are the aerial highways on which the spider travels to its struggling prey so that it can deliver a fatal bite.

Once it has spun its web, the spider patiently waits in the center. When something becomes entangled, the spider identifies the struggler by the vibrations it sends along the strands. A fly's wings vibrate at about two hundred times a second. And since a fly is a tasty treat for a spider, this frequency causes the spider to run down the web. Your tuning fork, vibrating at the same frequency as a buzzing fly, fools the spider.

Spiders are so tuned in to web vibrations they can even tell what kind of prey is trapped. You can see this by watching the way the spider approaches the struggling bug. A fly, which can't hurt the spider, brings the hungry hunter quickly and directly. When responding to a wasp, which is dangerous, the spider moves more slowly and cautiously so that it can zero in on the head and avoid being stung.

A SIGHT FOR SORE EYES

Staring at a waterfall makes you see trees rise up.

THE SETUP

First, find a waterfall. After you've admired the beauty of this natural phenomenon, create another one with your own eyes. Stare at the waterfall for about thirty seconds. Then shift your gaze to the nearby trees on a bank next to the falls. The trees will appear to move upwards. This illusion is not limited to trees. You can even move mountains.

INSIDER INFORMATION

In your eyes there are pairs of receptors that track motion.

Receptors for downward motion are paired with receptors for upward motion. When you look at a waterfall the downward-motion receptors are fired. Stare long enough and these receptors get tired. When you shift your gaze to a stationary object, these tired downward-motion receptors no longer fire. Strange but true, when one member of paired receptors is not firing, the other is activated even though nothing is moving. In this case, the upward-motion receptors are free to fire and you perceive motion when there is none.

If you're a city kid you can still have this uplifting experience by looking at artificial waterfalls or fountains.

You can also try this from inside your own personal waterfall—the shower. Gaze at the falling drops, then watch the rising tide in your soap dish.

GOO TO GO

Use the sticky goo from a pine tree to propel sticks across a pond.

THE SETUP

Pines and other evergreen trees produce a thick, sticky material called resin. To build an amazing racing boat, you'll need to collect a big blob of this resin. Check out nearby pine trees, and see if one has had a recent injury. If it has, you'll find dried, whitish gum on the trunk. This is the resin that you need. If you can't find an injured tree, pull off a small branch where it attaches to the trunk. Soon goo will ooze out of the wound. Take a small stick and collect a gob of goo on the end of it. (Be careful not to get any on your clothes or skin. It's hard to remove without using turpentine.) This goo stick is your racer and it is now all fueled up and ready to go.

Find a large puddle or pond and place the stick in the water with the

gooey end nearest the shore. The resin racer will shoot forward, without a push from you, sailing across the water at a steady pace.

If you have a friend with you, launch a resin-powered boat race.

INSIDER INFORMATION

The stick moves, but the propellant is not really the resin. It's the water itself. The molecules on the water's surface cling together like a skin. The force holding water molecules together at the surface is called the surface tension. Pine resin forms a film on the water breaking surface tension for an instant. The water's surface repairs itself, creating a turbulence which pushes the stick forward. Since the resin doesn't dissolve in water, the process is repeated over and over. This series of little pushes moves your boat steadily toward the finish line.

SLIME MOLD RACES

Stage one of the world's slowest races with mysterious creeping blobs.

THE SETUP

When people first saw slime molds they thought they were aliens from outer space. But these unidentified growing objects turned out to be a remarkable living thing. For a long time scientists didn't know how to classify them. But they were so entertaining that people kept them as pets. They even held slime mold races.

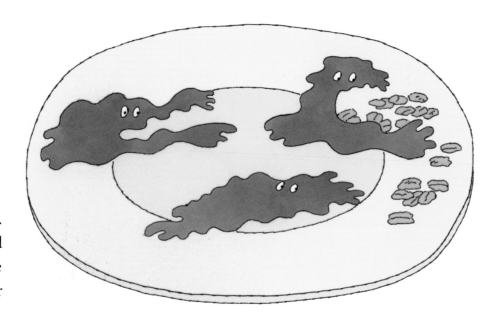

If you'd like to try, collect some slime mold from the woods. The best places to find slime molds are inside rotting logs and under the leaf litter on the forest floor. Look for a blob of yellowish goo that may have veins in it like a leaf. (There's little doubt why "slime" is its first name.) Pick it up in a plastic bag or small container. Don't worry about being "slimed." It's disgusting looking but harmless.

The race course can be a dinner plate. Put two or more small blobs of slime mold on one side of the plate. At the finish line, the other side of the plate, put some pieces of dry oatmeal, which is one of their favorite foods. With a speed approaching that of a snail, your slimy competitors will creep toward their reward. The pulsating slime mold engulfs the oatmeal like a giant amoeba.

INSIDER INFORMATION

Slime molds are truly weird. For starters, they have eighteen different sexes. They are not plants. They're not animals. And they're not fungi. But at different times during their bizarre life cycle they have characteristics of each of these living things. Scientists finally decided that they belonged in a separate kingdom called Protoctista.

Slime molds are still very much a mystery. But they sure are fun to play with.

SLUDGE BUSTERS

Clean up an oil spill by souping up nature's sanitation squad.

THE SETUP

An oil tanker on the rocks is not the only source of environmental contamination. Every day millions of cars, especially old ones, drip oil on roads and driveways. Rain washes these pollutants into the surrounding soil. If you look around your neighborhood you will probably find a small unsightly oil spill that is polluting the soil. This is your golden opportunity to help clean up the environment!

Get some liquid plant fertilizer—one that contains nitrogen. If the polluted soil is hard packed, break it up with garden tools so air can get into it. Spray or sprinkle the fertilizer on the sludge until the soil is dampened. **Be sure to wash your hands after you work around oil spills.**

It only takes a minute or two to pollute the environment but it's going to take longer to clean it up. You should start to see a difference after two weeks. If all the oil isn't gone, repeat the fertilizer treatment.

INSIDER INFORMATION

A spoonful of soil has been estimated to contain five billion bacteria. Some of these happen to like oil as food. At nature's pace it would take decades for them to eat your oil spill. If you can encourage their appetite, however, they will eat faster and clean up an oil spill quickly. The nitrogen in fertilizer stimulates the appetite of the sludge busters so they eat more. They digest the gooey oil, producing non-polluting carbon dioxide and water as waste products.

Using microorganisms to restore natural environmental conditions is called bioremediation. The first time it was used on a large scale was after the huge 1989 *Exxon Valdez* oil spill in Alaska. Of all the methods environmentalists tried to clean up the beaches, the most effective one was spraying them with ordinary farm fertilizer. Two weeks after treatment, scientists observed the area from a helicopter. Much to their surprise, the fertilized beaches looked clean.

Of course, not all soil bacteria have a taste for oil. There are specialists that thrive on a strict diet of petroleum. Bioremediation companies sell packages of oil eaters. They also sell bacteria to eat radioactive waste, sewage, and garbage. They have discovered microbes that can clean up over ninety percent of all hazardous chemical substances. The new science of bioremediation gets the job done better, faster and cheaper.

FLYING SAUCER

Send a paper plate racing up a kite string.

THE SETUP

Go fly a kite! It's fun. You can make it even more of an adventure with a line traveler. Use a paper plate and you've got a genuine flying saucer.

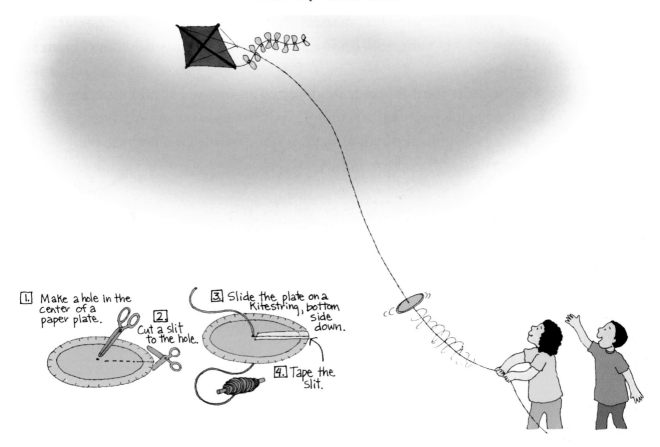

Aside from the paper plate you will need a pair of scissors and some tape. Unless you can tie your kite to something while you prepare for the launch, you had better enlist the help of an assistant.

Using the points of the scissors, make a small hole (a little bit bigger than the diameter of the string) in the exact center of the plate. Cut a slit from the edge of the plate to the hole. Slide the plate on the kite string with the bottom of the plate facing toward the ground. Tape the slit closed. Make sure the plate slides easily on the string.

Push the plate up the kite string until the plate catches the wind. It will travel up the string till it hits the kite. Sometimes, if the plate blows against the string, its journey is interrupted. When the wind shifts, your flying saucer continues climbing.

INSIDER INFORMATION

Line travelers, or kite ferries, as some people call them, are as old as kite flying, which is an ancient sport. Over the years kite fliers have invented some very clever variations.

Sometimes they put a stop, such as a cork, partway up the string. One kind of traveler releases a parachute when it hits the stop. Another has a trigger mechanism that collapses a sail and sends the kite ferry back down the line.

Kite shops sell travelers in many different styles including airplanes and butterflies. We think its more fun to invent your own.

One of the best things about a paper plate traveler is the puzzled look of passersby as they try to identify your very identifiable flying object. It is easier to believe in a flying saucer than a flying paper plate.

ANTI-GRAVITY GIZMO

Stay dry under an upside down container of water.

THE SETUP

You can't say there are no strings attached to this trick. Strings help you create a force greater than gravity. Take a quart-sized disposable plastic container and make three evenly spaced holes near the rim. Cut three two-foot lengths of string. Slip a piece of strong string through each hole and tie it securely. Knot the loose ends together. This is your anti-gravity gizmo. Fill it half-full of water. Swing the container back and forth like a pendulum, building up speed and the length of the swing. Your goal is to make a complete circle. The container will be upside down some of the time but the water will not fall out. Keep it moving and stay confidently dry.

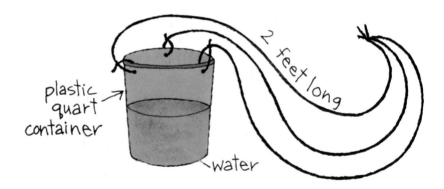

plastic quart container

water

2 feet long

INSIDER INFORMATION

There are two forces acting on the container. First, you exert a force to move the container away from you in a straight line. Second, the strings exert a force to prevent this from happening and pull the container toward your hand. The result of these two forces is that the container makes a circular path at the end of the string.

CAUTION!
Before you start swinging, make sure no one is standing too closely.

The combination produces a centrifugal, or away-from-the-center force, on the water inside the container, pressing it against the bottom. When the container is upside-down, you have obviously created an anti-gravity force that is stronger than gravity.

GRAVEYARD BEACH?

Test a beach and discover where it came from.

THE SETUP

It takes millions of years to make a beach. Those tiny grains of sand were once something else. Some are minerals that were originally part of larger rocks. Some are minerals that used to be part of living things. Some are even from outer space (check it out in the Cosmic Sand activity on page **89**). Some beaches have sand from only one source while others contain sand from a variety of sources.

One of the most common kinds of sand is made of limestone, known to scientists as calcium carbonate. The sources of limestone are shells and skeletons of marine life. If you want to know whether you are walking on the remains of dearly departed sea critters, test for limestone. To detect the limestone, you'll need distilled white vinegar and a paper cup or some other kind of small container. Put some sand in the bottom of the container. Pour in enough vinegar to cover the sand. Watch for bubbles. If they appear you know that your beach is a graveyard.

INSIDER INFORMATION

This test takes advantage of the fact that calcium carbonate reacts with acids. Vinegar is an acid—although a very weak one. However it is powerful enough to react with limestone.

When it does, carbon dioxide gas bubbles to the surface. The other kinds of sand don't react this way, so this is the acid test for limestone!

In nature, slightly acidic water dissolves limestone. Sometimes these limestone-water solutions drip into caves and the water evaporates, leaving behind stalagmites and stalactites made of calcium carbonate.

KNEAD A BALLOON?

Sand becomes an amazing plastic material inside a balloon.

THE SETUP

Make a sandbag. This is most easily done with a balloon. Take a funnel or a piece of paper rolled up like a funnel and stick it into the neck of the balloon. Pour in enough sand to almost fill the balloon. If the sand stops running into the balloon before the balloon is filled, squeeze it to let out air. Knead the balloon a few times to get the feel of the dry sand.

NOTE

If you don't have a balloon, you can try this with a plastic bag.

Now, pour enough water into the balloon to cover the sand. Again, you may have to release an air lock. Tie a knot in the end of the balloon. Squeeze the balloon a few times. The sand doesn't feel like it did before, does it? It is a plastic material now that is fun to knead.

1. Fill the balloon with sand.

2. Add water to cover the sand.

INSIDER INFORMATION

A mound of sand is made up of tiny rock crystals that are piled on top of one another in no real order. The spaces between the grains are filled with air. When you pour water over the grains, the water flows around the grains replacing the air.

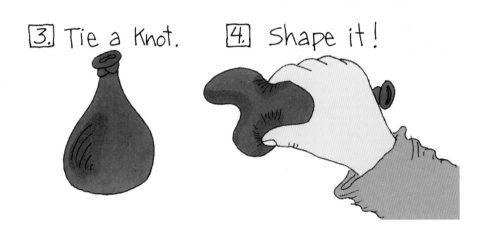

3. Tie a knot.

4. Shape it!

But water does what air can't. It lubricates the sand crystals. This allows the grains to move closer together and become densely packed.

Wet sand is a plastic—a material that is easily molded. Knead your sandbag and see all the shapes you can make. As every sand-castle builder knows, wet sand holds its shape even without a balloon.

A substance that allows a non-plastic to become a plastic is called a plasticizer. In this case, water is the plasticizer. Do you think another lubricant, such as salad oil, can do the same job? Experiment and find out.

FLIPPING SKIPPING STONES

Hard-packed sand puts a new spin on the skipping stone.

THE SETUP

Almost everyone has skipped stones across water. The best stones for throwing are oval flat ones about two or three inches long. The best throwing motion is side arm, snapping the wrist just before the release. The idea is to put a spin on the stone as it flies off roughly parallel to the water. In a good throw, the stone skips or hops repeatedly along the surface of the water. The world record is twenty-four hops. But records, of course, can be broken. Go for it!

If the water is rough when you're at the beach, try skipping stones on the sand. Near the water's edge, the sand is wet and hard packed. This is the perfect surface for the land version of this sport. Throw a stone there exactly as you would on water.

You'll notice that stones skip differently on sand. On water, the first hop is the longest; the others get progressively shorter. On sand, the first hop is short, followed by a much longer hop similar to the first hop on the water. Additional hops alternate between short and long. The evidence of this unusual pattern is marked in the sand.

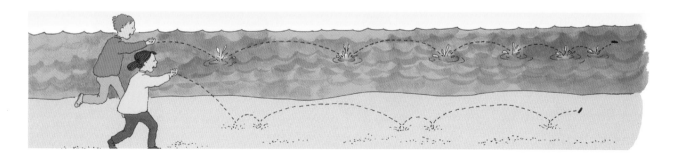

INSIDER INFORMATION

Friction causes the stone to flip over when it hits the sand, so the short hop is not a skip, it's a flip. Friction is a force between two surfaces moving against each other. It slows down motion. There's not as much friction on water so the stone doesn't flip. Instead, the back edge builds a wave in front of it, which gives added lift to its flight. As a result, you'll get a lot more skips on water.

COSMIC SAND

Find meteorites at the beach.

THE SETUP

Meteors, or shooting stars, are rocks from space that burn when they enter the earth's atmosphere. If they are not completely vaporized, as most are, and if they survive to land on the surface of the earth they are called meteorites. Finding a large meteorite is very difficult because they are extremely rare. But you can find tiny ones because meteorites are constantly falling on the earth's surface. They are everywhere, but the easiest place to collect them is at the beach.

Your high-tech meteorite collection kit consists of a magnet inside a plastic bag. Drag it through the sand. The tiny particles will stick to the magnet through the bag. To collect them, carefully turn the bag inside out so that the particles are trapped in the bag. Remove the magnet and shake the particles into another plastic bag. Continue "mining" the beach until you have as many space rocks as you want. Congratulations! You now own some extraordinarily ancient stuff. Your sand may be 4.6 billion years old. That's a billion years older than any earth rock.

INSIDER INFORMATION

The reason that you use a magnet as a meteorite collector is because meteorites are mostly iron. And, as you probably know, iron is attracted to magnets. All of the material you collected is not, necessarily, from outer space. Scientists have estimated, however, that about twenty

percent of the magnetic material on the earth's surface is from the cosmos. If you want to make sure that you have collected some cosmic sand, look at it with a strong magnifying lens or, better yet, under a microscope. Meteorite particles are nearly perfect spheres although in time some of them may be worn down by erosion and become irregular in shape.

Why are meteorites usually round? When meteorites enter the earth's atmosphere, air resistance causes them to heat up just like a reentering space ship. The iron becomes red-hot and melts. Liquids become spheres when they are falling freely. (Falling raindrops are spheres, not teardrop-shaped.) By the time the meteorite particles hit the ground, they have cooled and hardened in their spherical shape.

If you're not near a beach you can still collect cosmic sand. The roof of a house is a large surface area and a lot of meteorite dust lands on it. When it rains, the dust is washed into the rain gutters. If you place a plastic-bag-covered magnet in the stream of water that gushes out of the downspout, the magnetic dust will cling to it. The best time to collect the dust is as soon as water starts to flow from the roof after several days of dry weather.

3. GOING PUBLIC

There is some science you just can't discover unless you go public. You can detect the sway of a skyscraper only in a skyscraper's bathroom. You need your friends at school to discover why there are no singing weight lifters. And you need certain equipment you can find in school, like a public address system, to listen to your muscles.

All you need is an inquisitive mind and an adventurous spirit and a desire to visit public places. Besides school and a skyscraper this chapter has discoveries to be made in restaurants, elevators, libraries, amusement parks, playgrounds and planes, trains and automobiles. Fascinate friends, impress parents—and even teach your teachers. If knowledge is power, you can be a mighty source.

The world is filled with opportunities for discovery. Most people miss them, but you won't. You'll be in the right place at the right time with the right information—this book is the key!

MIRACLE AT THE MALL

Amaze a friend by extracting cola from an uncola drink.

THE SETUP

Pull a fast one on a friend the next time you're in a fast food restaurant. When your friend orders a drink, order a drink that's the same size but a different color. In other words, if your friend orders a clear drink, you order a cola. Let your friend carry the food to the table while you carry the drinks. Of course you'll have to make a stop to get straws. Unwrap the straws and stick one down to the bottom of each beverage. Put a finger over the end of each straw and pull them both out of the cups. You will be holding a sample of soda in each straw. Switch the straws—put the one with the uncola sample into the cola and vice versa. Keep your fingers tightly on the tops of the straws until both straws touch the bottoms of the cups. The setup is now complete and you can treat the cups as if there's nothing amiss.

Before your friend has a chance to drink the clear beverage, say, "Oh look, they've gotten some cola in your drink. Let me see if I can get it out." Reach over and wiggle the straw, pretending to gather up the contaminating cola. Then put your finger on the top of the straw and lift it out. Hold the straw over an empty cup and release your finger. Miraculously, or so it seems, cola runs out of the straw.

As in any situation, things can go wrong. If your friend starts drinking before you are able to work wonders, don't worry. Chances are he or she won't notice the change in flavors. In spite of what the advertisers say, one sweet fizzy soft drink tastes very much like another. Besides, you've got a back up—your drink. Just say, "Oh look, they've got some uncola in my cola…"

INSIDER INFORMATION

This is no miracle. This is science in action. Air pressure keeps the soda in the straw. When the straw is sitting in the drink the level of the soda in the straw is always exactly the same as the level of soda in the cup. The atmosphere presses equally on the surface of the liquid in the cup and in the straw. Cover the top of the straw and you cut off atmospheric pressure from above. The soda doesn't run out because the pressure on the bottom of the straw is now greater than gravity.

You might wonder why the cola in the straw doesn't mix with the uncola when you switch straws. It will … eventually. The reason it takes a long time to mix is that the only place where the two liquids are in contact with each other is at the end of the straw and this is a very small area. This gives you plenty of time to get your act together.

STRAW-WRAPPER SNAKE

Turn a soda straw wrapper into a writhing snake.

THE SETUP

To create this life-like creature you need a soda straw in a paper wrapper. Hold the wrapped straw in a vertical position and grasp the top end between your thumb and index finger. Slide your fingers down the straw. The wrapper will split at the top end and the paper will be scrunched together at the bottom. Pull off the wrapper, keeping it in its tightly compressed form. This is your new pet. Put it on a waterproof surface where it has room to grow.

Now dip the end of the straw into a beverage and cover the top of the straw with your finger to collect some liquid. You want to turn the straw into a dropper. You can control the amount of liquid that runs out of the straw by regulating the amount of air you let into it. Practice until you can release one drop at a time. Put a drop of liquid on the paper "snake." Water makes the snake move and grow. It will wriggle and squirm until it is completely wet.

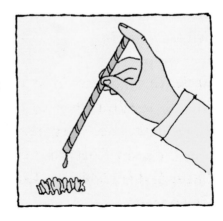

INSIDER INFORMATION

Paper is made up of thousands of tiny cellulose fibers. The fibers are bent when the paper is scrunched. Paper absorbs water easily. When this happens the fibers swell and straighten out.

GRASPING AT STRAWS

Others may grasp at straws, but you can hold one with a completely open hand.

THE SETUP

This is something you can do to amuse your dining companions in a restaurant that provides straws with paper wrappers. Tear off one end of the wrapper and push it up enough so that you can grasp the straw at the bottom. With your other hand, rapidly slide the paper wrapper up and down the straw. Five to ten times should be enough.

Remove the wrapper. Hold the hand that moved the wrapper in the position you would use to karate chop a brick. Place the straw against your open palm and let go with the other hand. Ta da! The straw sticks without any grasping.

INSIDER INFORMATION

You'll get a charge out of this explanation. In fact, by rubbing the straw and paper together you create an electric charge on both. Electricity produced by rubbing is called *static electricity*. Tiny negatively charged particles, known as *electrons*, rub off the paper wrapper onto the plastic straw. Since the straw now has an excess of electrons, it becomes negatively charged. The paper, having lost electrons, is now positively charged.

Electric charges are either positive or negative. Opposite charges attract each other. Like charges repel each other.

Your hand has no charge. But when you bring the negatively charged straw near it, the electrons on your skin are pushed away from the surface, giving a slight positive charge to your hand. The straw is now attracted and sticks.

The straw will continue to stick as long as it remains charged. It will lose its charge as it leaks its extra electrons to your hand or to the air. Water molecules attract electrons. If both the weather and your hand are dry you will be more successful than if your hand is moist and the humidity is high.

THE TILTED TOILET

How to detect the swaying motion of a skyscraper.

THE SETUP

Skyscrapers used to be called cloud scratchers. That's a good description for them because the tops of these tall buildings move back and forth in the wind.

Even on the top floors of a skyscraper, which sway the most, you can't sense the motion. But you are moving—and you can prove it. Go to a restroom and look in the toilet. Believe it or not, a toilet can be a scientific instrument. The water gently tilts from one side of the bowl to the other as the building sways.

Keep this discovery to yourself if you don't want to explain why you've been toilet gazing.

INSIDER INFORMATION

Things are not always what they seem to be. It appears that the water in the toilet is tilting from side to side. But it isn't moving at all. The toilet is moving around the water because the toilet is attached to the building and the building is swaying. Water, like all liquids, *always* has a surface that is parallel with the earth's surface. In other words, it is always level.

Modern skyscrapers are built to withstand forces. They are flexible enough to sway when the wind blows or an earthquake shakes them. The building's motion absorbs enough of the impact to prevent damage. In a really tall building the movement is not insignificant. The Sears Tower sways about six inches off center at the observation deck on the 103rd floor.

LEADFOOT AND LIGHTFOOT

See how elevator walking affects your weight.

THE SETUP

This is not a hands-on activity. We'd call it feet-on. Walk back and forth in a high-speed elevator as it accelerates upward. As you lift one foot, the other feels as if it is supporting more than its usual load. You'll also find that it's harder to jump when you're going up.

Going down, you'll no longer feel like a leadfooted walker but more like a lightfooted one. As in the upward journey, you can only feel these changes when the elevator is speeding up.

These feelings are not imaginary. The changes in weight can actually be measured. Bring along a bathroom scale. Stand on it and discover the ups and downs of weight watching.

INSIDER INFORMATION

When the elevator is rising, it is pushing up with a force that is greater than your weight. You feel as if you are heavier and so you push downward with a greater force than normal when you walk. The increased force is measured on the scale as an increase in your weight. The reverse happens when you are descending. The acceleration of the falling elevator is subtracted from the pull of gravity making you feel and walk lighter.

LIE OF THE LAND

Confuse a compass in the library.

THE SETUP

A library is a good place for finding things, but you wouldn't need a compass there. In fact, a library security system can make a compass monumentally unreliable.

To discover what a mess you can make of your compass, take it to a library that has a magnetic security system. You can recognize this type of security system by the archway at the exit. Inside the library, look at your compass and make a mental note of where north is. Then take your compass to the front desk and ask the librarian to stroke it over the device the library uses to prepare the books for checkout. Look at your compass again. The north-seeking end of the needle now points south. Many stores have magnetic security systems if your library doesn't.

Don't use your lying compass to find your way home.

INSIDER INFORMATION

You can find your way with a compass because the marked end of the needle always points north. The reason it does this is because it is a magnet and so is the earth. The north-seeking pole of the compass needle is attracted to the earth's North Pole.

Some libraries put a strip of metal that has been encoded with a magnetic signal in each book. When the detector in the archway reads this signal, an alarm rings, which can be very embarrassing. Part of the checkout process includes stroking the book over a strong permanent magnet. The magnet scrambles the signal in the strip so that it doesn't trigger the alarm. When you return the book, the librarian uses another device to demagnetize the strip, which reactivates the encoded signal.

The checkout magnet is so powerful that it can scramble the smaller permanent magnet that is a compass needle. This is not a random scramble. The magnetic field does a 180° flip. Librarians treat the super magnet with respect. It can erase magnetic tape, both audio and video, and damages mechanical watches.

Your compass is not broken. You can get it back on track with another pass over the super magnet.

BE A STILLIE PRODUCER

Make the opposite of a movie.

THE SETUP

A moving picture is an illusion. It is nothing more than a rapid sequence of still pictures. When the pictures are flashed at a rate of twenty-four images per second, you can't see the individual pictures. Instead, you see the sequence as continuous motion.

It is possible to make the opposite of a movie—a series of movements that produce a still picture. What do you call the opposite of a movie? We came up with "stillie" but maybe you can do better.

You will need:

- a slide projector or an overhead projector
- slide with an image on it
- sheet of paper
- yardstick
- overhead transparency film
- stiff piece of white paper or a foam board

You will need to project an image. A slide projector or an overhead projector will do. You don't however, need a screen. Position the projector so that the light beam goes out a window or through an open doorway. You want the light to go off into the distance and not fall on a surface.

Put a slide in the projector. Hold a piece of paper in the beam of light about five feet from the projector. Have a friend focus the image on the paper. Remove the paper. You can't see any picture now. But it's there. Prove it by rapidly waving a yardstick up and down at the same spot you held the piece of paper.

The image appears, hanging in thin air.

INSIDER INFORMATION

If you hold the yardstick in the light beam, you will see a very thin band of the image on the stick. By rapidly moving the yardstick up and down, you produce a series of bands, each showing a different part of the picture. After an image disappears, your eye retains it for about 1/30 of a second. If the yardstick makes a sweep from top to bottom in 1/30 of a second there are enough bands to fuse into a single image. By waving the stick up and down at least sixteen times a second, the fused image remains visible.

CAUTION!

Projectors use strong lights. Don't look directly at the light or you may damage your eyes.

When you wave the yardstick up and down you are creating a flat surface. What if you move it with a circular motion? You will get a distorted image. The picture will curve as if it were being projected onto a globe.

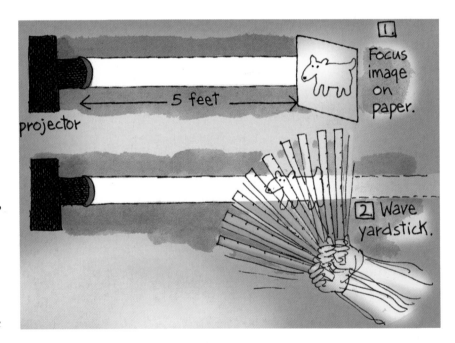

You can also make an imaginary cylinder from a flat circle. Draw a circle on overhead transparency film. Set up the experiment the same way as you did for the yardstick activity. This time, instead of a yardstick, use a stiff piece of white paper or foam board. Hold the paper or foam board in the light beam with the flat side toward the projector. Move it rapidly toward and away from the projector. Your motion makes the flat circle appear to be a cylinder.

LOONY TUNES

A computer monitor makes a rigid tuning fork wiggle weirdly.

THE SETUP

School is a good place to create this "metal bending" illusion because you are likely to find both a tuning fork and a computer monitor there. Borrow the tuning fork from the music room or from the science teacher. Take it to a computer monitor. Turn on the monitor and the computer. Create a white screen on the monitor by opening a new file.

Hold the tuning fork by its handle. Gently strike it against a desk to make it vibrate. Look at it as the tone sounds. Now move it in front of the monitor. Hold it vertically. The tines appear to be distorted with a wave-like motion. Hold it horizontally and you get a different effect—the tines appear to be vibrating slowly.

INSIDER INFORMATION

A computer monitor screen (or a television) looks like it is illuminated by a steady light but it's not. A tiny beam of light scans back and forth across the screen from top to bottom sixty times a second. Every point on the screen is illuminated sixty times each second. The rest of the time it is dark. But your eyes see this as a continuous light because they aren't sensitive enough to see such rapid flickering.

A rapidly flickering light is called a *strobe*. A strobe appears to slow down moving objects. When something moves in front of a strobe, the on-off flashes capture the object in multiple positions and it appears to be several objects instead of a single moving one.

A monitor is a complicated kind of strobe. Due to the scanning nature of the monitor's light, an additional illusion is created. This special effect is only visible when the tuning fork is held vertically and is vibrating faster than sixty times a second. It is especially visible when the vibrating frequency (measured in hertz) of the tuning fork is close to some whole number multiple of sixty. Then the solid metal of the tines appears to bend in a wave formation—and the waves appear to travel down the tines as the scanner moves from top to bottom. The multiple images of the vibrating tines are in different positions as the scanner moves down the screen. This causes the wave effect.

You can see a similar effect with a rubber band. Cut one open to make a rubber "string." Have a friend stretch it tightly and hold it vertically in front of a monitor. Pluck the "string" and watch what happens.

THE STRONG SILENT TYPE

Discover why there are no singing weight lifters.

THE SETUP

Have your gym teacher select an activity that requires upper body strength, such as push-ups, chin-ups, or weight lifting. Choose a song everyone knows and see if anyone is able to sing it while doing the chosen workout.

Instead of music, you'll get grunts.

INSIDER INFORMATION

When you want to lift a heavy weight, you need to tense the muscles in your chest and abdomen. You do this by holding your breath. It increases the pressure in your chest cavity and your ribs become a more stable platform for the muscles to pull against. This increases their lifting power. This strength enhancing technique is called the *Valsalva maneuver*.

During the Valsalva maneuver, a little flap called the epiglottis closes your windpipe. And the windpipe is directly related to your ability to sing because sounds are produced when air

moves past your vocal cords, which are located below the epiglottis. Since the epiglottis is closed when you are straining, no air can move. So you can't sing.

The song of strain is a grunt—a sound the dictionary says is "short, deep, and typical of pigs."

FALLING FOR BOYS

Most boys will fall for this trick but girls usually won't.

THE SETUP

This activity separates the boys from the girls. Do it with a large group and see what happens.

Each participant should kneel on the floor and bend forward with the elbows against the knees and the hands together in a praying position. Have an assistant stand a matchbox on end and place it in front of the fingertips. Everyone should go back to the original

kneeling position and clasp hands behind the back.

Now for the test. Each participant must lean forward and try and knock over the matchbox using only the nose.

Some participants will be able to knock over the matchbox. Some will fall on their face! In general, the boys will do most of the falling.

INSIDER INFORMATION

This is a balancing act. In order to keep from falling on your face, you have to keep your center of gravity from getting too far in front of your knees. In boys, the center of gravity is usually higher up than it is in girls. The males have more mass in their upper bodies than their lower bodies and this makes them somewhat top heavy. Girls have more of their weight in their hips. The heavier hips are a counterweight and allow females to lean out farther.

There will probably be exceptions in your test group. We've found that puberty is a big factor. In fact, this works really well with moms and dads. See if you can figure out why.

SMART BUBBLES

See bubbles avoid an electric shock.

THE SETUP

Begin your quest for smart bubbles by searching for a Van de Graaff generator. This machine, used to demonstrate electrostatic experiments, is often found in high school physics classrooms. If your school doesn't have one, perhaps your teacher can arrange to borrow one.

CAUTION!
Van de Graaff Generators can give you a shock. Do this with the help of an adult assistant.

When you've found a Van de Graaff generator, have your adult assistant turn it on. Blow a stream of soap bubbles toward it. They will be attracted to the negatively charged sphere until the lead bubble strikes it and pops. At this point, the others will turn tail and run away, as if they got the message "Electricity can be hazardous to your health."

INSIDER INFORMATION

If you think soap bubbles are smart, you may be a bubblehead. Obviously there is some other explanation for this unexpected bubble behavior. It's static electricity.

Here's what's happening. The Van de Graaff generator produces a strong electric field of force around itself by collecting electrons on its metal sphere. Since electrons are negatively charged particles, the electrostatic field of force is also negatively charged. When soap bubbles enter the field, their electrons move away from the generator because like charges repel each other. The side facing the generator becomes positively charged. Now the bubbles are attracted to the generator because opposites attract. When the first bubble strikes the generator, it instantly picks up electrons and becomes negatively charged for the rest of its extremely short life. But its influence extends after its bubble phase. When the lead bubble pops, droplets of the negatively charged soapy water spray onto the approaching bubbles. They in turn pick up the negative charge and are now repelled by the electric field.

MUSCLE TONES

Listen to the rumble, crackle, and pop of muscles.

THE SETUP

People have known about strange rumblings from inside the body for more than three hundred years—sounds that are different from the loud gurgles of the digestive tract. They heard them by putting their thumbs in their ears and clenching their fists. Try it. You, too, will hear faint rumbles and crunches. At first, no one knew these were the sounds of muscles working.

We have learned a lot about these sounds with the aid of modern technology. Scientists use an electronic stethoscope to hear muscle tones but you can use the microphone and speakers of a public address system.

Muscle sounds have been described as crackles, a series of clicks, and low rumbles. To hear them for yourself, have someone hold a two- to five-pound weight with an outstretched arm. (A weight makes the muscles work harder and maximizes their sounds.) Place a microphone against your assistant's biceps. You may have to move the microphone around to find the noisiest spot. Also, if your speakers are adjustable, set them to amplify the bass tones.

INSIDER INFORMATION

There are two reasons why it's hard to hear muscle tones without some electronic help. First, they aren't very loud. Second, their deep pitch is at the lower limit of human hearing. Although an ordinary stethoscope amplifies sound, we still miss many low frequencies. An electronic stethoscope doesn't, so it is able to pick up the muscle sounds. It makes them visible as lines on a screen.

Some animals hear low frequency sounds a lot better than humans. Sharks, for example. Recent studies have shown they are attracted to prey by the noise of their muscles, not their thrashing movements. That may be why they can locate even quietly swimming prey.

Sound travels much better in water than it does in air, so under water may be the best place to listen to your muscles. Submerge your head and open and close a hand near your ear. Now you can hear the sound of one hand clapping.

STRESS TEST

Two pairs of polarized sunglasses reveal hidden stresses.

THE SETUP

Lots of materials can get stressed out, and you know what happens then? Failure! Overstressed things tend to break. You can easily detect stress points in transparent plastic with polarized sunglasses.

Put on a pair of sunglasses. Hold the other pair in front of you and slowly rotate it clockwise. You will notice that there is a position where all the light is blocked and the lenses of the pair you are holding look black. Keep holding the sunglasses in this position.

Put a piece of transparent plastic in front of one of the lenses. (Good sources of plastic to stress test are jewel boxes for CDs, clear plastic forks or even torn plastic bags.) Look at areas that are bent, at edges, and at stamped designs. If you don't see any stress, apply some by bending, breaking, or tearing the plastic. In sunlight stressed areas will appear in a rainbow of colors with the most stressed areas appearing as black lines. Because the colors can interfere with the detection of the stresses, it is better to use a light source that is a single color, such as the sodium or mercury vapor bulbs in street lamps. Only the black stress lines will show up under these lights.

INSIDER INFORMATION

Finding hidden stresses may not seem like an earthshaking discovery to you but architects in California think it is. They worry about metal fatigue in the structures they design for earthquake zones. Before a design is finalized, a clear plastic model is subjected to forces similar to an earthquake and then examined with polarized lenses. The weak points in the model predict problems that could occur in a real building.

Materials that are not transparent can also be examined for stress—but not with polarized lenses. Airplanes and bridges, which can develop metal fatigue, are regularly inspected with X-rays.

QUICK COMEDOWN

Use a tiny dent to destroy the strength of a soda can.

THE SETUP

The thin wall of an empty aluminum soda can is strong enough to support your weight—if you weigh less than 250 pounds. However, it's only strong enough if your weight is evenly distributed on top of the can. You'll need a perfect can, too. One with no dents in it.

collapsing tool

Tap with this end.

This balancing act is a bit tricky. The easiest way to get up on the can is with the help of a couple of friends. Place one foot on top of the can. Hang onto your friends (always a good idea) and lift your other foot off the ground, gently transferring all your weight onto the can.

CAUTION!

Do this outside on a hard, level surface. Don't do this at home because you might slip off the can and send it—or yourself—rocketing into furniture or other breakable objects, including humans.

When you are balanced, have one of your friends tap the side of the can with the eraser end of a pencil. It doesn't take much of an effort. The can will instantly collapse. Talk about a quick comedown!

INSIDER INFORMATION

An aluminum can, with walls no thicker than two pieces of paper, can support eight thousand times its own weight. It is essential, however, that the center of the load be directly over the center of the can. Your weight may be heavy enough to cause the sides of the can to bulge. But it won't collapse as long as your weight is still evenly distributed.

A dent in the can creates a weak spot. Then the weight from above pushes the dent it further out of line and the can collapses into a nice flat pancake, ready for recycling.

Speaking of recycling, did you know that Americans use 100 billion aluminum beverage cans a year? That's one can a day for every man, woman, and child. You don't have to be a mathematician to see that it's important to recycle cans and reusing old cans is doubly good for the earth. This saves ninety-five percent of the energy it would take to manufacture new cans, plus we won't need to use aluminum ore to produce more cans.

SPIN DOCTOR

Speed up a merry-go-round by throwing your weight around.

THE SETUP

Get a high performance ride out of a playground merry-go-round—the kind you push. Beefing up the ride will take a few friends. (One for each triangular section of the merry-go-round.) Everybody needs to push, jumping on when the ride is moving as fast as you can get it to go. The riders should keep to the outside until your signal. Notice the speed before you do anything.

At the count of three, everyone should shift to the center. If you all move at the same time, the merry-go-round will spin faster.

INSIDER INFORMATION

A merry-go-round spins around a central post which is called the *axis of rotation*. The rate at which it spins is determined by the distribution of weight around the axis of rotation. The closer the weight is to the center, the faster the merry-go-round goes.

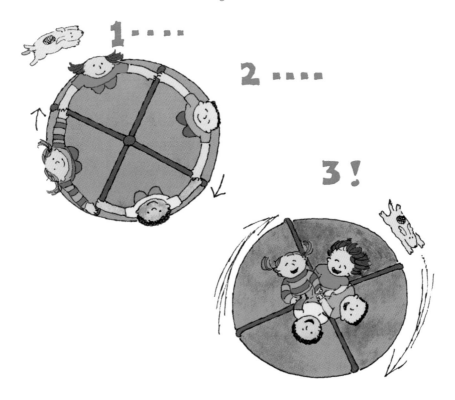

Spinning ice skaters take advantage of this physics principle. By pulling their arms close to their bodies they speed up and turn into whirling blurs. Gymnasts know the secret of rapid spinning, too. The tighter they tuck, the faster they can rotate and the more turns they can get into a flip.

SWING TIME

Discover which takes longer: swinging in a big arc or swinging in a little one.

THE SETUP

Take a guess. In a swinging contest who do you think would take longer to make two complete swings: a pumped-up high swinger or a gently swaying rider? You'd probably guess wrong. This is a no-win contest.

Some things just have to be seen to be believed. And this is one of them. You can use two swings side-by-side or a single swing to conduct the experiment. If you use two swings, it is important that they be the same length. It is not important that the swingers be the same weight. A watch that times seconds would be helpful. If one is not available you can count off the seconds by saying: One chimpanzee, two

chimpanzee, three chimpanzee, etc.

Get both swings going—one high and fast, the other slow and low. Quit pumping and let the swings move naturally. Time how long it takes for each rider to return to the starting place of the measurement and make one complete swing. There are no winners here. But, on the other hand, there are no losers either. Big arc swings and little arc swings take exactly the same amount of time.

INSIDER INFORMATION

To understand what is going on, you have to get physical. To a physicist, a swing is simply a pendulum. The time it takes to make one complete to-and-fro swing is called its period. The period of a pendulum is affected only by its length. The distance it moves or the weight it moves has absolutely no effect.

Before there were mechanical clocks, the Italian physicist Galileo discovered this law of pendulum motion. He noticed a swinging lamp in church and timed its period by using his pulse. He found that the period of the lamp remained the same as it slowly diminished the distance it swung. This seemingly useless bit of trivia was later used by clockmakers. Pendulums became the basis for measuring time. It's a good thing Galileo didn't get too excited by his discovery. If his heart has begun to beat faster and his pulse had speeded up, the march of science might never have been the same.

AIMLESS FUN

Experience the illusion of throwing a curve ball while remaining a straight shooter.

THE SETUP

A simple game of catch becomes a whole new ball game when you're going in circles. Try as you will, throwing the ball to a catcher isn't easy if you are on a merry go round.

Play catch with a friend when you are both on a moving merry go round. Aim carefully and throw. The ball will appear to curve away from your friend. It is helpful to have a retriever (human or canine) to get the "misses."

Another variation of aimless fun is a throw to a catcher standing a distance away from the merry go round. Again. A miss.

INSIDER INFORMATION

The path of the ball is determined by more than one factor. Take the first pitch—throwing to someone else on the merry go round. Your position relative to the catcher doesn't change. But you are both moving. When you release the ball, it travels away from you in a straight line. Your targeted catcher, however, is circling. In the time it takes the ball to reach the spot you aimed at, the catcher has moved. So the ball misses the target and appears to be traveling in a curved path. In reality, it's the background that's moving.

In the second pitch—thrown from a rotating merry go round to a stationary catcher—the ball has two forces operating on it which affect its path. One is the force you deliver with your mighty muscles. The other is delivered by the spinning merry go round. The two forces acting together throw off your throw.

To hit the target if you're going clockwise, aim to the right of a friend who's moving with you and to the left of a friend on the ground. With practice you can master merry go round catch.

RACING WITH THE MOON

Race the moon in a car or train and you'll never win ... or lose either.

THE SETUP

Look at the moon as you speed down the highway. You whiz by trees, houses, telephone poles, and people but you can't get ahead of the moon. Increasing your speed won't help at all. Neither will slowing down. The moon appears to be traveling along with you. And you can't shake it.

INSIDER INFORMATION

As you ride along, far away objects stay in view longer than nearby objects. At a distance of 239,000 miles from earth, the moon is definitely far away. So it is going to stay in your sight a very long time. You can't move far enough fast enough to change the angle of your view.

You can see this on a smaller scale on a playground. Position two friends, one behind the other in the middle of the playground. The farther apart they are from each other the better. Walk a path that is at right angles to an imaginary line connecting your friends, passing about ten feet in front of the closer one. Keep your head turned toward your friends as you walk. Your distant friend (a stand-in for the moon) will be in your line of sight much longer than your closer friend (a stand-in for the trees, houses, or telephone poles).

A lot of heavenly motion is actually going on while you are moon gazing. The earth is spinning on its axis making the moon rise and set. The moon is revolving around the earth, displaying different amounts of its illuminated surface over the course of a month. But neither of these motions is fast enough to make a difference in what you see when you look out your car window.

FALSE STARTS

You feel as if you're on the move, but it's only in your mind.

THE SETUP

Trains and planes have "windows of opportunity." Picture this. You are in a train waiting to leave the station. As you look out the window you see a moving train on the next track. However, it doesn't appear to be moving. Instead, you feel certain that *your* train is pulling out of the station. Uh-uh! Time for a reality check. One look at the platform and you can see that you're *not* going anywhere yet. But one more look at the other train and you will feel the illusion of motion again.

INSIDER INFORMATION

Your eyes are operating as they normally do as you view a moving object out the window of your stationary vehicle. They send information to the brain that lets you know something is in motion. But, because the moving object fills your field of vision, your brain is not getting all the information it needs to determine which object is moving: you or the train you see out the window. Normally some stationary object would give you an additional clue and your brain could make the correct decision. Without a clue, however, your brain is literally without a clue too. It often sends false signals that the motion is your own. It is easy to trick the brain when it expects to experience some motion. After all, that's why you are on the train in the first place—to go somewhere.

We have also had this illusion when looking out the window of a parked airplane. Instead of a passing train, the moving object that tricked us was a luggage carrier.

You may also experience this illusion in the IMAX theaters which surround you with a moving picture. The scenes of a roller coaster, dashing fire truck, or small plane were deliberately chosen to create the false start illusion and trick you into thinking that you are moving. Scientists call this little bit of brain confusion the *Duncker effect*, after the man who first described it.

NEW ANGLES ON FLIGHT

Measure changes in speed and altitude from your airplane seat.

THE SETUP

On your next airplane trip bring along about ten inches of string, a small weight (like a key or a washer) tied to the end of it, a protractor, and some tape. The protractor measures angles and is very similar to the device in "G" Whiz you used to measure G forces. Make sure you have a window seat.

While you're on the ground, tape the protractor, upside down, to the window with the flat edge parallel to the ground. Tape the string to the center so it hangs straight down, passing through the 90 degree mark.

Watch what happens as the plane starts accelerating during takeoff. Hold the string to measure the angle just before the wheels go up. (You suddenly feel the plane speed up with "wheels up.") Notice the string's position as you ascend to cruising altitude. When the string is again at 90 degrees you are at cruising altitude.

INSIDER INFORMATION

The angle of the string is a measure of the change in speed of the airplane and/or its tilt as it changes altitude. When there is no change in speed or altitude, the string hangs motionless at 90 degrees. This is in perfect agreement with Newton's First Law of Motion—there will be no change in the motion of the weight on the string unless acted upon by a force that comes from a change in speed or direction of the airplane. We found that the string was displaced between 15 and 20 degrees during take off and was a steady 10 degrees during the climb to cruising altitude. This is one cool way to play the angles when you fly!

BLOWN OUT OF PROPORTION

Discover what happens to a balloon in an airplane.

THE SETUP

The next time you go on an airplane bring along a balloon, a piece of string, and a marker pen. While you're waiting for takeoff, blow up the balloon. Inflate it about half way and knot the end. Wrap the string around the balloon. Make a mark on the string to indicate the diameter of the balloon. Also mark the balloon to show where the string was when you measured. You will need to measure in the same spot later.

When the plane has reached cruising altitude, measure the balloon again. You'll find that it has increased in size—just how much depends on your altitude at your take-off location and the amount of pressurization in the cabin. The balloon will show what your ears have registered all along—the air pressure has definitely decreased.

NOTE

If you don't have a balloon, just get a bag of chips at the airport and don't open the bag in the air. Just watch how the bag puffs up as you go up and deflates as you go down. However, you can't eat your chips and do this experiment, too.

INSIDER INFORMATION

Air pressure is the weight of a column of air from the earth's surface to the end of the atmosphere. At sea level, a one-inch square column weighs about fifteen pounds. As you go higher, there's less air above you so it weighs less. It's also thinner and there's less oxygen. An oxygen-starved flight is definitely a bad trip. To keep you comfortable, not to mention alive, airlines pressurize the cabin to about ten pounds per square inch or two-thirds of the pressure at sea level. It's as if you are at an altitude of about six thousand feet. But that's still enough to feel a difference.

Gases always obey the gas laws—anywhere, any time. One of them states that as the pressure on a gas decreases, its volume increases. In other words, as you go up and air pressure drops, the balloon expands. The reverse is also true. As you descend, the pressure increases and the volume decreases.

You can check out the differences with other things such as your ears or a bottle of carbonated beverage. Notice how the cabin attendants are always careful when they open drinks filled with pressurized gas. As soon as the cap or pop top is loosened, the gas is free to expand. Its exit is sometimes quite dramatic as the soda rushes out in a fizzy explosion. To see the reverse effect, bring along an empty water bottle (one made from soft plastic). It should have a screw top. When you are up in the air, open the bottle then shut it tightly again. When the plane has landed you will have a collapsed container. Air pressure on the outside is now greater than that on the inside.

Why do your ears react to a change in air pressure? There is air on both sides of your eardrums. However, the air inside your head does not connect directly to the outside. It must go through tiny tubes. When the pressure on one side of your eardrum is greater than on the other, you feel pain. There are tricks that will help you equalize the pressure. On the way up, it's helpful to yawn. Caution! Yawning is contagious. Check out "yawn trick" on page 41 to learn more about it. On the way down, hold your nose, close your mouth and blow very gently.

CAUTION!
Blowing hard may damage your ears.

UPSCALE FLIGHT

See your money increase as your plane takes off.

THE SETUP

Watch your money carefully during takeoff. Coins get heavier as your plane climbs to its cruising altitude. The increase in weight is, unfortunately, only temporary. It is, however, measurable.

Bring a postage scale and some tape with you on a flight. Before takeoff, tape an ounce or more of coins on the scale—four quarters make an ounce. The reason for the tape is to keep the coins from vibrating off the scale. Hold the scale on your armrest. Nothing will happen until the plane leaves the ground. As it climbs to its cruising altitude, watch the scale. You will see a small but noticeable increase in the weight of the coins.

INSIDER INFORMATION

As it accelerates upward, the plane is working against gravity. There is an increased upward force that you feel as the cushion presses against the seat of your pants. The increased force also causes the scale to push harder up against the coins. This is the same as saying that the coins are pushing down on the scale with increased pressure which shows up as the weight gain. The weight gain only occurs when you are climbing. At a level altitude you will have lost your increased wealth. Easy come, easy go!

Some skyscrapers have high speed elevators that will also increase your money. They have an advantage over an airplane as a testing area because you can see a weight loss as you go down. Planes descend too gradually for you to measure with such an imperfect instrument as a postage scale.

LAW-ABIDING BALLOON

See how a balloon behaves differently in a car than you do.

THE SETUP

Which should you trust: a balloon or your brain? Normally, we'd say, "Trust your brain." But sometimes a balloon is a better indicator of what's really happening.

Take a helium-filled balloon on a car ride. Sit in the rear seat and hold the string so that the balloon floats freely without touching anything. The balloon experiences a completely different trip than you do. When the car speeds up, you feel as if you are pressed against your seat back. The balloon, however, moves forward. If the car abruptly slows down, you feel yourself thrown forward. Only the seat belt saves you from going through the front windshield. The balloon, on the other hand, moves to the rear. When the car makes a right turn, you are thrown left but the balloon goes right. A left turn and the balloon moves the way the car moves. You tilt right.

INSIDER INFORMATION

The balloon is observing the laws of physics. And in spite of the way it looks, so are you. When the car accelerates, everything that's not attached to the car resists the change in speed. That includes you, the air and the balloon.

You are not easy to push around. Your weight resists the change in speed long enough for you to feel as if you're moving in the opposite direction. The air offers so little resistance that it accelerates at just about the same rate as the car. The helium-filled balloon, the lightest object in the car, is pushed forward by the speeding air. In fact, it actually goes slightly faster than the car. If the balloon were not on a string, it would keep going until it hit the windshield.

When the car maintains a constant speed, the string keeps the balloon in its original position. The force that displaces the balloon only occurs when the car is changing its speed or direction.

FAKE LAKE

See a mirage on the road.

THE SETUP

Mirages are famous for luring thirsty desert travelers, who stagger toward an oasis only to discover that it doesn't exist. You don't have to be in a desert to see a fake lake. And you certainly don't have to be thirsty. The illusion of water in the distance can even trick a camera. This mirage has been photographed many times.

The best place to see a fake lake is on an asphalt road on a hot, sunny summer day. When you get to a place where the road is straight, look ahead for a patch of shimmering "water" in the distance. Oncoming cars can drive through this "desert carwash" without making a splash. In fact, you can see a car's reflection in the fake lake. As you approach, the phantom puddle disappears only to be replaced by another one farther down the road.

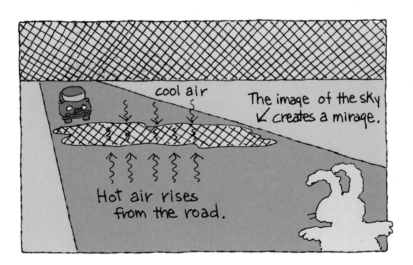

cool air

The image of the sky creates a mirage.

Hot air rises from the road.

INSIDER INFORMATION

Light bends when it travels from one transparent material to another. When you look at your feet in a swimming pool they are not where you expect them to be because the image is bent when it passes from the water to the air. Hot air acts as if it were a different material from cooler air. Air rising over an asphalt road bed is hotter than the air above it. Light from the sky bends at the boundary between the hot and cooler air. Instead of continuing in a straight path down to the road, it is bent toward your eyes. What you see is an image of the sky on the ground. Water reflects an image of the sky in the same manner. When you look at the mirage your brain says, "I've seen this before. It's water." You can't tell the difference between a bent light image of the sky and a similar image reflected from water.

Your brain isn't finished fooling you with this illusion. When there is a car in the distance, it can sometime appear to be traveling on a mirror. Because there are no waves and you see an undisturbed upside down image of a car, you realize it can't be water. What can it be? Your past experience says it could be a mirror.

4. FLUID FEATS

Which of these are fluids: molasses, air, glass? (Hint: A fluid is anything that will flow unless it is restrained by a container.) If you answered all three, you're right. But you probably didn't guess correctly because glass is a fluid fooler.

In most ways, glass is like a solid. You could call it a fluid, though, because it flows. Glass wouldn't win any flowing contests, however. It makes molasses look like a speed demon since it might take a hundred years to move one inch. But move it does, and in time you can see it in places like old windowpanes, which are much thicker at the bottom than the top.

Just so you know a fluid when you see one here are:
MOTHER NATURE'S RULES
AND REGULATIONS
GOVERNING FLUIDS

State of matter: liquid, gas, and an occasional offbeat solid
Color: any or none
Temperature range: from nearly absolute zero to more than the heat of the sun

Weight of one liter (about one quart): from less than a gram to more than fourteen kilograms (more than thirty pounds)

Time necessary to move one centimeter: From a split second to hundreds of years

Are you thoroughly confused about fluids? We thought you would be. This description of fluids is so strange that it looks like Mother Nature was out to lunch while fluids were being designed. So much the better for creating a challenging puzzle for scientists to unravel.

Most of the fluids you are familiar with, such as air and water, share other properties as well. For one thing, they exert pressure in all directions including *upward*, which surprises some people. Another fooler is the fact that fluid pressure is equal in all directions. Unexpected behavior like this makes a perfect setup for a con game. So we have included lots of "pressure tactics" in this chapter.

People are so familiar with air and water that they don't expect surprises. An egg climbing up a waterfall sure surprised us—a case of going *against* the flow. Most people think a bubble will break when you poke it. We've got a fluid fooler guaranteed *not* to burst your bubble.

Fluids also stick together. This clinging tendency, called "cohesion," is strongest at the surface where it acts like an invisible skin. And as soon as you've got invisible anything, you can fool people.

Fluids are adhesive, too. This ability to stick to other things is often totally unexpected. In this chapter, we'll show you how to make water act just like glue. You'll be stuck for the answer!

Don't forget: Fluids are the creepiest things on earth. They creep uphill, downstream, underground, and even creep into each other's spaces. Master them and be the king of the creeps.

Con games depend on inside information. This chapter is overflowing with it.

WATER TOWER

Bet you can lift water in an upside-down glass!

THE SETUP

This is a good trick to do in the bathtub. Fill a tall glass by completely submerging it in water. Get all the air out. Then turn it upside down under the water. Lift it, bottom up, above the surface until only the mouth of the glass is under the water. The water will stay in the glass, rising high above the surface of the bath.

INSIDER INFORMATION

If you had a taller glass you could lift the water even higher. You could lift it thirty-three feet if you had a glass that tall. Air pressure holds up your water tower. There is no air in the glass, so nothing is pressing down on the water in the glass. But air pressure is pressing down on the surface of your bath, and this allows the column of water to rise thirty-three feet from the surface. An Italian physicist, Torricelli (1608–47), discovered this in 1643. He tried the same trick using mercury, which is thirteen times heavier than water. He found that the air pressure could support a column of mercury 760 millimeters high and that this length varied according to the weather. No kidding. On sunny days it was higher than on rainy days. In case you haven't guessed, Torricelli's mercury column was the first barometer or weather predictor.

MAKE A SUCKER OF SUCKERS

Bet you can't suck soda through two straws!

THE SETUP

Put two straws in your mouth. Stick the free end of one in a glass of soda. Keep the second straw outside the glass. Now try to drink the soda through the straw.

INSIDER INFORMATION

You can suck till your cheeks meet but the soda will not reach your mouth. Ordinarily, when you drink through a straw, your mouth becomes a vacuum pump, lowering the air pressure in your mouth. Because air pressure tends to equalize, the now greater air pressure of the atmosphere pushes down on the surface of the drink, pushing it up the straw into your mouth.

In this stunt, the open straw keeps you from forming a vacuum pump with your mouth. Vacuum pumps won't work if they are not airtight. The straw is a leak in the system. Since the pressure in your mouth remains the same as the atmospheric pressure, the drink stays in the glass.

NOTE

It is considered cheating to put your tongue over the end of the straw that's outside the glass or to cover this straw with your finger.

ANOTHER BET FOR SUCKERS

Bet you can't suck water from a jar!

THE SETUP

Make a hole large enough for a straw in the screw top of a jar. Insert a straw and seal the connection with clay or putty. Fill the jar to the brim with water. Screw on the cover with the straw in place. Now try to drink the water through the straw!

INSIDER INFORMATION

In this stunt you *can* make a partial vacuum in your mouth. But you won't suck up the water because the surface of the water is not in contact with the atmosphere, so no air pressure can push the water into your mouth. A strong mechanical vacuum pump might be able to draw out the water, but the straw would probably collapse first. Your mouth can never create enough suction to win this sucker bet.

Soda carry-out containers, the plastic lids with holes in the center, are not airtight. That's why you can still sip through the straw.

INFLATION?

Bet you can lift a dime with a straw!

THE SETUP

Dip the end of a plastic straw in water. Set the straw down on a dime and suck in hard. Lift while inhaling.

Wipe the dime dry and ask a friend to try the trick without water. The dime stays firmly on the table.

INSIDER INFORMATION

Without water, this trick won't wash! Water makes it work because of several different phenomena. First, the force of *adhesion* allows the water to be attracted to both the straw and the dime. In addition, water sticks to itself. This is the force of *cohesion*. And last, water seals the joint so that when you inhale through the straw, you reduce the air pressure inside the straw. Air pressure on the underside of the dime pushes it up against the straw. This, combined with the water "glue," is enough force to get your dime off the ground. Too bad its value doesn't go up as well.

GRAB BAG GRABBER

Bet you can push a plastic bag in a jar so no one can pull it out!

THE SETUP

You could even get the best of King Kong with this trick. It shows that "easy in" does not always mean "easy out." All you need is a plastic bag, a jar with a mouth wide enough for your hand, and a rubber band.

Put the plastic bag inside the wide-mouth jar with the edges of the bag hanging over the mouth of the jar. Make an airtight seal by putting a rubber band over the bag. If the jar has screw ridges, place the rubber band below the ridges. Now try to pull the plastic bag out of the jar.

INSIDER INFORMATION

The grabber here is air pressure. To pull the bag out of the jar you would have to create a vacuum inside the jar. Human hands are just not strong enough to create this pressure. Nor is the bag strong enough to resist the force needed to pull it from the inside of the jar without tearing. This is a situation where you are "stuck" for a solution!

COLD-BOILED

Bet you can "boil" water without heat!

THE SETUP

For this weird illusion you will need a small handkerchief and a juice glass about three-quarters full of cold water. Wet the center of the handkerchief and put it over the mouth of the glass so it curves slightly into the glass. Now cover the mouth of the handkerchief-covered glass with your right palm. Lift the glass with your left hand, keeping the mouth tightly pressed to your right palm. Invert the glass. The water should not leak out.

Grasp the glass with your left hand near the mouth. Hold the glass and handkerchief firmly and briefly lift the glass off your right hand.

To make the water "boil," slide the handkerchief up the sides of the inverted glass with your left hand and press down on the bottom of the glass with your right hand. As the handkerchief tightens on the mouth of the glass, bubbles form and come to the surface. It looks as if the water is boiling.

INSIDER INFORMATION

Of course, the water really isn't boiling. But it does give a very good imitation of it. When the glass of water is inverted, a partial vacuum is created in the space above the water. When you tighten the handkerchief across the mouth, air rushes into the glass through the holes in the cloth to fill the vacuum. This produces bubbles that make the water appear to be boiling.

A BREATHTAKING CHANCE

Bet you can't blow a wad of paper into a bottle!

THE SETUP

Place an empty soda bottle on its side. Put a small wad of paper in the neck. Try to blow the paper into the bottle.

INSIDER INFORMATION

Not only won't the wad go in, it will fly out at you instead! When you blow into an enclosed space like a bottle, you increase the air pressure inside. Since pressure will equalize when it can, the air rushes out of the bottle, taking the wad of paper with it. Amazing, but that's the way it flows!

THE ODDS AGAINST BLOWING UP

Bet you can't get two balloons to share air equally!

THE SETUP

You will need two identical balloons that you have blown up a few times so you know they inflate easily, a four-inch length of rubber or plastic tubing from an aquarium store, a clothespin or other type of pinch clamp, and two small rubber bands. Fold the tube in half and pinch the halves together with the clamp. This creates an airtight seal. Blow up one of the balloons so that it is almost fully inflated. Attach the neck to one end of the tubing with a rubber band. (This may take several tries before you get an airtight connection.) Inflate the second balloon slightly and attach it to the other end of the tubing with the remaining rubber band. Open the clamp, allowing the air to pass freely from one balloon to the other.

INSIDER INFORMATION

It isn't magic but a scientific law that keeps the two balloons from ending up the same size. The small balloon will always empty its contents into the large balloon.

Fluids in a flexible container assume a shape that has the smallest surface area. A single large sphere has less surface area than two smaller spheres whose contents equal the single large one. Since one large balloon has less surface area than two balloons containing the same amount of air, the small balloon empties its contents into the larger one.

CORK SCREWY

Bet you can sink a cork without touching it!

THE SETUP

Float a perfectly normal cork in a bowl of water. Never at any time will your hands touch the cork, but still you can make it sink below the surface of the water.

INSIDER INFORMATION

The secret sinker here is air! Turn a large glass upside down and carefully lower it into the water over the cork. As it sinks below the surface of the water, so does the cork. The water level

in the glass is lowered by the compressed, and the water level of the bowl is increased. Soon you will have a cork "floating" underwater. A sneaky feat if ever there was one!

PROTECTIVE COVERING

Bet you can put a piece of paper underwater without getting it wet!

THE SETUP

Stuff a tissue in the bottom of a six- or eight-ounce glass. The tissue should stay in place when you turn the glass upside down. Now hold the glass perfectly straight in an upside-down position and submerge it into a basin of water. Remove the glass and feel the tissue. It's nice and dry, in spite of its trip.

INSIDER INFORMATION

Air is the protective covering in this stunt. As you lower the glass into the water, there is no way for the air to escape. The water presses up against it and the gas compresses. This makes the air push back against the water. So the tissue remains dry.

A diving bell works on this principle. Divers take an air supply with them in

a bell-shaped container over their heads. They can stay underwater as long as the diving bell doesn't tip and fill with water or they go so deep that all the air is squeezed into a tiny space where they can't fit their noses.

DRY CLEANING

Bet you can make a dry spot in two liquids!

THE SETUP

Put a tablespoonful of water on a china saucer. Color it if you wish with a few drops of food coloring. Pour a few drops of rubbing alcohol in the center of the water. Lo and behold, the water rushes away from the alcohol,

leaving a dry spot in the center of the plate.

INSIDER INFORMATION

This stunt is a battle between the "skins" of two liquids. If you don't believe that water has a skin, then watch the baglike drop form on a faucet. The shape of the drop is due to surface tension in the "skin," where the water molecules cling together with quite remarkable strength. Alcohol also has a visible surface tension, but it is not as strong as that of water. On the shallow dish where the two surfaces meet, there is a tug-of-war between the surface tension of alcohol and the surface tension of water. Since the surface tension of water is stronger, it pulls away from the alcohol and destroys the weak surface film of the alcohol, leaving an empty and quite dry spot behind.

I CAN'T BELIEVE I DID THE "HOLE" THING!

Bet you can hold water in a sieve!

THE SETUP

A metal strainer, some clear paraffin wax (the kind used for sealing jelly jars), a double boiler made from an aluminum pan and a larger pot of water, and a piece of paper. You need to use the stove for this trick so check with an adult first.

Put the paraffin in the pan and melt the paraffin over hot water in the pot. (Do not put directly on the stove.) When it is completely melted, quickly dip the sieve into it. Shake the sieve as you remove it so the holes don't fill up with wax. Let the wax harden around the wires.

Put a piece of paper into the bottom of the sieve. Pour cold water into it so that the paper breaks the force of the falling water. When you have filled the sieve about half way, remove the paper. There are many holes, but the water mysteriously stays inside.

INSIDER INFORMATION

The sieve holds water because the water doesn't wet the waxed surface and each tiny hole is sealed by the surface tension of the water. The combined surface tension of all the holes is enough to keep the water in the sieve. This works only when the holes are small.

LOADED WORDS

Bet you can't flip a newspaper into the air with a ruler!

THE SETUP

Lay several sheets of full-sized, broadsheet newspaper (not the tabloid size) on a table. Choose a smooth-surfaced table, not one with a tablecloth. Position the paper so that the long edge runs along the edge of the table. Put a wooden yardstick or ruler under the newspaper so that half of it sticks out over the edge of the table. Smooth the papers flat. Now try to flip the newspaper two feet into the air by striking the ruler with a single, quick blow like a karate chop.

INSIDER INFORMATION

That newspaper is not going anywhere. Here's why. When you smooth the newspaper flat against the table, there is almost no air underneath it. All the pressure of the air is not on top of the paper and it's considerable. The total weight of air pressure on the surface of a single sheet of newspaper is about 10,000 pounds. The fast motion you need to flip the paper pits the ruler against the full 10,000 pounds of air, and the ruler breaks.

Of course, you can lift the paper by slowly pressing down on the ruler. When you do this, air seeps under the paper, the pressure equalizes, and the paper can easily be lifted. However, a gentle tap on the ruler will never flip the paper.

THE LEAKPROOF HOLE

Bet you can't make water leak out of a hole in a bottle!

THE SETUP

Get a pair of scissors and a plastic bottle with a screw top. Make a small hole in the side of the bottle near the bottom with the point of the scissors. Cover the hole with your finger while you fill the bottle with water to the brim. (Do this over the sink.) Screw on the top, making sure there is no air in the bottle. Take your finger away from the hole. Stand back and watch for the water to come pouring out!

INSIDER INFORMATION

No water? That's because the odds were stacked against it. For water to leak out the hole, the air pressure pushing on the water has to be less than the force of gravity. Usually the pressure on top of a liquid is equal to the air pressure pushing on the hole. The two forces cancel each other out; gravity wins and the water rushes forth. (Open the top of the bottle and see this happen.) But as long as the surface of the water is protected from air pressure by the bottle cap, air pressure works to keep the water *in* the bottle. Air pressure then wins because it is stronger than the force of gravity!

You have something else working against you here, too. It's the surface tension of the water. It acts like a skin and holds the water together. It's a weak force, but it works for you when you have a small hole.

BLOWING A CHANCE

Bet you can't blow up a balloon in a bottle!

THE SETUP

Select a balloon that is easy to blow up. Put it on an empty soda bottle and stretch the neck of the balloon completely over the mouth of the bottle. Try to blow up the balloon so it fills the bottle.

INSIDER INFORMATION

So you thought this one would be easy? It's not only difficult, it's downright impossible. To inflate the balloon, you would need to compress the air trapped between the balloon and the bottle. To compress air requires force. Human lungs are not strong enough to inflate the balloon *and* to compress the trapped air.

WASTED BREATH

Bet you can't blow out a candle through a funnel!

THE SETUP

Hold a candle so the flame is in the center of the wide end of a funnel. (Don't try to put the flame into the funnel.) Now try to blow out the candle.

INSIDER INFORMATION

No matter how you huff and puff, the flame doesn't go out. Instead it strangely flickers *toward* the funnel!

Many fluids have a tendency to flow along a surface. In this case, the air that is blown into the funnel spreads out and hugs the surface of the funnel. Almost none of your breath travels through the center. This is why the flame is not extinguished.

The flame flickers toward the funnel because of another strange fluid phenomenon called the Bernoulli principle. According to this principle, moving air creates lower pressure along the surface next to the current. When you blow into the funnel, air rushes along the sides and creates a low pressure area in the center. Any time a low pressure area exists, air will rush in to equalize the pressure if it can. The flame is in the path of this rush of air, so it leans toward the mouth of the funnel. The next five tricks are also based on the Bernoulli effect.

BLOWOUT PROOF

Bet you can't blow a Ping-Pong ball out of a funnel!

THE SETUP

Put a Ping-Pong ball in a funnel. Tilt your head back and try to blow the ball out of the funnel. Blow with a steady pressure or with short bursts but make sure that you don't move the funnel so that gravity helps you out. That's cheating.

INSIDER INFORMATION

The most frustrating part of this bet is that the harder you try to blow the ball out, the more firmly it stays in place! This stunt is a classic example of the Bernoulli effect. Moving air exerts decreased pressure at right angles to the direction of motion. In this case, the rushing air coming out of the funnel hits the surface of the ball. Air rushes around the ball, creating lower pressure on the underside of the ball. The greater pressure of the atmosphere becomes immediately apparent. It holds the ball in the funnel. So the harder you blow, the more you reduce the pressure under the ball and the more firmly the ball is pushed by the atmospheric pressure into the funnel.

There *is* a way to blow a Ping-Pong ball out of a funnel. But you have to change something. Here's what you can't change: the funnel, the ball, and the way you hold the two so gravity can't get at the ball. What you *can* change is the direction you're blowing. Blow straight down on the ball from above. Surprised? The best way is to blow horizontally across the top of the funnel. The Bernoulli effect of air rushing across the top of the ball, lowers the downward pressure so air pressure from underneath easily pops the ball out.

NO WINDFALL HERE

Bet you can't blow a piece of paper off the end of a spool!

THE SETUP

You will need a two-inch square of paper, a straight pin, some tape, and a spool of thread. Put the straight pin through the center of the paper and tape it in place. Insert the pin in the center hole of the spool of thread. Tilt the spool upward slightly as you put the open end to your lips. Try to blow the paper off the end of the spool! Blow with steady pressure, not short bursts.

INSIDER INFORMATION

The Bernoulli effect makes this an impossible task. The harder you blow, the more securely the paper is drawn against the top of the spool. Air rushes out of the hole, spreads between the paper and the spool, and, as in the last two tricks, reduces the air pressure. The greater atmospheric pressure on the other side of the paper presses down and holds it firmly against the top of the spool. You lose.

UP AGAINST THE ODDS

Bet you can't blow a strip of paper down toward your toes!

THE SETUP

Cut a strip of ordinary paper about eleven inches long and two inches wide. Hold one end just below your lower lip against your chin. Blow down on the paper. Try to make it point toward your toes.

INSIDER INFORMATION

The paper is going to rise toward your nose, not droop toward your toes! This apparently simple gimmick is the key to flight. It demonstrates the lifting properties of the Bernoulli Effect. Air rushing across the top of the paper reduces the pressure. The air under the paper, at the greater pressure of the atmosphere, pushes upward and lifts the paper.

Engineers use this principle in the design of airplane wings. A wing is shaped so that air rushes over the top of the wing faster than it passes under the bottom. The greater pressure on the underside of the wing lifts the plane into the air.

LOOK, MA—NO HANDS

Bet you can keep a ball in the air for an hour without touching it!

THE SETUP

All you need to perform the seemingly impossible is a Ping-Pong ball and a hair dryer—the "gun" kind. Turn on the dryer and hold it so that the stream of air is pointing straight up.

Place a Ping-Pong ball in the stream of air. It doesn't blow away but sits so securely that you can tilt the hair dryer to an almost horizontal position.

You don't really have to hold the hair dryer for an hour to see that this trick is going to work. A few minutes are long enough to see this spectacular effect.

But if you really want an even bigger show, try floating several items in the airstream at the same time. Put a Ping-Pong ball closest to the dryer, then add a balloon, and over that a larger balloon. Try some plastic Easter eggs. See how long a line of floaters you can manage.

INSIDER INFORMATION

The invisible ballplayer is air. In this case what you see is the result of the Bernoulli Effect. Bernoulli, an Italian physicist who lived in the eighteenth century, discovered a peculiar property of moving fluids. He showed that moving air loses pressure in a direction at right angles to its motion. This means that air from the dryer moves faster around the sides of the ball than air on top of the ball, which is still. Lower pressure on the sides of the ball makes the air next to the ball rush in to fill the vacuum, thus holding the ball in the airstream. The Bernoulli Effect is the reason that heavier-than-air planes fly. Air rushing over the tops of wings exerts less pressure than air under the wings does. As a result, the under air pushes up to give planes a lift.

BLOWING UP TOILET PAPER

Set a speed record for unrolling t.p.

THE SETUP

A roll of toilet paper can become a flying streamer of immense proportions. All you need is a strong enough wind. A leaf blower is a home-grown hurricane. It produces a wind of 150 miles an hour, well into the hurricane range on the Beaufort scale.

You will need:

- roll of toilet paper
- a broomstick
- a leaf blower
- a friend

Blowing up toilet paper requires two people.

Go outside (that's where hurricanes belong, after all). Put the roll of toilet paper on a broomstick and hold the broomstick horizontally so that the toilet paper unrolls over the top. Unroll a few sheets and let them hang down. Now for the action. The person holding the leaf blower should aim the airstream so that it rushes over the top

surface of the roll. Keep the direction of the airstream parallel to the direction you want the paper to go. The hanging t.p. rises and the roll begins to unfurl, rapidly becoming an airborne banner.

INSIDER INFORMATION

There are two things happening here: the toilet paper unrolls and the unraveling paper flies. It unrolls because the enormous force of the airstream pushes against the top of the roll, making it spin. The unrolling paper takes off because the air passing over the top surface of the paper lowers the air pressure on that surface. The air pressure under the paper is now greater and

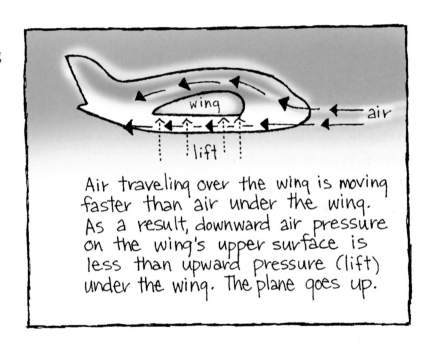

Air traveling over the wing is moving faster than air under the wing. As a result, downward air pressure on the wing's upper surface is less than upward pressure (lift) under the wing. The plane goes up.

the paper rises. The faster the air moves over the top surface the smaller the downward pressure becomes.

Bernoulli's principle explains how an airplane is able to stay up in the air. Plane wings are shaped so that air moves faster over the top surfaces. As long as the engine moves the plane forward, the air underneath the wings will lift up the plane.

SUM IS LESS THAN MORE

Bet you can't mix one quart plus one quart and get two quarts!

THE SETUP

You will need a large measuring cup, a three-quart pot or bowl, a spoon, a quart of rubbing alcohol, and water. Put a quart of water in the pot. (Four cups equal one quart; measure carefully!) Pour in one quart of rubbing alcohol. (Again measure carefully!) Stir the mixture well. Now measure the volume of the mixture with the measuring cup. Did you get two quarts?

INSIDER INFORMATION

If you didn't get two quarts, it's not because you are a sloppy measurer. The two liquids combine to measure noticeably less than two quarts! Why?

The disappearing liquid is due to the space between the molecules of water and of alcohol. When these two particular liquids are mixed, the alcohol molecules slip between the spaces of the water molecules, making a smaller combined volume for the two liquids. Not all combinations of liquids will give this strange shrinkage, but water and alcohol are good foolers.

WATERTIGHT

Bet you can't pull apart two wet glasses!

THE SETUP

You will need two heavy plastic water glasses that are the same size. Put one inside the other. Drip water around the rim of the outer glass so that a thin layer of water forms between the two glasses. Try to separate them by pulling them apart.

INSIDER INFORMATION

The water acts like glue, holding the glasses together. Nature has put in a double fix here. The first is *cohesion*, which is the force pulling water molecules together. The second is *adhesion*, which is the attraction between water and the glass. Only in a tiny place like the one between the glasses can they combine to form such a powerful bond.

Since you have those two glasses stuck together, it's only fair play to tell you the secret of how to get them apart. Cool the inner glass by filling it with ice water. While the water is still in the inner glass, run hot water around the outside glass and **immediately** pull them apart. If you don't act quickly, the glasses will stick even more tightly. The outer glass expands from the heat and the inner one contracts from the ice water. The small difference in size is large enough to break the seal of the water so you can pull the glasses apart.

If all else fails, just wait. Sooner or later, the water making the seal will evaporate and then it's a snap to pull dry glasses apart.

FLOATING ODDS

Bet you can't make a cork float near the edge of a glass of water!

THE SETUP

Fill a glass with water. Now overfill it by adding water slowly until the surface rises over the edge of the glass. Gently set a cork afloat near the edge. Try to keep it there!

INSIDER INFORMATION

The cork is going to move toward the center no matter how many times you push it toward the edge. If you look at the surface of the water of an overfilled glass, you will see that the surface is curved. The highest point is at the center. The surface tension is pulling toward the center. On a flat surface, the buoyant force of the liquid is straight up and down. But a curved surface tilts the cork slightly and makes the cork move to where the surface is the highest and the pull the strongest—the center not the edge.

Now as long as you're fooling around with that cork, try this one:

Bet you can't make a cork float near the center of a glass of water!

THE SETUP

Empty some of the water from the overfull glass so that the surface of the water is well below the rim of the glass. Gently put the cork in the water. Guide it toward the center if you like. Try to keep the cork there.

INSIDER INFORMATION

The cork is always going to migrate to the edge. If you look at this surface from the side you will see that it is curved but now the curve is concave. The water at the edge, next to the glass is higher than the center. Again the cork tries to float at the highest point because the surface tension is pulling toward the edge.

COMING UP EMPTY

Bet you can't pour water through a hose!

THE SETUP

You will need a garden hose that is at least five-eighths of an inch in diameter, a reel for storing the hose that is at least one foot in diameter, a funnel, a bucket of water, and an empty bucket. Coil the hose at least five times around the reel. The hose should be completely empty and have no kinks. Put one end of the hose in the empty bucket. Hold the other end several feet above the reel. Insert the funnel in this end and pour in the water. Watch for it to come through the other end.

INSIDER INFORMATION

You could watch forever! Nothing will ever come through. Water just overflows the funnel end and nothing ever empties into the bucket. This is a scientist's nightmare. There are several theories as to why the water doesn't run through the hose. It should, according to all logical explanations. But it doesn't. *Scientific American* magazine asked scientists to write in and explain it. None wrote in. But we bet that someone, maybe you, will come up with the answer someday.

NOTHING TO SNEEZE AT

Bet you can part a pepper sea!

THE SETUP

Fill a glass or a bowl with water and sprinkle pepper liberally on the top. Stroke a path through the pepper with your index finger and try to make the pepper "clear the road."

INSIDER INFORMATION

You can't do this unless you dip your finger in soap. The soapy finger then will make a clean sweep through the floating pepper. Soap weakens the surface tension of the water, and the pepper no longer is able to float on the surface but sinks into the water below.

WATER ON A TIGHTROPE

Bet you can pour water sideways!

THE SETUP

Wet a string about three feet long and tie it to the handle of a pitcher or measuring cup. Fill the pitcher about two-thirds full of water. Pass the string from the handle over the mouth of the pitcher and its spout to a glass about two feet to the side of the pitcher. Hold the pitcher a foot above the table. With your left hand hold the end of the wet string inside the glass. Make sure the string is taut between the pitcher and the glass. Pour the water down the string. It will cling to the string as it moves sideways down to the glass. Not a drop will spill on the table.

INSIDER INFORMATION

There are two forces with you here. One is the attraction between the water and the surface of the string. Water wets the string and sticks to itself. The attraction of water for itself creates a stream. Together these two forces are greater than gravity, which is pulling the water toward the ground.

WHAT A GAS

Bet you can extinguish a flame by opening a bag of potato chips!

THE SETUP

Check with an adult before you do this as it involves a candle. Light a candle. When the flame is well established open a bag of potato chips so that the gas inside gently floods the area around the candle. Don't squeeze the bag. That just blows out the flame. With a silent shudder, the flame is out. Instantly!

INSIDER INFORMATION

That's not air puffing up a bag of potato chips. It's pure nitrogen. As you may know, nitrogen makes up almost eighty percent of the air, oxygen about twenty percent, and a few other gases in very small amounts. Oxygen supports burning and it also combines with the oil in potato chips to make them taste stale. So potato chips manufacturers preserve the shelf life of chips by packing them in pure nitrogen. The puffy bag also protects them against breakage.

By the way, when you blow out a flame, you also deprive it of oxygen by creating a partial vacuum according to the Bernoulli Effect.

TAP-DANCING EGG

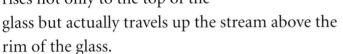

Wanna bet you can make an egg climb a waterfall?

THE SETUP

Use the nearest waterfall. Make it in your kitchen sink. Fill a glass of water and put an egg in it. Notice that the egg sinks. (If it doesn't, it's rotten.) Place the glass under your kitchen waterfall. The stream doesn't push the egg against the bottom of the glass as you might expect. Instead, the egg rises not only to the top of the glass but actually travels up the stream above the rim of the glass.

INSIDER INFORMATION

This is a real fooler. Scientists have not been able to explain exactly why it works. We do know that the water must be very turbulent. Without violently rushing water, the egg will only rise to the top of the glass. Turbulence causes it to climb the waterfall. You may have to experiment a bit with the flow to get the effect eggsactly right.

SUCKER BET

Wanna bet a bottle will suck up a wad of paper?

THE SETUP

Earlier, we challenged you to blow a small wad of paper into an empty soda bottle (see A Breathtaking Chance on page 127. We told you to rest an empty soda bottle on its side,

place a small wad of paper in the neck, and try to blow the paper into the bottle. We were right—it didn't work.

You can't do it with your breath, but the forces of Nature can. The catch is in the setup, which is just a little bit different. You must use a plastic bottle. Squeeze the bottle in the middle to make a dent. Hold the bottle horizontally and place the wad of paper in the neck. Squeeze the soda bottle to make the dent pop out. The wad of paper flies into the bottle. Don't blink, because the bottle is one fast sucker.

INSIDER INFORMATION

Denting the bottle gives it a smaller volume. A dented bottle contains less air than an undented one. Some of the air is forced out. There's a well-known saying that nature hates a vacuum. When you release the dent, you create a partial vacuum. When the bottle returns to its original shape and volume, there is less air in it. Instantly, air from the room rushes into the bottle to fill the partial vacuum. It carries the lightweight paper wad with it.

MESSAGES IN THE MIST

Wanna bet you can write with a potato?

THE SETUP

Future spies take note. You can write secret messages with a piece of raw potato. Cut a potato and write on your bathroom mirror with the cut surface. The message will be practically invisible until someone takes a shower. Then the message appears in the misty mirror.

INSIDER INFORMATION

This is nothing to get steamed up about. Water vapor forms tiny droplets when it comes in contact with a cool mirror. Droplets form because the force of attraction between the

water molecules is stronger than the attraction between the water molecules and the glass molecules. This clouds the mirror and you can't see in it.

The raw potato contains a substance that the water molecules "like" almost as much as they "like" each other. Instead of forming little balls that reflect light, the water vapor over the message forms a thin sheet that's easy to see through. The writing appears as clear spots surrounded by the foggy dew.

It is possible to use potatoes as emergency windshield wipers. If your wipers break, rub a piece of raw potato across the windshield and the raindrops will turn into thin sheets of water that you can see through.

DON'T TAKE THIS LYING DOWN

Wanna bet you can make a cork float upright?

THE SETUP

Place a cork in a bowl of water so it floats on its end. Don't waste a lot of time trying. The cork will float only on its side. But this rule applies only to a single cork. You can get a cork

to float upright if it's part of a group. Here's how. Hold three or more corks underwater until they are thoroughly wet. Gather them at the surface of the water in an upright position. Make sure the sides are touching each other. Slowly remove your fingers. The cork raft will float with all the members upright.

INSIDER INFORMATION

A single cork floats on its side because its center of gravity is at its lowest point in this position. If you stick the corks together, they float upright because, for a raft, this is the position where the center of gravity is lowest. In this trick, water acts like glue. The water is attracted to the surface of the corks and also to itself. The bond that forms is strong enough to create the raft.

POKING FUN

Wanna bet you can stick your finger through a soap bubble without popping it?

THE SETUP

Soap bubbles are about the thinnest thing you can see with the unaided eye. Because they are thin, they are fragile. You can't stick your hand through one without bursting your bubble. Not unless you make a bubble with a hole in it.

We know a way to do it.

You will need some bubble solution and a "magic" wand. Any bubble solution will do. Buy it or make it with our recipe. The wand, however, is special. Bend some wire into a large circle. Make a circle of thread a little larger than your finger. Suspend it in the center of the wand by attaching it with strings at opposite points on the wire circle. Pour bubble solution into a shallow pan and dip the wand into it. Remove

the wand and pierce the soap film in the loop of thread with a pencil. The loop of thread springs open, forming a circular hole you can stick your finger through.

Recipe for bubble liquid:

- 1/3 cup dishwashing liquid (Joy or Ajax work well)
- few drops of glycerin (optional)
- 1 quart warm water

Mix the dishwashing liquid in the water. Adding the glycerin will produce longer-lasting and stronger bubbles.

INSIDER INFORMATION

The thread loop forms a barrier that prevents the entire soap film bubble from bursting. The thread opens into a circle because the soap film pulls evenly on all sides.

LITE DETECTOR

Wanna bet you can pick a can of regular cola from a can of diet cola blindfolded?

THE SETUP

This is a science experiment you can drink after you are finished. You will need a can of regular cola and a diet cola of the same brand. Make sure the cans are identical with

the same amounts of liquid. Fill the bathtub to a depth of at least eight inches. Put on a blindfold and get a friend to hand you the two cans. Hold both cans underwater with the bottoms resting on the tub. Let go. The can of diet cola will float higher than the regular cola. You can feel the difference, even with your eyes covered.

INSIDER INFORMATION

Believe it or not, diet drinks really are lighter! When you read the label you will see that each can contains the same number of fluid ounces. Fluid ounces are a measure of volume, not weight, though. A twelve-ounce can of regular cola contains about ten teaspoons of sugar. They dissolve in the liquid without increasing its volume. The molecules of sugar spread evenly between the water molecules where there's a lot of empty space. There are now more molecules in the cola, making the liquid more dense. Diet colas are usually sweetened with aspartame, which is 160 times sweeter than sugar. Obviously, ten teaspoons of sugar weigh more than a pinch of aspartame. The cans are the same size but the densities are different. The can that contains the lower-density liquid will float higher.

There is one other way you can tell the two colas apart. Ask a bee. Bees are not the least bit interested in the diet cola. They must not be worried about their weight.

SODA FOUNTAIN

Wanna bet you can shoot a geyser of cola ten feet up in the air?

THE SETUP

Setting off a Diet Coke geyser has been all the rage on the internet the past few years. The trick is to deliver ten Mentos Mints all at once to a two-liter, freshly opened bottle of Diet Coke. Set up your bottle outside on a lawn. Roll up a piece of paper to make a tube slightly larger than the diameter of a Mentos Mint candy (about one inch in diameter). Tape the tube closed. Stack ten candies in the tube, keeping the bottom covered so that they don't fall out. Cover the end of the tube with the index card, so that the candies can't fall out. Place the tube over the open bottle so that you can slide out the card and all the candies will fall into the bottle.

MOVE OUT OF THE WAY FAST!

Almost instantly a fifteen-foot geyser will shoot out of the bottle.

INSIDER INFORMATION

What really happens when the candy hits the soda? Carbon dioxide gas is dissolved in soft drinks. Some of this dissolved gas is released when you open the bottle and the pressure on the solution quickly lowers. The release of the dissolved gas is increased with the introduction of a surface that contains sites that break up the surface tension of water and allow bubbles to form. These are called "nucleation sites" and the surface of a Mentos Mint contains thousands of them. Since the candies sink, introducing a lot of candies all at once gives the carbon dioxide in the soda lots of places to rapidly form bubbles. (Put one Mentos Mint in glass of clear soda and see a laboratory version of nucleation as bubbles stream off the surface of the candy.) The huge rush of gas is enough to forcefully propel an explosion of soda out the narrow mouth of the bottle in a powerful but short-lived spurt. You can do this with regular cola but since it contains sugar, it's stickier to clean up.

Nucleation sites are not exclusive to Mentos Mints. If you've ever made an ice cream float, you'll see lots of bubbles foaming around the nucleation sites on the ice cream. Add sugar or salt to soda and you'll see extra bubbles form. The geyser forms because there is a rapid gas build-up forcing the liquid out of a relatively small opening.

EGG BEATER

Wanna bet you can make an egg stand on end?

THE SETUP

Try to stand a raw egg on end. Can't do it, can you? It *is* possible, but you have to scramble the egg inside its shell. Shake it vigorously for several minutes. Then hold it for a few seconds with the bigger end on a table. Carefully remove your hand. Ta da! The egg is standing on its end. If it isn't, shake some more and try again.

INSIDER INFORMATION

An egg normally rests on its side. In this position the center of gravity is closest to the shell.

Weight is not evenly distributed inside an egg. The yolk is denser than the white, and there's a tiny pocket of air at the broad end. But the center of gravity is pretty close to the geometric center of the egg because the yolk is held in place by two twisted strands of protein that anchor it to the shell. When you shake the egg, one of two things happen: either the yolk breaks free and sinks or all the contents, including the air, become scrambled. In either case, the contents are now free to flow inside the egg. When

you hold the egg upright, the center of gravity shifts, and you can then balance it on its end. It takes a few seconds for the contents to settle and the air to rise to the top.

A REALLY BIG SUCKER

Suck through an extremely long straw.

THE SETUP

Find out how big a sucker you are. Can you drink through a one foot straw? A two footer? A five footer? If you're good, you may have to stand on a chair!

You will need:

- plastic straws
- scissors
- tape
- a beverage, preferably a dark color so you can see it through the straw

To test your pucker power, make a maxistraw by joining plastic straws together. Because it is important that you get an airtight seal, make two half-inch slits in the ends to be joined. Mesh the straws to that they overlap. Then tape the joint securely.

Start testing your lung power with a three-piece straw. Put the straw into your beverage and suck away. If you get a few good swallows, add a straw. Keep adding straws until you reach your limit. Vicki's last straw was number six. Kathy was not as big a sucker.

INSIDER INFORMATION

You suck a liquid up a straw by lowering the air pressure in your mouth. You aren't pulling up the liquid, it is being pushed up the straw by the greater pressure of the atmosphere pushing down on the liquid outside the straw.

There's a limit to the height water can rise. If there were a perfect vacuum above a column of water, that column would rise about thirty feet. You, however, are not a great vacuum pump. You can make only a partial vacuum in your mouth. In order to suck liquid through a three-foot straw, you must lower the atmospheric pressure in your mouth by one tenth. A six-foot straw means you've lowered the pressure to four-fifths of an atmosphere. Six feet is probably close to the maximum pressure reduction the human mouth and lungs can make.

THE FLYING TEA BAG

Burn a tea bag so it floats in the air.

THE SETUP

If someone shows us a better mouse trap, we'll use it. There's an old parlor trick that allows the ash from a burning column of tissue paper rise up into the air. It is tricky and dangerous. Here's a new twist to this stunt that's somewhat safer and surefire. It comes from our friends down under in Australia.

You will need:

- a Bigelow flow-through tea bag
- a metal pie pan
- matches

Remove the staple (or the string) from the tea bag. Unfold the bag and dump out the tea. (Since the Boston Tea Party, dumping tea has been an American tradition. You don't have to throw away the tea, however. Put it in a cup of hot water and drink it.) Use your fingers to open the paper so that it becomes a tube. Set the tube in the middle of the pie plate so it looks like a little chimney. Light a match and set fire to the top of the tube.

The tea bag paper quickly burns from the top down. When the flame reaches the bottom, the ash-tube rises and floats in the air.

INSIDER INFORMATION

As the paper tube burns, a column of hot air forms inside. Warm air rises. As cooler air rushes in to replace the rising column of warmer air a *convection current* forms. This current of air is strong enough to lift the lightweight ash that remains after the teabag is almost finished burning. The teabag ends its burn as it rises. Cool!

A Bigelow tea bag works better than other types. First, it's already the right shape to make a column of hot air. Second, the special filter paper contains enough additives, such as the clay, to make a significant ash to float in the air. Some teabags are made from paper that is almost pure cellulose. They don't leave enough ash to make an impressive flying teabag carcass.

It will burn quickly.

There is one warning, however. If the teabag falls over while it's burning, it will not fly. So do this in a room where there are no drafts. This trick is one of Vicki's most popular demonstrations at school visits.

ONE COIN CLAPPING

Make a coin clap without touching it.

THE SETUP

Ever wonder about the sound of one hand clapping? Now you can give a hand for the amazing clapping coin.

You will need:

- an empty two-liter plastic soda bottle
- a quarter
- a freezer
- water

Put the empty un-capped soda bottle in the freezer for about twenty minutes. Wet the quarter thoroughly. Take the chilled bottle from the freezer and immediately cover the top with the wet quarter. Wait. Within a few moments the coin will start moving up and down, clacking on the top rim of the bottle.

INSIDER INFORMATION

The volume of air depends on temperature. When temperature goes down, air contracts (put an inflated balloon in the freezer if you don't believe us). When the temperature rises, the volume of a gas increases. When you put an open bottle in the freezer, the bottle soon is full of cold air. You seal the air in the bottle with the wet coin. Water acts like a weak glue.

As the air in the bottle warms up to room temperature, it expands, pushes against the quarter until it breaks the seal of the water glue. A small amount of air escapes and the coin falls back, making a sound as it hits the rim. This will continue until the air in the bottle is the same temperature. It's worth a round of applause.

THE SELF-PAINTING PICTURE

Make modern art in milk.

THE SETUP

This art may not be to your taste but it is not hard to swallow. Your canvas is white milk. Your paints are liquid food colors.

You will need:

- a glass of milk
- liquid food colors

Put a glass of milk on a counter or table and let it settle. It's important for the milk to remain still so don't move the glass or shake the table while your picture is painting itself.

Put a drop of each color somewhere on the milk near the side of the glass. Wait. The colors will swirl and mix while you watch. This, however, is not art for eternity. If you wait too long the colors blend completely and you'll have one yucky color. Better drink up while it still looks good.

INSIDER INFORMATION

Even when a liquid appears to be still it is in motion. The molecules in milk and every other liquid are constantly moving. Food coloring is a highly concentrated substance. When food coloring and milk come in contact with each other, molecular motion causes them to mix without any outside help. No stirring or shaking required. The self-mixing process is called *diffusion.*

During diffusion molecules move from a crowded area (food coloring) to a less crowded area (milk). The path of the diffusion creates designs in the milk. Each glass of

designer milk has a unique pattern. But the final result of all diffusion is the same: an even mixture of one color.

ANTIBUBBLES

Make liquid-filled bubbles.

THE SETUP

An antibubble is not something we made up. It's similar to the kind of bubble you're familiar with—it's round and it breaks when you poke it. A regular bubble is a skin of water (and sometimes soap) surrounding air; it can exist in either air or water. An antibubble is a globule of water surrounded by a skin of air; it exists only underwater.

You will need:

anti bubbles

- a glass bowl or jar
- water
- measuring spoons
- liquid dishwashing detergent
- a glass measuring cup
- food coloring
- a clean, empty squeeze bottle with a hole about 1/8" in. diameter (an Elmer's glue bottle, a contact lens solution bottle, or a ketchup or mustard squeeze bottle will do nicely)
- salt (optional)
- honey or corn syrup (optional)

To make antibubbles, fill a bowl with water and squirt about a teaspoon of liquid dishwashing detergent into it. Keep a thin thread of water running into the bowl while you sweep off the foam at the top. When the foam is gone, pour enough of the soap-and-water mixture into a measuring cup to fill the squeeze bottle. Then put a few drops of food coloring into the measuring cup, and stir gently. Fill the squeeze bottle with the colored liquid. Add water to the bowl until it is almost full again.

Squirt the bottle over the surface of the water in the bowl. Some of the water globules will skitter across the surface of the water before they break, leaving a trail of color behind. Some globules will be pushed beneath the surface of the water. These are your antibubbles.

It takes a bit of practice to create antibubbles. Experiment with different angles and try squirting with different pressures. A gentle squeeze seems to work best.

How can you spot an antibubble? Look for color or for bubbles that rise to the surface very slowly. With practice you can produce a steady stream of antibubbles. We made particularly big ones by holding the squirt bottle vertically and placing one water globule directly on top of another.

INSIDER INFORMATION

An antibubble has liquid both inside and outside with a thin layer of air in between. A regular bubble has air inside and out with a thin layer of liquid in between. When you pop an antibubble the liquid inside the bubble joins the surrounding liquid and the air layer forms a tiny regular bubble that quickly rises to the top. When you pop a regular bubble, the inside air joins the surrounding atmosphere and the liquid skin forms a tiny drop that falls to the ground.

In water, antibubbles, like air bubbles, rise to the surface. However, since antibubbles are mostly water with a very thin skin of air, they are just slightly lighter than the surrounding water. As a result, they take a much longer time to rise to the top. If the fluid inside the antibubble is heavier than water, the bubble will actually sink. Salt water is heavier than regular water. So if you add salt to the water in your squeeze bottle, you can create some sinkers. When they hit the bottom of the bowl, they will break. If you want to prolong the life of your antibubbles, put a layer of honey or corn syrup on the bottom of the bowl to cushion the landing.

ANTIBUBBLE GIZMO

Make this antibubble toy.

THE SETUP

Once you've met the challenge of making antibubbles in water, try making them in other liquids. Endless numbers of antibubbles and waves are easily produced in this portable, perpetual antibubble gizmo.

You will need:

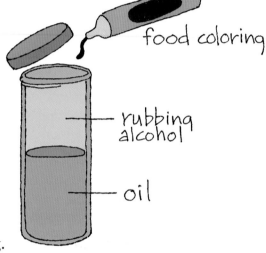

food coloring

rubbing alcohol

oil

- an olive jar (or any other tall, thin jar) and screw top
- vegetable oil
- rubbing alcohol
- food coloring

Remove the label by soaking the jar in hot water. Wash and dry the jar. Pour oil into the jar until it is half full. Then add rubbing alcohol until the jar is as full as it can be. Put in a drop or two of food coloring. Screw on the top. Check to make sure there are no air bubbles by turning the jar upside down. If there are bubbles, open the jar and add more rubbing alcohol.

Shake the jar and you will produce many patterns of antibubbles in the oil layer.

INSIDER INFORMATION

You know that you've produced true antibubbles in your gizmo for two reasons. Because the jar is full, there is no air present, so you can only produce a "liquid in a liquid" bubble. The food coloring detects the presence of rubbing alcohol which forms the skin.

The antibubble gizmo has no known practical value. However, staring at it has a mysterious soothing effect. Just be sure you don't leave it where it might be mistaken for a soft drink.

DIVING DUCK SAUCE

Sink packets of sauce without touching them.

THE SETUP

Command packets of sauce to dive in a bottle of water. Amazingly, they not only obey you but return to the surface when you tell them to.

You will need:

- a clear plastic 1 liter soda pop bottle
- duck sauce, soy sauce, ketchup or other sauces in individual packets
- water
- bowl of water

Collect the candidates for your diving team the next time you're in a takeout or fast food restaurant. Unopened packets of soy sauce, duck sauce, ketchup, mayonnaise and mustard all have potential. Select your divers by putting the packets of sauce in a bowl of water. Choose the ones that are barely floating.

Prepare the diving chamber by removing the label from the one liter bottle. Fill the bottle with water almost to the top. Force one or two packets of sauce into the bottle. Add water until the bottle is filled completely. Screw on the top and you're ready.

Place your hands around the bottle and squeeze. The packets will head for the bottom if you've applied enough pressure. Release the pressure and the divers return to the surface. Once you have mastered the pressure regulation, you can even get the divers to stop half way. When you entertain your friends, command the divers to "sink" or "swim." If you don't let them see you squeeze the bottle, the way your divers follow instructions will seem mysterious.

INSIDER INFORMATION

Just like fish, each of your divers has a swim bladder. The sauce packet contains a bubble of air that keeps it afloat. When you squeeze the bottle, the pressure on the bottle is transmitted through the water, causing the bubble to shrink. The smaller bubble is less buoyant and the packet sinks. When you release the pressure, the bubble gets bigger and the packet floats. Fish change the size of the bubble in their swim bladder to regulate their depth.

It doesn't matter where you squeeze the bottle. The divers will dive because pressure to one part of the water in the bottle spreads evenly throughout all the water in the bottle. This ability of a liquid to transmit pressure evenly has lots of practical applications. Hydraulic lifts in service stations and hydraulic brakes in cars are two examples.

1. Force the packets into a bottle of water. one liter bottle

2. Fill the bottle to the top with water and screw on the cap.

3. SQUEEZE.

4. RELEASE.

5. ENERGY ENTRAPMENTS

In nature, there's no such thing as an energy crisis. Big shocker! There will never be more energy on earth than there is right now. But you don't need to alert the media—the planet is *not* going to run out of it. In fact, there won't ever be any less energy than there is right now. So why, then, is everybody going around crying that there is a crisis and telling us to save energy?

There's a law that states that energy can't be created or destroyed, it can be changed from one form to another. Heat, light, sound, electricity, the energy in molecules (called *chemical energy*), and that in atoms (called *nuclear energy*) are all forms of energy. When people talk about the energy crisis, what they're really talking about is running out of fossil fuels. These are the natural gas, oil, and coal that formed millions of years ago from decaying plants and animals. Engineers and scientists know how to transform fossil fuels into energy we can use, like electricity. They haven't yet figured out enough inexpensive, renewable, nonpolluting alternatives to fossil fuels to meet future energy requirements. The world may run out of fuel, but it won't run out of energy. Does this surprise you? There's a loophole in the law that can trick you: nature doesn't care what form energy takes.

Heat, light, sound, electricity, and motion are all forms of energy. One can be changed into another. Rub your hands together and feel motion transformed into heat. Your experience tells you that flames do damage. Heat energy can destroy. In this chapter you'll meet a flame that doesn't scorch. Your experience tells you that light makes things visible. But we've got a trick that makes something disappear in broad daylight. Light moves faster than anything else in the universe. Marvel at its acrobatic bends and bounces. Watch it rotate through a rainbow. Your experience tells you that you can detect the direction of a sound. We can move that sound with a dish and stump you. We're going to teach you how to make electric spit. That ought to warm you up so you can create lightning in your mouth. Then we'll introduce you to a renewable fuel source that's pretty nutty.

Microwaves are an invisible form of light energy or *electromagnetic radiation*. The original use of microwaves was for military purposes. Radar detects enemy craft with microwaves. When a radar engineer discovered a melted candy bar in his pocket, he realized that microwaves could be used to heat food. His company then produced the first microwave ovens, called Radaranges.

In an oven, penetrating microwaves cause the water molecules in food and other materials to vibrate. And a vibrating molecule is a hot molecule. The other chapters in this book have some really cool stuff. But we know that this one has the hottest tricks of all.

Energy is defined in science as the ability to do work. Physicists measure it in terms of mass moved through a distance. For your entertainment, we are going to take energy and bend it, twist it, bounce it, burn it, and even extinguish it. Here's our law: Energy generates fun!

NOT A BURNING QUESTION

Bet you can't keep a match burning over a glass of soda!

THE SETUP

Check with an adult in your house before doing this trick, which involves fire. You will need a fresh bottle of carbonated soft drink and a match. Pour the soda into a glass. Light a wooden match and hold it over the glass. Be careful not to burn your fingers!

INSIDER INFORMATION

The warning about burning your fingers is our little joke. There is no chance your fingers will get burned. The match is quickly extinguished when you hold it close to the soda. This is because the soda contains carbon dioxide gas under pressure. When the bottle is opened, the bubbles of gas burst at the surface and the area just above the glass becomes rich in carbon dioxide and poor in oxygen. Fire is heat and light energy that is released with a fuel is combined with oxygen. Remove the oxygen and the reaction stops. In this case, the match quickly burns up whatever oxygen there is in the vicinity and only carbon dioxide, which won't support combustion, remains. So the match goes out.

NOTE
This trick requires a bottle of freshly opened soda. The wager will fall flat if the beverage is flat!

FOLLOW THE BOUNCING BALL POINT

Bet you can't get a SuperBall to bounce as high as a pen!

THE SETUP

They will both be dropped onto the same surface, from the same height, and with the same force. You will need a SuperBall and a ball-point pen. Stab the point of the pen into the SuperBall. Insert it deeply enough so that the ball won't drop off when you hold only the pen, but don't jam the entire tip into the ball.

Hold the end of the pen at arm's length. The ball should be facing down.

Now you are ready. Drop the pen. **WATCH OUT!** Which bounced higher—the ball or the pen?

INSIDER INFORMATION

The pen rockets out of the ball. If you are indoors, it will hit the ceiling. The SuperBall either doesn't bounce at all or just a fraction of what it normally does. Usually the SuperBall bounces to ninety percent of the height it was dropped from, losing very little of its *kinetic*

WARNING!
You must take two safety precautions at this point; first, check to make sure you are not standing beneath a ceiling light fixture, and second, cover your eyes with your hand and peek out through a tiny crack.

energy, or motion energy. But when it is dropped in tandem with the pen, the collision affects both the ball and the pen. If there were no pen, the kinetic energy of the impact would show up in the bounce of the ball. In this case, some of the kinetic energy of the ball is transferred to the pen, which really takes off. This happens because the pen has a smaller mass (weight) than the ball. Thus, it can travel nine times as high as the ball from the same amount of kinetic energy.

NO STRAINING ALLOWED

Bet you can't make a flame pass through a strainer!

THE SETUP

Check with an adult in your house before doing this trick, which involves fire. You will need a candle and a wire strainer. (Do not use a plastic strainer because it could catch on fire or melt.) Light the candle. Hold the strainer over the flame. Try to make the flame pass through the wire grid. There are plenty of holes, so this should be easy. Right?

INSIDER INFORMATION

It's not easy. In fact, it's impossible. The strainer may be full of holes, but the flame stops beneath it. A visible flame is a combination of both heat and light energy given off the by the burning gases. But the metal strainer absorbs the heat energy. Without heat energy, the gases cannot maintain kindling point (the temperature necessary to initiate combustion) and all the combustion is done below the source of heat diversion (the strainer). View the effect from the side. You will see that the light of the flame stops at the wire strainer, but smoke from the burning gases passes freely through the holes.

Back in the nineteenth century candles were used by miners to illuminate mines. This was very dangerous because there were lots of inflammable gases that a candle could ignite. So a scientist, Humphry Davy, invented a miner's lamp that contained a candle inside some wire gauze. The heat of the candle couldn't reach the dangerous gases yet the light came through the gauze.

A COLD FACT

Bet you can't cut an ice block in two with a wire!

THE SETUP

Remove the separator from an ice cube tray and fill the tray with water. Freeze it overnight. Remove the block of ice from the tray and suspend it between two cans. Do this in the sink or a flat pan because there will be dripping water. Tie a loop of very thin wire around the ice. Hang a brick or other heavy weight to the wire. The wire will slowly cut through the ice. When it cuts through, do you have two pieces?

INSIDER INFORMATION

Surprisingly, the wire passes completely through the block but it still remains in one piece. The wire cuts the ice because of pressure, a force over an area that is transformed into heat energy. As the wire presses against the ice, the part directly below the wire melts. The melted ice directly above the wire refreezes, even when the air temperature is well above the freezing point.

The water is able to refreeze because the inside of the ice block is several degrees below the freezing point. The heat of the melted ice is transferred to this cold area, refreezing the ice.

Ice skaters get a smooth ride because the pressure of the blade and the friction from the moving skate melts the ice briefly. The water under their skates "lubricates" their tracks. The next trick is another variation of this one.

HEAVY PRESSURE

Bet you can cut through an ice cube and it will seal itself behind you!

THE SETUP

You will need almost ten inches of fine wire, two spoons, a soda bottle, and an ice cube. Wind each end of the wire around a spoon handle. Leave about four inches of wire between the spoons. Rest the ice cube on top of the bottle. Put the middle of the wire across the spoons. This isn't a quickie. It takes about ten minutes for the wire to pass completely through the ice cube. But the ice cube will be whole again as the wire passes out of the bottom.

INSIDER INFORMATION

Pressure on the wire melts the ice just underneath it. As the wire moves down, the ice melts. Then the water above the wire refreezes as the heat is removed from the tiny amount of melted water by the surrounding ice.

ODDS THAT ARE OUT OF SIGHT

Bet you can't see a penny through a glass of water!

THE SETUP

Fill a glass with water—right to the brim. Then place it on top of a penny. Cover the top of the glass with a saucer. Can you see the penny?

INSIDER INFORMATION

Don't strain your eyes! You won't see the penny. In order to see something, light reflected from the object must reach your eyes. Since light can pass through water, it's puzzling that there is no spot where we can see the penny.

Actually, there *is* a spot—but it is covered by the saucer. The light rays are bent as they pass from one transparent substance to another. This moves the image of the penny upward (that's why the bottoms of pools seem shallower than they really are). When the penny is under the glass, you can't see it unless you look straight down. The saucer prevents this.

For a very strange illusion, remove the saucer and view the surface of the water from the side. The image of the penny will appear on the surface of the water.

COOL UNDER FIRE

Bet you can't raise the temperature of ice water by heating it!

THE SETUP

For this wager, ice water is defined as water with ice in it. To begin, you will need a tray of ice cubes, a saucepan, a weather thermometer, a spoon, and some water. Put the ice cubes in the saucepan with five or six inches of water. Stir the mixture with the thermometer until the mercury stops moving. It should read 32° F or 0° C. Make sure that the bulb of the thermometer is completely submerged and that it is not touching the sides or bottom of the pot.

Place the pan over a low flame for a minute. Turn off the stove and stir the ice water thoroughly. Again take a temperature reading, making sure the bulb is suspended in the liquid and not touching the pan. If the temperature has not been raised, heat the mixture again until the ice is almost melted. Stir and take another temperature reading.

When the ice is melted, you are finished. The mixture is no longer ice water.

INSIDER INFORMATION

As long as there is ice in the water, the temperature will stay 32° F or 0° C . The heat you put into the pot, however, did not just disappear. All of the energy was used to melt the ice. Not a single bit went to warm the water. When the ice is gone, of course, the heat will produce a change in the temperature of the water.

PLAYING WITH FIRE

Bet you can burn a handkerchief without hurting it!

THE SETUP

First, check with an adult before you do this and perform it over the kitchen sink. Take a small handkerchief or, even better, use a three-inch square of clean, old rag. Soak it in a mixture of four tablespoonfuls of rubbing alcohol and four tablespoonfuls of water. Hold the wet cloth over the sink with tongs. Light the bottom of the cloth with a match. Be prepared for a substantial flame that will last a few minutes. When it's finished burning, your cloth will be undamaged. It won't even be singed.

NOTE
Water will extinguish an alcohol flame in case of an accident.

INSIDER INFORMATION

The secret is in the mixture of alcohol and water. There is enough alcohol for a flame but enough water to wet the cloth. The heat from the flame must cause the water to evaporate before it can burn the cloth. There is too much water in the mixture for this to happen.

SOUND ADVICE

Bet you can make an echo in a dish!

THE SETUP

You will need two identical soup bowls and a ticking watch. Sit at a table and place one soup bowl in front of you. Hold the other soup bowl upside down over one ear. Hold the watch about an inch above the bottom of the soup bowl on the table. Move your body so that the bowl over your ear is above the bowl on the table. The watch now sounds as if it is ticking in the soup bowl by your ear and not in the one on the table.

INSIDER INFORMATION

The fix is an echo. Sound bounces off surfaces. Bouncing sounds or echoes can be collected by dish-shaped objects, much like the way a light is collected by the dish-shaped mirrors or antennae of telescopes. The dish shape focuses the echo of the ticking watch. You are hearing the echo, not the original sound.

HEARING AID

Bet you can hear a watch ticking across the room ... with your ears covered!

THE SETUP

Find a long solid piece of wood, like a dining-room table or a stair rail. Place a watch at one end. Put your ear tightly against the other end. Place your hand over the other ear. Listen.

INSIDER INFORMATION

You can hear the watch ticking loud and clear. This strange hearing aid really is quite simple. Sound waves travel through the wood more directly to your ear than through air because there are fewer things in the way to deflect them. In the air all sorts of currents keep the sound from reaching your ear. So you can hear the watch ticking through the wood when you can't hear it in the air.

LIQUID LAMP

Bet you can pour light!

THE SETUP

You will need a tall, slim jar with a lid (like olives come in), several sheets of newspaper, a flashlight, a hammer, and a large nail. Use the nail and hammer to make two holes in the lid: one large hole near an edge, and a smaller hole near the opposite edge. Fill the jar three-quarters full with water and screw on the lid. Turn on the flashlight and place it at the end of the jar so the light shines into it. Roll both the jar and flashlight in newspaper. (You may need a friend to help you wrap the paper around the two items.) If you are alone we suggest a bit of Scotch tape over the holes until you have the apparatus wrapped securely. The purpose of the newspaper is to make a light-tight tube.

To pour the light, tilt the jar so the water spurts out of the big hole into a basin. Do this in a darkened room. If you stick your finger into the stream of water, light will fall on it. This happens if you put your finger in the water near where it comes out of the jar or in the curved part of the stream near the basin. The light is completely contained in the curved stream of water. Light pours!

INSIDER INFORMATION

It is true that light travels in a straight line. But there are exceptions to every rule, and this is one of them. The light remains inside the stream of water because it is reflected internally by the water at the boundary of the stream and the air. This phenomenon also occurs in fiber optics, where light is contained in a flexible glass fiber. Fiber optics and the phenomenon of internal reflection can direct light waves anywhere a wire can go. Sending messages on light waves contained in cables of fibers revolutionized communications. It can even be used to direct light into dark, small places in the human body.

A LONG LOOK

Bet you can see into infinity!

THE SETUP

For this truly puzzling trick you will need two mirrors, some modeling clay, and a knife. Use the clay to make a stand so the mirrors can stand vertically. In the center of the back of one mirror, scrape away a circle of slivering with the knife to make a peephole about half an inch in diameter. Set the mirrors parallel to each other a few inches apart, with the reflecting surfaces facing each other. Put an object between them. When you look through the peephole, you will see the image of the object reflected an infinite number of times.

INSIDER INFORMATION

A mirror is a surface that reflects light. This means that light bounces off it. When such light bounces to another surface that also is reflective, you will see an infinite number of images as long as the mirrors are parallel. If they are at an angle, you'll see a lot of images but at some point the angle will keep you from seeing to infinity.

CLEARLY NOTHING

Bet you can make a glass disappear in a glass!

THE SETUP

Check with an adult before you do this trick as you'll need to handle the paint remover carefully. You'll need a large glass jar and a smaller one that fits into it easily. Put one jar inside the other. Now fill both the inside jar and the space between jars with paint-and-varnish remover (petroleum distillates). Amazingly, the inner jar disappears.

INSIDER INFORMATION

An object is transparent because light passes through it. Each object has its own particular speed of light transmission. When light travels from one transparent object to another (such as from air to glass), it is bent at the boundary because of the different speeds. Bent light is what lets you see the transparent object.

In this trick you replace air with a transparent liquid (the petroleum distillates) through which light moves at about the same speed as it does through glass. Light doesn't bend at the boundaries, so the boundaries are invisible. Presto! The smaller jar disappears right in front of your eyes.

OUT ON A LIMB

Bet you can fill a stocking with an invisible leg!

THE SETUP

This eerie illusion works best on a cold, dry day. It may not work for you if it's hot and muggy. To make a "ghost" leg you will need a woman's nylon stocking—the shiny kind, not the kind with elastic in it. And you must have a piece of wool (a sweater, sock or scarf). Hold the toe of the stocking in your left hand. Grasp the piece of wool in

your right hand and place it around the stocking close to your left hand. Pull the stocking through the wool-clad hand. Repeat this, rubbing the nylon in the same direction each time. Soon it will be "charged" up. Hold the opening of the stocking in your right hand. It will appear to inflate with an invisible leg.

INSIDER INFORMATION

Rubbing the nylon gives it an electrical charge known as static electricity. The entire stocking picks up the same charge, and since like charges repel each other, the opposite sides of the stocking move away from each other leaving room for the phantom limb.

VAMPIRE FIRE

Wanna bet you can make fire with blood?

THE SETUP

Dracula didn't invent this trick, but he would have loved it! Since it requires the use of fire, have a grown-up stand by.

Pour about an inch of hydrogen peroxide (the kind you buy at the drug store) into a wide mouth container. Take a long wooden match or bamboo barbecue skewer and light the end. Blow out the flame and hold the

glowing end close to the surface of the peroxide. Nothing happens. Wait. This isn't the trick. We just wanted to prove to you that peroxide alone won't affect a glowing stick. You need to make a bloody mess before it will burst into flame.

Now for the gory part. You will need a source of blood! Add a pinch of very fresh (bright red) hamburger or a piece of fresh liver to the peroxide. Light the stick again and blow it out. Put the glowing ember near the now bubbling peroxide and it will burst into flame.

INSIDER INFORMATION

Fire is energy that results when a fuel (wood in this case) combines with oxygen. Air only contains about twenty percent oxygen. If you increase the amount of oxygen, the energy is released faster.

Hydrogen peroxide contains a lot of oxygen and it is very unstable. If you look closely you can see tiny bubbles of oxygen as they slowly move to the surface. Blood (yours included) contains an enzyme, called *catalase*, which speeds up the release of the oxygen, turning the peroxide into plain water. Oxygen bubbles out of the peroxide so rapidly that it forms a froth as it escapes into the air. In the oxygen-rich environment, the dying fire blazes again.

SWEETNESS AND LIGHT

Wanna bet sugar glows in the dark?

THE SETUP

This should spark your interest. You can make mini-lightning with cubes of sugar. Take two sugar cubes into a closet or very dark room. It is very important to you wait five to ten minutes

so your eyes can adapt to the darkness. Rub the two cubes rapidly together or strike one against the other as if you are striking a match. You will see a faint glow where the cubes meet.

INSIDER INFORMATION

The glow is lightning on a very small scale. Lightning is a stream of electricity that excites nitrogen molecules in the air. Excited nitrogen releases as light the extra energy it gets from the electricity. When sugar crystals are crushed, the pieces become positively and negatively charged. That makes the electricity jump through the air between the pieces of sugar, exciting nitrogen molecules and making them emit light.

Chemical energy is stored in all kinds of molecules. In some substances, chemical energy can be changed to light energy by pressure. Sugar crystals have this unusual property. When you squeeze, press, or crush the crystals, they give off electricity called *piezoelectricity* (*piezo* means pressure).

More energy is released from the sugar than meets the eye. The next trick taps into this invisible energy and is guaranteed not to leave you in the dark.

THE ELECTRIC LIFESAVER

Wanna bet you can make sparks fly in your mouth?

THE SETUP

Rubbing sugar cubes may not be one of the all-time great tricks, but candy that flashes lightning in your mouth is. You've gotta try this one—you may develop quite a taste for it.

Again, you must go into a dark room and wait for your eyes to adapt to the darkness. You can observe the mouth lightning with a mirror or take turns creating it with a friend. Hold a Wint-O-Green Life Saver between your teeth and watch as you bite it. Sparks of blue-green light leap out wherever your teeth crack the candy. If you are not allowed to bite hard candies, use a pair of pliers.

INSIDER INFORMATION

This trick begins where the last one left off. The same scientific principle is working here. Piezoelectric sugar in the candy provides the energy. Some of it is emitted as the glow you saw in the sugar-cube experiment, but a lot of it is released as ultraviolet light that the human eye can't detect. Wintergreen is a substance that absorbs the ultraviolet energy and transforms it into visible light. This process is called *fluorescence*. The excited wintergreen molecules emit a bright blue-green light that is stronger than the glow from sugar alone.

The same phenomenon is at work in certain adhesives. Check out Flashy First Aid on page 234.

This trick will not work with candies made with sugar substitutes. You'll get no light from lite candy!

A NUT CASE

Wanna bet you can toast a marshmallow with a nut?

THE SETUP

When you consider the high price of oil, you might not think it grows on trees. Surprise, it does! This is a nutty trick, but we are not crazy when we suggest burning a Brazil nut. Nuts contain oil, and a single, shelled Brazil nut burns long enough to toast several marshmallows.

Since this trick involves fire, have an adult present before you begin. Stick a Brazil nut on the triangular, pointed end of a metal can opener and place it in the center of a pan. Light a long candle or a fireplace match and hold it under the nut until it begins to burn, then extinguish the candle or match. Wait until the nut is burning steadily before you toast your marshmallow.

INSIDER INFORMATION

Brazil nuts are large seeds that are sixty-seven percent oil. Brazil nut trees use the energy of sunlight to manufacture oil. The oil is a source of stored chemical energy that can be released later. The Brazil nut seedling uses this energy to grow. When you eat a Brazil nut, your body uses this energy. You can also release the energy stored in oil by burning it. So the light energy of the sun can be transformed into energy used by living things or into the heat and light of fire.

Brazil nuts are not the only oily nuts. You might want to try toasting marshmallows with a walnut, a cashew, or even a macadamia nut.

Unlike petroleum, nut oils are a renewable resource. Theoretically, there could be peanut-powered cars in our future.

ELECTRONIC SPIT

Wanna bet you can taste electricity?

THE SETUP

Although this trick involves electricity, it is not a shocker. Believe it or not, electricity has a flavor all its own. To find out what it tastes like, you will need aluminum foil and a piece of silver. Touch the foil to the tip of your tongue. Then taste the silver. Notice the flavor of each. Put them together and touch your tongue to the place where they overlap. The tangy taste that tingles your tongue is electricity.

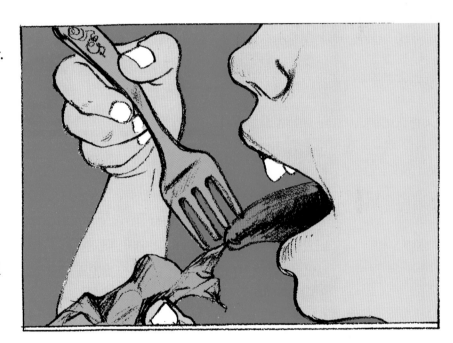

INSIDER INFORMATION

You have made a battery with your tongue. Batteries produce electricity, a stream of tiny negatively charged particles called *electrons*. In your tongue battery, electrons move from the aluminum through your saliva to the silver and then directly back to the aluminum. As the moving electrons cross your tongue, they stimulate the nerves in your taste buds. Now that you have tasted power, are you hungry for more?

A SICK JOKE

Wanna bet you can fake a fever with a TV remote or a flashlight?

THE SETUP

Thermometer strips are an inexpensive, modern way to take your temperature. You can get them in almost any pharmacy. When you place one against your forehead, it changes color, showing whether or not you have a fever.

You can make these strips register a fever even when you don't have one. Try placing a TV remote-control device against the thermometer strip and clicking the on-off switch. Vicki's clicker didn't work, but Kathy's did. So, if yours doesn't work, shine a small flashlight on the strip instead, and you may get the same hot news.

INSIDER INFORMATION

Sometimes it takes high tech to beat high tech. The

temperature strip contains an unusual kind of matter, a liquid crystal.

Normally a crystal is a solid. Ice, diamonds, emeralds, and salt are examples of crystals. The molecules in all crystals have a regular arrangement that scatters the light that strikes them. Sometimes scattered light gives a crystal its color. When a crystal melts and changes into a liquid, the molecules are no longer held rigidly in a regular pattern and the crystal no longer scatters light the same way.

A liquid crystal has a regular arrangement of molecules like a solid, but it also flows like a liquid. When heat energy is applied to the liquid crystal, the structure of the molecules continually changes. Each change scatters a different color of light. So you see the chemical go through a series of colors: red, yellow, green, blue, and violet. When it cools, the colors show up in reverse order. Heat, however, is not the only kind of energy that will affect the liquid crystal. Infrared radiation that comes from the TV clicker and ordinary light from a flashlight also do the job.

NOTHING TO GET STEAMED UP ABOUT

Wanna bet you can't boil water in boiling water?

THE SETUP

There's an old saying that a watched pot never boils. That's because it seems to take forever to come to a boil when you're in a hurry. But in this trick it *would* take forever. The water truly never boils.

Have an adult present before you do this trick, since you will be using the stove. Put some water into a small jar. Find a way to suspend the jar in a pot of water so that it doesn't touch the sides or the bottom. If you use a two-handled pot, hang the jar from a wire that is fastened to the handles. Heat the pot on the stove. The water in the pot will soon come to a boil, but the water in the jar never will.

INSIDER INFORMATION

This may come as a bit of a surprise. After all, the water in the jar is the same as the water in the pot. To make water boil and turn into steam requires an input of heat energy. The heat energy of the stove makes the temperature of the water in the pot rise until it reaches 100° C (212° F). At that point, the stove's heat changes the water into steam—the water boils. The conversion of water to steam keeps the temperature from rising above 100 degrees. The water in the jar, however, is kept separated from the source heat, the stove. So it never gets enough heat to boil.

A double boiler works on this principle. It is used to cook foods that should not boil, like chocolate pudding.

A TV FLOP

Wanna bet you can watch TV upside down on a piece of paper?

THE SETUP

You can turn any TV show into a flop. All you need is a magnifying glass and a piece of white paper. Turn on the tube and cut the lights. Stand about ten feet from the set and hold the magnifying glass between the TV and the paper. Both the paper and the lens should face the screen and be vertical. Position the paper about six inches from the lens. Move the lens back

and forth until you see a focused image of your TV picture projected on the paper.

INSIDER INFORMATION

Your image is tiny, upside down and backward. The magnifying glass bends light that passes through it and focuses the emerging light to form an image. The light from the left side of the screen is bent to the right, and light from the top of the TV is bent to the bottom, and vice versa.

HOME GROWN TV

Wanna bet you can make a big screen TV with a shaving mirror?

THE SETUP

Can't afford a big screen TV? Why not grow it yourself. Here's how you can get the big picture. All you need is an ordinary TV with a wall behind it and a magnifying shaving or makeup mirror. Turn the TV on and the lights off. Hold the shaving mirror about two feet in front of the screen and tilt it slightly upward to project the image on the wall. To focus the image, move the mirror either closer or farther away from the TV. Moving the TV away from the wall will let you make an even bigger picture.

INSIDER INFORMATION

There's one very good reason why the homegrown large screen TV hasn't caught on. You'll notice it immediately. This is yet another flop. Your favorite program is upside down and backward.

A magnifying mirror has a curved surface. Like all mirrors, it reflects light. But the curved surface spreads the reflected light so that it projects an enlarged image. Any mirror reverses left and right, but the curved mirror also reverses top and bottom.

FAR OUT REMOTE CONTROL

Wanna bet you can control your TV from another room?

THE SETUP

For this trick you need a TV with a remote control unit, several mirrors, and some friends. Notice that the TV has a small light detector, a square or a circle, on the front panel. This is your target. Stand outside the TV room. Have a friend hold a mirror so that you can see the TV in the mirror. Aim the remote control at the image in the mirror. Fire! The TV obeys your command.

INSIDER INFORMATION

The remote control device is an invisible-ray gun that shoots infrared light. This invisible light bounces, or reflects, off a mirror, just like the light you can see. The reflection of light from a mirror is very predictable. If *you* can see a person in a mirror, that person can also see you in the mirror. The light detector in the TV is like an eye. If you can see the TV in the mirror, it will get the message sent by invisible light. You can make your remote control even more remote. Just add mirrors and friends to hold them. If everything is properly lined up, there's no telling how far you can go.

NO PLACE TO HIDE

Wanna bet you can see through a mirror?

THE SETUP

For this trick you will need a pair of mirrored sunglasses. Normally when you look at someone wearing mirrored sunglasses, you see the whites of your own eyes, not theirs. It is possible to see through this mirror, though. Take them off and put a light behind them. What was once an impenetrable mirror is now transparent.

INSIDER INFORMATION

Most mirrors don't transmit light. They only reflect the light that strikes their surfaces. Mirrored sunglasses, however, have a special surface that allows light to pass through. If they didn't, they wouldn't be much use as glasses.

They are not one-way mirrors. There's no such thing. If light can go through one way, it can go through the other way, too. When people wear mirrored sunglasses, there isn't enough light between their eyes and the lenses for you to see their eyes from the mirrored side. If you hold the mirrored side to your eyes, though, you'll see right through. The transparency of either side depends on where the greatest amount of light is.

Two-way mirrors have been used to con people for years. When magicians make objects appear and disappear, it's often done with the aid of these mirrors. They also make an ideal "cover" for spies. To check out suspicious mirrors, turn out the lights and put your eyeball right up to the mirror.

READING OTHER PEOPLE'S MAIL

Wanna bet you can read a letter through the envelope?

THE SETUP

It's the business of spies to see things other people don't want them to see. A good spy knows how to read a message without opening the envelope. It is illegal to read other people's mail. Spies don't care. We'll show you how to do it, but we don't want you to get into trouble—and blame us. Have a friend write you a message and seal it in an envelope. You can read the message right through the envelope if you spray it with hair spray or artist's fixative spray (matte-finish Krylon).

INSIDER INFORMATION

Light passes through transparent materials. Although it is made of two transparent materials, cellulose fibers and air, paper is not transparent. Light travels at different speeds through different transparent materials. When it passes from one transparent material to another, it bends at the boundary because of the different speeds. (That's why the magnifying glass focuses the image of your TV screen.) Instead of passing through paper, light is bent at the boundaries of cellulose and air and scatters internally. When you spray the envelope with a fixative, the air spaces are filled with a material that transmits light at about the same speed as cellulose. The light has a more uniform material to pass through, so it doesn't bend and scatter. The paper becomes transparent.

Oil makes paper transparent for the same reason, but a spy wouldn't use oil because the envelope would remain transparent. Tampering would be obvious. Hair spray evaporates quickly and doesn't leave a clue.

THE MILKY WAY

Wanna bet you can see a sunset in a glass of water?

THE SETUP

Ever wonder why the sky is blue and sunsets are red? Create your own Milky Way to discover the answers. Stir a half teaspoon of milk into an eight-ounce glass of water. Shine a flashlight through the side of the glass. Notice the bluish color of the water-milk mixture. Now look directly at the flashlight bulb through the side of the glass. It looks yellow. Shine the flashlight up through the bottom of the glass. When you look down on the flashlight bulb from the surface of the liquid, it looks orange.

INSIDER INFORMATION

The milk-water mixture is a model of the atmosphere. The earth's atmosphere is made up of gas molecules, water vapor, and dust particles. When light travels

through the atmosphere, the particles scatter the light. Sunlight is white light that is made up of all the colors of the rainbow, called the *spectrum*. Blue light is scattered the most, making the sky appear blue. The milk particles, suspended in the water, scatter blue light from the flashlight in the same manner.

When you see the sun during the day, you see what's left of the spectrum after the sky has scattered the blue light; the remaining light from the sun's surface is a mix of green, yellow, orange, and red, but it appears yellow.

The sun is closest to you at noon, when it's directly overhead. At sunset the sun is near the horizon. Now the light source is farther from you, and sunlight has to pass through more of the atmosphere and it hits more particles. Now, the blue, and the green and yellow light is scattered as well, leaving behind an orange or red sun. When you look at the flashlight from the top of the glass, the light passes through more of the mixture than it does from the side. More colors are scattered, leaving behind an orange bulb—a sunset in your glass.

COLOR BLIND

Wanna bet you can't find a blue gumball?

THE SETUP

Put gumballs of different colors (white, red, blue, green, etc.) in a box. View them through a filter made of eight layers of red cellophane. The red gumball and all the other colors that reflect a lot of light will appear white. The green and blue gumballs will look black.

INSIDER INFORMATION

When white light strikes a red object, the object reflects the red part of the spectrum and absorbs all the other colors. When you look through a red filter, the light you see is red. When the red light strikes the red gumball, most of the light is reflected and you see it as white. When red light strikes a blue gumball, there is almost no blue light for the gumball to reflect. All the red light is absorbed and it appears black. Green gumballs also look black. You won't be able to tell the blue from the green. There's no need, however, for others to know of your defeat. Eat the evidence!

TIME OUT

Wanna bet you can make time disappear?

THE SETUP

To do this trick you need a pair of polarized sunglasses and a watch with a liquid crystal display (LCD). Put on the sunglasses and look at the time display. Slowly rotate the watch and the numbers will magically disappear. Keep turning and they'll reappear again. This also works for computer screens. If you wear the polarized sunglasses, the picture will disappear as you tilt your head.

INSIDER INFORMATION

Light travels in all directions. Polarized sunglasses are filters that allow only light that's traveling in a vertical direction to pass. Glare travels horizontally and is stopped by polarized lenses. When you look through two polarized lenses that are at right angles to each other, all the light is blocked. The top of a liquid crystal display has a polarizer on it. You can't see anything in the watch when your polarized glasses are aligned at right angles to the watch's polarizer.

Substitute an LCD calculator for the watch and instead of killing time you can eliminate math.

AH, SWEET MYSTERY OF LIGHT

Wanna bet there's a rainbow hidden in syrup?

THE SETUP

All the colors of the rainbow can be seen in a glass of clear corn syrup. To see the light show, you will need two polarized lenses that you have removed from a pair of sunglasses, (check with the owner before you pop the lenses) a clear drinking glass, Karo syrup, a light source, and a helper.

Look down at the light source through one lens, the drinking glass, and the second lens. Rotate the top lens to find the darkest position. Keep looking while your helper slowly pours syrup into the glass. One by one, beginning with blue, the colors of the spectrum appear.

INSIDER INFORMATION

Corn syrup has the ability to rotate polarized light. When you look through two polarized lenses that are at right angles to each other, light is blocked. By adding syrup, light emerging from the bottom lens is rotated slightly. This light is no longer at an angle that is stopped by the top lens, so some of it passes through. The emerging light shows up as a single color. The color that you see is the one that is rotated into a position that lines up with the top lens. As you increase the thickness of the syrup, you increase the rotation of polarized light so the next color moves into the line-up. When you see red, stop pouring. You're at the end of the spectrum. Now, if you rotate the top lens you will be able to see all the colors again, one by one in order.

There are other optically active syrups. Check out honey and pancake syrups.

A BRIGHT IDEA

Wanna bet you can write secret messages with laundry detergent?

THE SETUP

You will need colorless liquid laundry detergent containing brighteners, a "black" light bulb from a hobby or novelty store, and a cotton swab. To write a secret message, use the cotton swab as a pen, the laundry detergent as the ink, and your arm as the paper. When the message dries, it will be invisible. To reveal it, look at your skin under the black light. The message will glow!

INSIDER INFORMATION

Most laundry detergents contain fluorescent chemicals called brighteners. Although a "black" light appears dim, it's giving off a lot of light that you can't see, called *ultraviolet*. When ultraviolet light strikes fluorescent materials, it is changed into visible light. That's why the message glows.

Ultraviolet light is present in sunlight. Small particles of the brighteners remain in your clothes after washing. They transform the ultraviolet light from the sun into visible light and make the colors look brighter.

Sunscreen is an ultraviolet blocker. It is designed to protect your skin from the damaging ultraviolet rays of the sun. Instead of fluorescing, like brighteners, it absorbs UV light. You can use it to write secret messages, too. White paper is especially

CAUTION!

Microwave ovens produce heat. The following experiments *must* be done with adult help. Have potholders handy, and use them whenever you handle hot dishes. And don't leave your experiment unattended in the microwave. Not only will you miss the fun, but also you need to be ready to shut off the oven in case of an emergency. If a fire should occur in the microwave oven, leave the door closed and turn off or unplug the oven.

striking. Under the black light, the paper, which contains brighteners, glows and the sunscreen message is dark. A message on your skin doesn't show as much contrast but it can still be read.

MAP YOUR MICROWAVE

Nuke fax paper.

THE SETUP

Some spots in a microwave oven get hotter than others. That's why manufacturers recommend that you rotate food during cooking. Want to know the best place to put your food? Fax the answer to yourself.

You will need:

- a piece of thermal fax paper
- scissors
- a microwave oven
- a marker

CAUTION!

When you see dark areas appearing on the paper, turn off the oven. The paper may catch on fire if you nuke it too long. If this does happen, leave the door closed and turn off or unplug the oven.

Get a piece of thermal fax paper from a fax machine or office supply store. Put a small mark on the shinier side, the side facing up as it comes from the machine. This is the only side that is heat sensitive. Cut the fax paper to fit the bottom of your microwave oven. (If your oven has a rotating table, remove it for this experiment.) Place the paper in the oven with the marked side up. Nuke on high for about seven minutes.

thermal fax paper

You now have a thermal map of your microwave. The hottest spots are the darkest, the cooler areas are white.

If your oven does have a rotating table, nuke another piece of fax paper while it's rotating and see what happens to your pattern.

INSIDER INFORMATION

Microwaves are really waves. Like water waves they bounce off surfaces, such as the oven walls. When a bouncing wave encounters an incoming wave, the two waves combine to form a larger wave called a *standing wave*. Standing waves stay in the same place. In a microwave oven, the standing waves form hot spots. Each microwave oven has its own pattern of hot spots. You've mapped your oven floor. But it you place the paper above the level of the floor, you may get a different pattern.

Now you know where to put your food so it cooks the fastest!

ERUPTING SOAP

Transform an ordinary bar of Ivory soap into an erupting volcano of foam.

THE SETUP

You will need:

- a regular-size bar of Ivory soap
- a paper plate
- a microwave oven

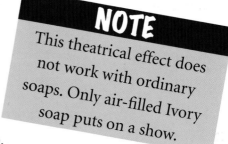

NOTE
This theatrical effect does not work with ordinary soaps. Only air-filled Ivory soap puts on a show.

Begin your experiment into the world of slow motion explosions by unwrapping a regular-size bar of Ivory soap. Place the soap on a paper plate in a microwave oven, preferably one with a glass door so that you can watch the eruption.

Nuke the soap for two minutes on full power. Your previously firm bar of soap is now a light and fluffy mound of frothy, expanded soap foam.

INSIDER INFORMATION

Your soap eruption is courtesy of two industrial accidents.

The first was the discovery of the heating properties of microwaves as described in the Map Your Microwave experiment on the previous page.

The second accident created Ivory soap. A machine that mixed soap was inadvertently left on during lunch. When the machine operator returned he found that the overly mixed batch of soap he had, had air beaten into it. The resulting soap floated. People liked the floating soap, and the mistake turned into a marketing success.

How do two accidents equal one volcano? Ivory soap, like all soaps, contains water. Microwaves cause water molecules to vibrate. The faster they vibrate, the hotter the water gets. When they vibrate fast enough, the water molecules turn into steam. Unlike other soaps, Ivory soap is honeycombed with thin-walled air spaces. The pressure of the steam breaks down the walls of the air spaces and a big puffball of soap grows until all the steam has escaped.

This experiment will not harm your microwave oven although it does tend to make your kitchen smell like a laundry. Speaking of laundry, your soap volcano doesn't have to go to waste. Press the puffball and ta da!—Ivory flakes that you can use for washing. You have made a significant discovery in the field of good, clean fun!

MONSTER MARSHMALLOW

Toast a marshmallow from the inside out.

THE SETUP

Picture a toasted marshmallow. Black and brown on the outside, white and gooey on the inside. Toasting a marshmallow in a microwave oven is a totally different experience.

You will need:

- a marshmallow
- a paper plate
- a microwave oven

Put a marshmallow on a paper plate and nuke it. The length of
time will depend on the strength of your microwave oven.
(Ours took one minute and
thirty seconds on high.) As
the microwaves bombard the
marshmallow it appears to
become a living thing: It grows to
three times its original size, it moves and sways.

Remove the monster marshmallow from the oven. **But don't touch the monster
marshmallow—it's very hot.** Give
it a few minutes to cool. Watch
as it slowly shrinks and shrivels.
The outside is white and looks
uncooked. Break it open. The
inside is brown. You've toasted
your marshmallow from the
inside out!

Eat your experiment when it's
cool. It is crunchy and delicious.

INSIDER INFORMATION

Microwave ovens cook by making
water molecules in the food
vibrate. The faster the molecules
vibrate, the hotter the food gets.
When the water gets hot enough,
it changes into steam and escapes.
This causes the tiny air spaces in
the marshmallow to expand.

Unlike a campfire, which cooks
from the outside in, microwaves
penetrate the marshmallow and
cook it all at once. The inside

temperature of the marshmallow gets hot enough to brown the sugar. The outside surface is cooled by escaping steam so it doesn't get hot enough to turn brown. The marshmallow will turn brown and burn after all the steam has escaped, so stop the microwave oven as soon as the puffing has stopped.

A new wrinkle on this trick is to nuke those fluffy marshmallow chicks called Peeps. They really blow up! In fact, a nuking Peep show has been featured on YouTube.

FIREWORKS FROM A GRAPE

Nuke a grape.

THE SETUP

Would you believe pyrotechnics from a grape?

You will need:

- a green seedless grape
- a sharp knife
- a microwave-safe plate
- a microwave oven

To prepare a grape for this heat-and-light show, carefully slice it almost in half leaving the halves attached by skin. Place the grape on a microwave-safe plate with the cut sides down. Place the plate in the center of a microwave oven. Nuke it on high for thirty seconds. Watch it through the door.

Within five seconds, sparks shoot between the grape halves. Three to four seconds later lightning arcs over the skin bridge and the force blasts the two halves of the grape apart, ending the show.

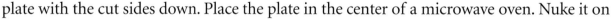

At this point turn off the microwave to prevent any damage to the oven or further damage to the grape.

INSIDER INFORMATION

There isn't a simple explanation for the grape explosion, but here's what some of the best minds around think happens:

1. Grape juice conducts electricity.
2. Microwaves not only heat the water in the grapes but force a small amount of electricity back and forth through the skin bridge. This heats the bridge hot enough for it to catch on fire.
3. The microwaves begin to pass through the flame, which can also conduct electricity. This kind of electric current forms a brilliant light arcing back and forth between the grape halves. By the time this happens the bridge has been burned, so to speak.
4. The arcing current is strong enough to blast the grape halves apart.

Not bad for a fruit that's just one of the bunch.

SUPERHEATED WATER

Use sugar to make water boil.

THE SETUP

How can you tell when water is boiling? Easy—just look for the bubbles rapidly rising to the surface of the pot. But boiling water in a microwave oven is different. It can be boiling without a bubble in sight!

You will need:

- a one-cup Pyrex measuring cup
- water
- a teaspoon
- sugar
- a microwave oven
- a potholder

CAUTION!
Since this trick involves not only a microwave oven but also boiling hot water, an adult assistant is definitely required.

Put water in a glass measuring cup and place it in the microwave oven. Nuke the water on high for two minutes and thirty seconds. The water is now hot enough to boil.

Remove the cup from the oven, using a potholder if necessary. Sprinkle a teaspoon of sugar across the surface. Within seconds a rush of tiny bubbles foams over the surface of the water.

INSIDER INFORMATION

Water boils when water molecules move fast enough to escape from the liquid into the air as steam. When you boil water in a pot on the stove, the water is heated from the bottom up. The hottest water molecules join together to form bubbles of steam on the bottom of the pot. Then the bubbles break loose and rise to the top.

In a microwave oven all the water in the cup is heated at the same time but not evenly. (Remember those hot spots in your oven.) Although some molecules are moving fast enough to escape, they can be trapped by slower moving surrounding molecules which prevent them from getting together to form a bubble. The sharp edges of the sugar crystals have tiny points around which bubbles can form. This is another example of *nucleation*, where rough spots in this case cause bubbles to form. For other experiments involving nucleation see Soda Fountain on page 15 and A Supercool Trick on page 215.

INSIDE JOB

Blow up a balloon inside a bottle.

THE SETUP

It's not possible for a person to inflate a balloon inside a bottle with lung power. However, you can do it with steam power.

You will need:

- a tablespoon
- water

- an empty 12 ounce glass bottle with label removed
- a microwave oven
- oven mitts
- a small balloon

Put a tablespoon of water into a clear glass bottle. **Do not use a plastic bottle. It will melt in the microwave.** Place the uncapped bottle in a microwave oven (if your microwave is too small, turn the bottle on its side). Nuke it on high. Set the timer for three minutes but watch the bottle through the window. Stop the oven when the water is **almost** boiled away. At this point the bottle is very hot and full of steam.

Have your adult assistant **use oven mitts** to remove the bottle and set it on a counter. Be careful not to knock the bottle over.

Your assistant should then take off the oven mitts and immediately stretch the neck of the balloon over the mouth of the bottle. Watch as the bottle cools. The balloon will be sucked into the bottle and will inflate until it fills the interior of the bottle.

You have now created a mysterious object. See if anyone can figure out how it was made.

Stop when the water is almost boiled away.

Have your helper place the hot bottle on a heat resistant surface.

INSIDER INFORMATION

The microwave oven heats the water so that it boils and changes into steam. The steam drives out all the air in the bottle. If you left the bottle alone, the steam would have cooled and condensed back into a very small amount of water. Air would have pushed into the bottle to replace the space left by the condensing

Stretch the balloon over the bottle mouth.

steam. Since you put a balloon over the bottle while it was full of steam, the returning air pushed against the balloon, inflating it inside the bottle.

You got around one impossibility only to create another: Bet you can't remove the balloon without breaking the seal!

6. MATTER OF MYSTERY

Want to be let in on the biggest get-rich-quick scheme of all time? Sure you do. Well, it was not the plunder of King Tut's tomb or an attempt to break into Fort Knox. But it did have to do with gold. The plan was to take all kinds of cheap metals and turn them into gold.

This bright idea was worked on back in the Middle Ages by men called alchemists. The only trouble was it didn't work. They took all kinds of matter and burned them, boiled them, beat them, and mixed them together. But no matter what they did, they never made gold. Their work was not a total loss, though. They discovered many of the properties of matter.

Modern chemists began where the alchemists left off. Modern chemists didn't make gold either, but a lot of money was made with materials they discovered. Some properties of matter can let you do surprising things. Five hundred years ago, Columbus discovered the natives of a Caribbean island playing with balls made out of something quite mysterious.

Unlike balls the Europeans had seen before, these balls bounced! The natives made the bouncing balls from the sap of a tree. They also dipped their feet in the sap. When it dried, their feet were waterproof. This bouncy, waterproof stuff is probably not a mystery to you. It's good old rubber.

It took a different kind of explorer, the laboratory scientist, to show how rubber could be put to good use. Natural rubber gets sticky in hot weather and brittle in the cold. Charles Goodyear, in 1839, figured out how to make rubber usable in any temperature.

Scientist-explorers not only alter materials, sometimes they discover brand new ones. These materials are as mysterious to us as rubber was to Columbus. We've taken some of these high-tech materials and created tricks that exploit their weirdness. Would you believe there's a bouncing liquid, a thirsty powder that drinks eighty times its weight in water, or a metal that can be trained to remember? We also added a "bomb," an explosion, blood, and acid—all presented for your experimenting pleasure. Once scientists know what stuff is like engineers can figure out useful things to do with it or … as in this chapter some useless but entertaining applications. Causing a coin to appear to pass through a solid or making tonic water glow are only two of the "apps" you've just gotta try.

This chapter is devoted to discovering the properties of materials. Discover them. You'll be richer for it.

BOUND TO WIN

Bet you can make a ball perform a delayed leap.

THE SETUP

Cut an old tennis ball in half. You can use scissors after you have punctured the ball with a knife. Cut around one of the half balls until you have a two-inch diameter. Turn the disc inside out. Set it on the ground inside out so the dome is up. Wait.

INSIDER INFORMATION

Suddenly and explosively, the piece of ball will fly into the air. When you retrieve it you will notice it has turned itself right side out again. It will take a little experimenting with the size of the disc and the kind of ball to use. If the disc is too small you will not even have time to get your hand away before it performs its inside-out leap. If the disc is too large, it might take hours before the flying leap occurs.

Rubber is a substance made up of long molecules that are folded

in accordion fashion. Each molecule acts like a spring. For this reason, rubber has the very interesting property of springing back to its original shape after it has been distorted. This elastic property gives rubber its bounce. This stunt will give you a kick.

QUITE A RIBBING

Bet you can balance a sheet of newspaper on its edge!

THE SETUP

Crease a sheet of newspaper across its diagonal. Fold back each side about an inch from the crease to form a rib, as shown in the picture. Now the newspaper will stand up on edge when you balance it on your hand.

INSIDER INFORMATION

Folding materials often makes them stronger by deflecting and diverting force. Engineers and architects make use of this fact in the design and construction of buildings. Another common use is the corrugated (or folded) paper used in boxes. Even animals, like bees, are aware of the fact that the shape of a structure affects the strength of the building material. A honeycomb cell—a perfect hexagon—makes walls stronger.

ASHES, ASHES, WE DON'T FALL DOWN

Bet you can hang a pop top on ashes!

THE SETUP

Soak about a foot of cotton string (make sure it's cotton by reading the label) in a solution of one tablespoon salt in a half a cup of water. (Heat the solution until almost all the salt is dissolved.) Remove the string and let it dry. Cut a length of string about six inches long. Tie one end to the ring of a soft-drink pop top. (You can remove the ring from the can by bending it back and forth until it breaks off.)

Make a stand out of a wire coat hanger by bending the curved hook so that it is at right angles to the triangular part. The triangle is placed flat on a surface as a base. Since this stunt uses fire, check with an adult before performing it.

Place the hanger stand on a fireproof surface like a stove top or in the sink. Tie the free end of the salt string to the hook with the pop top ring hanging down. All set? Now, light the string.

INSIDER INFORMATION

POP TOP   COTTON STRING

The string flames away and burns out. The pop top is left hanging by the ash.

The ash is strengthened by the salt crystals, which don't burn but give the minerals left in the cotton ashes just enough strength to cling together. Don't breathe heavily on the structure. Ashes are not your basic strong support.

SWEETNESS AND LIGHTNESS

Bet you can make a sugar cube float!

THE SETUP

This is a "do ahead" trick because it takes a bit of doctoring to make a sugar cube float. At the drugstore buy some New Skin, which athletes use to cover blisters. It is mostly a chemical called collodion. Pour some of the New Skin into a small paper cup. Hold the sugar cube with tweezers, dip it completely into the collodion, and hold it there for about twenty seconds. Remove it and set it in a warm place to dry. Wait about twenty-four hours before attempting to "float" it.

Drop an untreated sugar cube into some hot water or tea. It sinks and lies on the bottom of the glass until it dissolves. Now drop your treated cube into the water. Disappointment! It drops to the bottom too. But don't despair. It will slowly surface and float like a cork.

INSIDER INFORMATION

The collodion has the ability to coat the surface of the sugar crystals both inside and out. It fills in the spaces in the cube. So when the cube is put into hot water, the sugar dissolves but the collodion framework remains behind, and it is buoyant enough to float. And the bonus is it still looks just like a sugar cube. Don't, however, try to eat it.

LEAKPROOF

Bet you can stab a pencil through a water bomb without "exploding" it!

THE SETUP

Fill a polyethylene bag with water (You can add a few drops of food coloring for a more dramatic effect). Make sure it says "polyethylene" on the box. Twist it closed with a twist tie, or zip it if it's that style bag. Now stab a sharp pencil through the water bomb so that it goes in one side and

out the other. Leave the pencil in place. Despite the fact you have made two pencil-size holes, not one drop of water leaks out.

INSIDER INFORMATION

Polyethylene is a thermoplastic (one that melts with heat) that has the peculiar property of shrinking its molecules together when it is torn. When you puncture the bag with the pencil, the polyethylene shrinks around the opening, closing it off so no water escapes. This same property is used to make tires that can't blow out if punctured by a nail.

SMOKE BUT NO FIRE!

Bet you can make smoke come from your fingertips!

THE SETUP

This is another one of the fire stunts, so you should get the okay of an adult. You will need to use matches. Gather a metal pan, two new books of matches or a small box of "strike on" wooden matches, and a pair of scissors. Cut the striking surface off one side of the box or one of the books of matches. Fold it in half lengthwise. (You may have to peel off some of the cardboard from the back of the striking surface to get it thin enough to fold.) Put it upside down, like a tent in the metal pan. Light the cardboard behind the striking surface and let it burn in the pan until it goes out. When it has finished burning, you will notice a reddish-brown residue in the pan. Rub this stuff onto the tips of your finger and thumb. Now when you rub your finger and thumb together, smoke will come from your fingertips.

INSIDER INFORMATION

The striking surface of a matchbook contains a compound of red phosphorus that ignites at a low temperature. When you burn the striking surface you release red phosphorus onto the surface of the metal. This substance has the strange property of "burning" at a low temperature. The warmth created by the friction from rubbing your fingers together sends the smoke signal of oxidation into the air. Truly a magical effect!

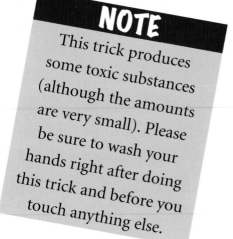

NOTE
This trick produces some toxic substances (although the amounts are very small). Please be sure to wash your hands right after doing this trick and before you touch anything else.

DIRT CHEAP

Bet you can make a black nail turn silver!

THE SETUP

Under adult supervision for the fire part of this trick, please! Hold a nail with a pair of pliers. Place it just over a candle flame. The nail removes heat from the flame so the burning is not complete. This is called a "dirty" fire. Some of the unburned material, in the form of carbon, coats the nail. This coating of black powder is called soot. Drop the soot-covered

nail in a glass of water. Look at it from the side. Instead of the pitch-black carbon, it gleams like pure silver. Too bad you can't bank on it.

INSIDER INFORMATION

Carbon is an element that has the peculiar property of attracting air to its surface. When you put it under water, the water does not wet the finely divided carbon soot. A very thin layer of air lies between the water and the soot. This layer of air causes the silvery look.

HANGING BY A THREAD!

Bet you can lift an ice cube with a thread that's not tied on to it!

THE SETUP

Curl the end of a piece of thread on an ice cube. Sprinkle generously with salt. Wait about a minute. Now lift the cube. The string is frozen to the cube and provides a handy handle.

INSIDE INFORMATION

Salt lowers the temperature at which ice freezes. The ice near the salt melts. The string now is surrounded by water. The water refreezes because it is surrounded by ice that's at a lower temperature, which removes heat from the water. The thread now is frozen to the cube. This is a short-time operation, though. If you wait too long, the entire cube will melt and you will have only one wet thread. The next trick cashes in on these same principles.

SLICK TRICK

Stack ice cubes to see how easily success can slip away.

THE SETUP

You're not going to build an ice castle. The object of this slick trick is just to pile ice cubes one on top of another. Good luck! Ice cubes are not bricks. They slip off each other as the tower grows.

You will need:

- ice cubes
- a plate
- table salt

There is a way to build a cool tower (more than three cubes high). Before you try stacking the ice cubes, let them sit on a plate at room temperature for two or three minutes. Then generously sprinkle salt on the top surface of a cube before putting another cube on top of it. Put a layer of salt between ice cubes as your stack grows. Practice and you may beat our record of five.

INSIDER INFORMATION

There are two reasons why the ice cubes don't slip in your salted stack. First, salt lowers the freezing point of water. The ice melts around each grain of salt as the salt dissolves. As a result, the ice is unevenly eaten away, forming a pitted, nonskid surface. (This is why salt is used to melt ice on roads and walkways.)

Second, the water, now salted, refreezes on the surface of the ice cubes, joining them together. This happens because the insides of the

A HANDY HANDLE!

ice cubes are much colder than the freezing point of water. They are cold enough to draw heat out of the newly melted water, and it refreezes.

REKINDLED CANDLE CAPER

Bet you can get a blown-out candle to relight itself!

THE SETUP

This is a fire trick. Do it over aluminum foil to catch the drips. And ask a grown-up to supervise.

Light two large candles. Hold them sideways with one flame about an inch and a half above the other. Blow out the lower flame. Hold the candles steady. The lower candle now will relight itself without any help from you.

INSIDE INFORMATION

This trick won't wait long, so be quick with the candles! When the lower flame is blown out, the hot gases continue to rise as smoke from the extinguished wick. When these gases reach the upper flame, they act as a wick. The flame burns down the gases and relights the lower

candle. The fire now has the three ingredients it needs to continue burning: fuel, oxygen, and the kindling point.

NO ATTRACTION HERE

Bet you can "kill" a magnet (so it loses its power of attraction)!

THE SETUP

Put a small magnet on the burner of the stove. (Check with an adult before you do this.) Turn on the burner. Heat the magnet for about five minutes. Turn off the burner and let the magnet cool for about fifteen minutes before you touch it. Now try to pick up some nails or metal paper clips.

INSIDER INFORMATION

The magnet now is dead as a doornail and just about as magnetic as one. Magnetism is caused by the regular alignment of iron atoms. When you put heat energy into a magnet, you cause the atoms to vibrate. This shakes them out of their magnetic alignment. Magnets can be "killed" using other means too. One is with a sharp blow. Hit the magnet with a hammer and you will jiggle the alignment. High-voltage electric power also will do the job.

A SUPERCOOL TRICK

Bet you can freeze water in your hand!

THE SETUP

This can be a bit tricky to get to work but if it does, you look like a magician. Take an unopened bottle of water that has been sitting around for a while and pour out half of it. Put the cap back on and place in a freezer.

NOTE

Do the freezing when no one opens or closes the refrigerator. We don't want the bottle to be shaken.

Leave undisturbed for about two or three hours. The time will vary depending on how cold your freezer is. Carefully open the freezer door and check to see that the water is still liquid. Remove the bottle and give it a shake. The water freezes in your hand!

INSIDER INFORMATION

Everyone knows that water freezes at 32° F or 0° C. But, if the water is very pure and in a container with very smooth walls, it's possible to chill water to a temperature *below* the freezing point without it turning into ice. Such water is said to be supercooled and it's just waiting for an opportunity to form solid ice crystals. In order for solid crystals to form, there must be a *nucleation point*—an irregularity in the surface or in the liquid or on the walls of the container, which start a chain reaction of crystal building. Even an air bubble can be one. That's why you want water that's been sitting around and has no air bubbles in it. Shaking the supercooled liquid does the trick. Cool! Verrry cool! Supercool!

TIGHT WAD

Bet you can stuff two handfuls of cotton into a full glass of water ... with no spills!

THE SETUP

Fill a juice glass almost to the top with water. Get two large handfuls of cotton. Be sure to use real cotton, not a synthetic material (read the box). Put the cotton bit by bit into the glass of water. Fluff each piece as you wet it so that it is thoroughly saturated. Water may begin to bulge over the top of the glass, but if you are careful you can get the entire wad packed into the glass without spilling a single drop of water.

INSIDER INFORMATION

You can add all the material to an already full glass because cotton fibers are made of hollow plant cells filled with air. The water penetrates into the hollow areas, displacing the air. There is so little solid material in the cotton that it is able to fit into the glass.

SPARK-A-PEEL

Wanna bet you can make fireworks with a lemon?

THE SETUP

You need a lighted candle for this trick, so be sure to have an adult nearby before you start. Cut a thin slice of rind off a lemon. Hold the outside of the rind near the flame and squeeze the inside surfaces together. You'll see mini fireworks between the rind and the candle flame.

All oils are flammable, and lemon rind contains tiny pockets of oil. When the rind is squeezed, the skin breaks and tiny jets of oil squirt out. Lemon oil burns in a brief but bright sparkle when it is ignited.

OLD NEWS

Wanna bet you can make paper last two hundred years?

THE SETUP

You can write a message to your great-great-great-great grandchildren or you can preserve today's newspaper for them to read. You'll need our anti-aging formula because some paper becomes so brittle that it falls apart when it gets old. The formula for paper preserver is nine tablespoons of milk of magnesia and one quart of club soda. Mix them in a shallow pan and soak your paper in the solution for an hour. Remove it carefully and blot it between sheets of paper towel. Let it air dry. It is possible that this treatment might not last the full two hundred years, but we can't wait to find out.

INSIDER INFORMATION

In the presence of acid, oxygen breaks down the cellulose fibers of paper. Since acid is used in the manufacture of most paper, it contains the seeds of its own destruction. The anti-aging formula contains magnesium carbonate, which forms when the magnesium hydroxide in milk of magnesia combines with the carbon dioxide of club soda. The magnesium carbonate neutralizes whatever acid is present in the paper. It leaves a residue, so any acid that might form in the future will also be neutralized.

BENT OUT OF SHAPE

Wanna bet you can tie a knot in a bone?

THE SETUP

A chicken drumstick bone can be as flexible as a rope—but not without a conditioner. Vinegar is a good one. Place the bone into a jarful and soak it overnight. Test it in the morning. If the bone is still stiff, let it soak some more. When it is good and rubbery, tie your knot.

INSIDER INFORMATION

Bones are stiff because tiny crystals of calcium compounds are embedded in a framework of flexible protein fibers. Vinegar is an acid. When it combines with the calcium compounds, the mixture forms a new substance that dissolves in the liquid. Only the flexible part of the bone is left. Your ears and nose are made of a similar material called cartilage.

BALLOON ACUPUNCTURE

Wanna bet you can skewer a balloon without popping it?

THE SETUP

Blow up a balloon and let a little air out before you tie it off. There should be a small bulge of unstretched rubber in the "end" opposite the knot. This is your target. Your acupuncture needle is a bamboo skewer. Dip the point of the skewer in some oil, for a smooth insertion. Then poke it into the target area, with a gentle twisting motion.

The balloon will not pop. Push the skewer clean through the balloon, exiting through the unstretched rubber next to where the neck is tied. Again, no pop.

INSIDER INFORMATION

As any good acupuncturist knows, it's where you stick the needle that counts. A balloon is made of a thin sheet of rubber. Stretched rubber is weaker and thinner than unstretched. A pinhole in a stretched area of a balloon quickly becomes a tear as air rushes out. The rubber around a hole in an unstretched area is strong enough to resist the force of the escaping air. If you remove the skewer, air will leak slowly out of the tiny holes you have made. Prove that this is no trick balloon. Jab the skewer in the side. Ruptured rubber results! Easier done than said.

HINGE ON THE FRINGE

Wanna bet you can cut and glue paper at the same time?

THE SETUP

In this trick, as you cut two pieces of paper, the cut edges stick together. First you have to doctor the paper. Spread a thin even coat of rubber cement on it and allow it to dry. The paper will feel tacky. Spread talcum powder on the paper and gently rub it over all the dried cement.

Cut two one-inch strips from the paper. Place one strip over the other with the powdered sides touching. With a sharp pair of scissors, cut across the strips close to the end. Holding the uncut end of the top strip, gently raise it. Instead of two strips, you'll find that you have one long one. If you cut the two strips on a 45° diagonal, they will form a right angle when you raise the top strip.

INSIDER INFORMATION

The talcum powder covers the cement so that the strips do not stick together. When you cut the strips, you expose glue at the freshly cut edge. Molecules of rubber cement have a strong attraction for one another. They form a hinge strong enough to hold the strips together.

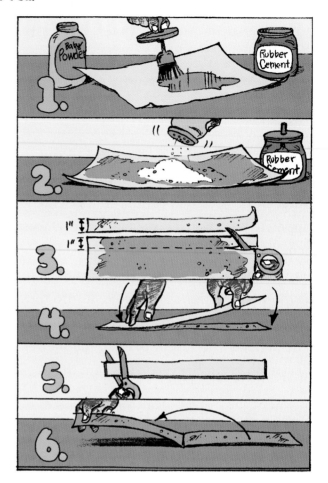

POWER OF MONEY

Wanna bet you can attract a dollar with a magnet?

THE SETUP

Hold a dollar bill by one end. Bring a strong magnet near the other end. The bill will be attracted to the magnet.

INSIDER INFORMATION

The ink used for United States currency is made with chemicals that contain iron. As everyone knows, magnets attract iron. Dollar-changing machines have a magnetic sensor

that "reads" the pattern of the ink on bills. It rejects forgeries, as well as old bills from which some of the ink has been worn off.

MUNCHABLE METAL

Wanna bet there are iron filings in your breakfast cereals?

THE SETUP

Iron is good enough to eat. In fact, you do eat it. Breakfast cereal manufacturers often add bits of iron to their products. The pure iron is ground up so fine that you don't notice it in the cereal, but a magnet can remove it.

Empty a packet of iron-enriched instant Cream of Wheat into a plastic bag. Make sure that it provides one hundred percent of the daily requirement. Crush

the cereal and add water. Place a clean magnet in the bag. Shake well for a few minutes. As you remove the magnet, try to touch as little of the magnetic surface as possible. If you look closely, you'll see tiny iron filings clinging to the magnet. Carefully wipe the particles onto a sheet of white paper. To see them well, put the magnet under the paper and move it around to make the filings "dance." You will collect only a tiny amount, but you don't need much to provide your body's total daily requirement.

INSIDER INFORMATION

Who would have thought you could eat pure iron, the stuff people pump in the gym? *Hemoglobin*, the red protein in the blood that carries oxygen, must have iron to do its job. Since the pure metal can be used as easily as iron compounds, the government permits very fine iron filings to be added to food. The words "iron fortified" on the package simply mean that ground-up iron has been added to the cereal.

We've heard that you can remove iron embedded in some flaked cereals such as Total. Crush the flakes and add water. Then go fishing with your magnet.

NUTTY PUTTY

Wanna bet you can transform glue into something completely useless but fun?

THE SETUP

In the early 1940s, a substance was invented that was so weird it couldn't be classified. In some ways it's like a liquid. In others it's like a solid. It flows. It bounces. It stretches when pulled slowly but breaks when pulled quickly. Its inventor called it

"Nutty Putty," and you can make your own version.

A Recipe for Nutty Putty

- 1 tablespoon borax (you can get borax in the detergent section of a supermarket)
- 1 tablespoon white glue (such as Elmer's)
- 1 1/4 cups water

Put the glue in a small container. Mix in one tablespoon of water. In another container, dissolve the borax in a cup of water. Add a tablespoon of the borax solution to the diluted glue and stir. Nutty Putty happens.

INSIDER INFORMATION

Nutty Putty was created by General Electric scientists who were trying to make an inexpensive substitute for rubber. Nutty Putty, a flexible goo, stretched farther, bounced higher, and resisted mold and decay better than rubber. However, there were a few drawbacks. It never held a shape and it broke when you hit it.

It did make a small fortune as a toy called Silly Putty. Lots of people wrote letters to the manufacturer with suggestions on how to use it. It could lift print off newspaper, collect cat fur and lint, clean ink off typewriter keys, and level wobbly furniture. But after more than fifty years, no one, including some of the world's leading engineers, ever came up with a really practical use for it.

Our version is not exactly the same as commercial Silly Putty, but it has the same properties. White glue is made up of long, string-like molecules called *polymers*. These molecules are so long that they interfere with each other, making the glue thick and slow to pour. Borax cross-links the polymer chains together. Cross-linked polymers get even more tangled, trap water, and form a gel-like material. The substance has new properties that make it fun to play with.

ELEPHANT WIRE

Wanna bet a wire remembers its shape?

THE SETUP

Elephants never forget and neither do some wires. A wire with a built-in memory is used by orthodontists for braces. Ask your orthodontist or dentist for a piece of arch wire so that you can see metal memory in action. It's also used to make jewelry and is carried by some bead stores.

Arch wire is programmed to remember the U shape of your jaw. Bend it and twist it into a different shape. Pour some hot tap water into a container. Drop the twisted arch wire into the hot water. At the speed of sound (720 miles per hour), it will pop back into its original shape.

INSIDER INFORMATION

The secret is a high-tech material made of two ordinary metals: nickel and titanium. The process by which they are combined gives three unique properties: It "remembers" its original shape and will quickly spring back when heat is applied; it stretches one-hundred times more than ordinary wire; it absorbs sound.

It is great for braces because it stretches and then remembers its original shape. Braces made of arch wire never have to be tightened when the teeth move. Arch wire has only a one-way memory but memory metals can be "trained" to have a two-way memory. Springs made from them are placed in shower heads. When the water gets hot enough to scald you, the spring opens and cuts off the water. When the water cools, the spring "remembers" its closed position and lets the water flow again. Its sound-absorbing property is used to make machinery less noisy. Maybe you can suggest school bells be made from Nitinol. They will never ring!

Your arch wire is an "untrained" wire. To get a two-way memory you have to train it. Here's how. Get a nut and a bolt. Wrap the wire around the bolt and make a spring. Tighten the nut so that it clamps the wire. Dip it in a bowl of hot water and then in a bowl of cold water. Repeat the water treatment fifty or more times. The amount of training your metal will need depends on the difference between the temperatures of the two bowls of water, but fifty double dips should do it. Take the nut and the wire spring off the bolt. Now when you dip it in the hot water it will take the original shape of the arch wire and when you dip it into the cold water it will form the coiled spring.

Plastics with a memory have been developed. They have many of the unusual properties of memory metals. We were going to include a trick with them, but we forgot.

MEMORABLE PLASTIC

Wanna bet you can make coasters from cups?

THE SETUP

Actually we didn't forget about the plastics with a memory! That's what the next trick is about. Since you will be using the oven, check with an adult before you do this. You should use an oven with a window. A toaster oven is fine. Preheat the oven to 450° F. You will need a clean empty yogurt cup that is marked with a PS on the bottom with the three arrows in a triangle that shows they are recyclable. The numeral "6" should be in the center of the triangle. Put a cup right side up in the center of a cookie sheet. Put it in the oven. Watch as it amazingly returns to its roots.

INSIDER INFORMATION

Would you believe that a yogurt cup was once as flat as cookie? It hasn't forgotten its origins. This proves it. Polystyrene is a plastic that Styrofoam is made from. It is a thermoplastic with a memory. Yogurt cups are manufactured from flat sheets of polystyrene that are placed over a hot mold. Pieces called plugs push up on the sheet. High pressure air on one side of the mold and a vacuum on the other also help shape the plastic. After the molded polystyrene has cooled, the many yogurt cups are cut apart. You can see the sharp edges of the cut on the "coaster" you have made. The cups are then printed with the graphics that are so nicely shrunk on your coaster.

SUPER-SLURPER

Wanna bet you can't pour water out of a glass?

THE SETUP

The secret of this trick is a super-slurping plastic you can get out of a disposable diaper. To collect the super absorbent, cut the edges off a toddler-sized disposable diaper. Discard the plastic covering. Rip the padding into small pieces and put them into a large plastic bag. Seal the bag and shake it. After a few minutes, remove the padding. There will be about one-half teaspoon of grainy powder in the bottom of the bag. The best way to get it out of the bag is to shake it into a corner and cut off the corner.

Place the powder in a small glass. Add about one third of a cup of water. You hardly have to wait. Turn the glass over. Ta da! Nothing pours out.

INSIDER INFORMATION

The super-absorbent plastic in the diaper is called *sodium polyacrylate*. It can absorb about eighty times its own weight in liquid by trapping water molecules in a gel. Diaper ads on television show water being poured into the diapers. Since salt makes polyacrylate less absorbent and urine is salty, the ads are a bit deceptive. Add salt to your gel and check this out yourself.

Super-slurpers are also used to help hold water in the soil around the roots of plants.

INSECT LIFESAVER

Give artificial respiration to a fly.

THE SETUP

Have you ever seen a drowned fly in a glass of water or soda? It's not necessarily dead. You may be able to revive it although most people will probably wonder why.

You will need:

- a drowned fly
- salt

Waiter, there's a fly in my soup!

Don't worry, sir! I'll save it!

Fish out the unfortunate fly. Place it in a dry spot and shake some salt on it. The resuscitation may be instantaneous or may take as long as fifteen minutes. After that, sign the death certificate.

INSIDER INFORMATION

Flies and other insects don't have lungs. They breathe through tiny air tubes called *spiracles* which are located along the sides of their abdomen.

spiracles

Flies drown when their spiracles fill up with water. Salt draws the water out of the spiracles. This happens because the salt dissolves in water on the surface of the insect's body. Since water flows to an area of higher salt content it is drawn from the breathing spiracles.

A PLASTIC EXPLOSION

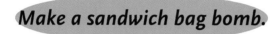

Make a sandwich bag bomb.

THE SETUP

This "bomb" isn't powerful but you'll get a big bang out of it anyway!

You will need:

- a heavy-duty Ziploc sandwich bag
- water
- scissors
- a sheet of paper toweling
- a measuring spoon
- baking soda
- a liquid-measuring cup
- vinegar
- a friend

Check the plastic bag for leaks by filling it with water. A leaky bag makes a dud of a bomb.

Cut or tear a paper towel into a six-inch square. Put two tablespoons of baking soda in the center of the square.

Fold one third of the paper over the baking soda and the fold the other third of the paper over it.

Fold the two ends up to form a packet.
Pour a quarter cup of warm water and a half cup of vinegar in the plastic bag.

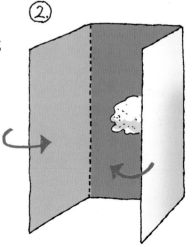

Now comes the tricky part. You have to assemble the "bomb" without letting it "explode" prematurely. This means that the vinegar and baking soda cannot come in contact with each other until the bag is completely sealed. Do this part outside or over the sink, and with a helper if possible. One of you holds the bag and starts zipping it. The other inserts the baking soda packet with one hand and holds it with the other hand from the outside. The packet should be held above the vinegar while the bag is sealed tightly.

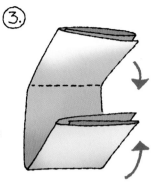

Once the bag is closed, release the packet and shake the bag. Drop the bomb in the sink or on the ground outside.

As the vinegar and baking soda mix, the bag inflates, plastic straining on all sides. Something's got to give. And it does, with a satisfying bang.

INSIDER INFORMATION

The destructive power of an explosion comes from expanding gases. In this case the gas is carbon dioxide produced from a chemical reaction between baking soda and vinegar. As the gas is produced the pressure builds inside the plastic bag. Finally, the bag gives way at its weakest point—usually the Ziploc seal. The gas rushes out at a very high speed causing an audible shock wave. *Pop!*

$\frac{1}{4}$ cup warm water + $\frac{1}{2}$ cup vinegar

This bomb will not cause a fiery explosion. In fact, just the opposite. Carbon dioxide extinguishes flames. If you would like to test this for yourself, get help from an adult assistant. Have him or her light a match and lower it into the exploded bag. The flame will go out.

Since carbon dioxide is heavier than air the gas will remain there for a while even if the bag stays open.

A GAS BOMB

Explode a film canister.

THE SETUP

Who would think you could make an explosion with a stomach remedy? Well you can. Alka Seltzer is powerful stuff. You don't even need a whole tablet. A half will do.

You will need:

- water
- a plastic film canister and lid
- an Alka Seltzer tablet or generic effervescent stomach remedy
- safety goggles
- an adult

Pour water into an empty film canister until it is half full.

Break an Alka Seltzer tablet in half. (Don't worry if the two pieces aren't equal.) Drop one of the halves into the film can.

Quickly, snap the lid on tightly and place the "bomb" on the ground. Move away six or seven feet.

Pow! The lid flies off, landing several yards from ground zero.

CAUTION!

An adult assistant and safety goggles are required because the canister flies apart with considerable velocity. Do this experiment outside and away from people and animals.

film canister

water

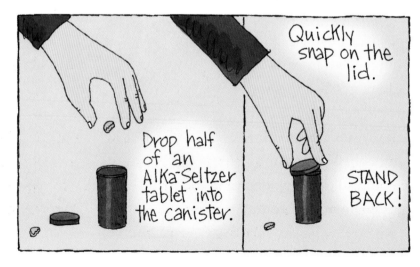

Quickly snap on the lid.

Drop half of an Alka-Seltzer tablet into the canister.

STAND BACK!

This is so cool we're sure you won't let the other half of the Alka Seltzer go to waste. You gotta try this again!

INSIDER INFORMATION

The propellant for this bomb is carbon dioxide gas, which is produced by a chemical reaction when the Alka Seltzer and water mix. The Alka Seltzer tablet contains baking soda and dehydrated citric acid. Both of these substances are necessary to produce the gas but they won't

react in a dry state. It is when you add water that the acid springs into action. This is the same reaction as mixing vinegar and baking soda. We tried making a baking soda and vinegar bomb in the canister but we couldn't get the lid on the film can fast enough. Alka Seltzer makes so much more gas it doesn't matter if some escapes.

The chemical reaction produces a lot of gas in a closed space, and this creates pressure. The gas build-up breaks the container at its weakest point—the lid. You have created an IFO—an identifiable flying object.

FLAMELESS FIRE

Make a homemade chemical handwarmer.

THE SETUP

You can get inexpensive chemical handwarmers at many winter sports stores. Chemical handwarmers are the small packets of material that become hot after you rip open the outside wrappers and expose them to the air. They're just the right size to insert in your mittens and can keep your hands warm for five or six hours. But with our secret recipe, you don't have to buy them, you can make them yourself.

You will need:

- 2 tablespoons iron powder (available from a machine shop, chemical supply house, or hobby shop)
- 2 tablespoons pulverized, *activated* charcoal (available at pet stores, used for aquarium filters)
- 3 tablespoons fluffy, fine sawdust (ask at your local lumberyard or try the shavings from a pencil sharpener)
- 2 tablespoons vermiculite (available at garden stores or other places where plants are sold)
- 1 teaspoon salt
- 2 tablespoons water
- measuring spoons
- a sandwich-sized self-closing plastic bag

plastic bag

2 Tbsp. iron powder
2 Tbsp. activated charcoal
3 Tbsp. sawdust
2 Tbsp. vermiculite
1 Tsp. salt
2 Tbsp. water

If you read the list of ingredients on the labels of commercial handwarmers, you'll see there is nothing exotic or magical in them. It may be a bit of a scavenger hunt to locate all the ingredients. If you can't get exactly what you need, you can improvise. For instance, if you can only get coarse activated charcoal, put some in a plastic bag and smash it to a powder with a hammer.

Mix all the ingredients together in an open plastic bag. We didn't put air on the list but it is absolutely necessary so don't squeeze the bag tightly when you close the top. It only takes a few minutes for the heat to turn on. Your homemade handwarmer will generate heat for hours. Put the bag in your pocket. When it starts to cool, open the bag and shake the contents to add more air and then reseal the bag.

INSIDER INFORMATION

The heat comes from a chemical reaction when iron combines with oxygen to form rust. The same kind of reaction occurs when fuels burn, only they give off heat rapidly enough to produce a flame. Rusting is a much slower reaction. These reactions are called *exothermic* because they emit heat.

Each ingredient has its own special role in the chemical reaction. The iron, of course, is the fuel. The salt and the activated charcoal speed up the reaction. The water brings the reacting materials together. The vermiculite holds and distributes the water evenly. The sawdust is a heat insulator to hold the heat in.

The reaction will continue until all the iron has rusted. Most of the heat is given off in the first few hours. After twenty-four hours the reaction is completed. Dead handwarmers, commercial and homemade alike, are environmentally friendly. They are nontoxic and biodegradable. You can feed the contents to your iron-loving azalea or holly plants.

A COOL REACTION

See a cool chemical combination.

THE SETUP

If you tried A Plastic Explosion on page 228 or A Gas Bomb on page 230, you know that baking soda and acid react to produce carbon dioxide gas. You may not have noticed how *cool* this reaction really is.

You will need:

- water
- a liquid-measuring cup
- a digital meat thermometer
- measuring spoons
- vinegar
- baking soda
- a spoon

Pour about a half cup of warm water in the measuring cup. Take the temperature. One hundred to 120° F works well. Leave the thermometer in the water. Add about two tablespoons of vinegar. Add a teaspoon of baking soda and stir. Watch the thermometer as the bubbles form. When the bubbles stop, stir in another teaspoon of baking soda. Add another tablespoon of vinegar when the reaction dies down. Watch the temperature drop. We're such cool scientists that we got a twenty-degree drop in about one minute.

Cool!

INSIDER INFORMATION

Some chemical reactions, like the one in Flameless Fire on page 231, or like fire itself, give off energy in the form of heat. Other reactions use heat from the surroundings. They're called *endothermic* reactions. This reaction between baking soda and an acid (vinegar) is an example. Baking soda is a home remedy that relieves the burning of an upset stomach. It reacts with excess stomach acid and neutralizes it. In the process it lowers the body temperature too, adding to the cooling effect of the medicine.

FLASHY FIRST AID

Create light with a strip bandage.

THE SETUP

You don't need to wait until you're bleeding to produce light from a bandage. And you won't be wasting the bandage. The flash is in the wrapper.

You will need:

- a Curad strip bandage (don't use any other brand)
- a room that is completely dark

Take a bandage into a dark room and wait a few minutes for your eyes to become dark adapted. Keep your eyes on the bandage even though you can't see it. Grasp the wrapper tabs and quickly pull them apart. A flash of light comes from the wrapper. Exciting!

INSIDER INFORMATION

You're not the only excited thing. Believe it or not, the wrapper adhesive is also excited. That's what made the light.
The glow is called *chemiluminescence*. When you pull the wrapper apart, you break the bonds between the adhesive molecules. The mechanical energy of the ripping, compliments of you, is transferred to the adhesive molecules. Scientifically speaking, they are now in an excited state. As you know, excitement can't last forever, and the added energy is released as the molecules return to their resting state. This energy is released as light, which comes a split second after you've finished ripping open the wrapper.

Save the bandage by resealing the wrapper.

Claims have been made that you can see chemiluminescence with other adhesives. Try self-stick envelopes or electrical tape. The light flash can create enough heat under some circumstances to cause an explosion. A heavy-duty lead-acid battery that was being recharged in a restricted space once exploded when an operator peeled off some nearby electrical tape. For another sparkling activity, see The Electric Life Saver on page 179.

SECRET INFOAMATION

Kill the head on root beer with a secret ingredient.

THE SETUP

Some people like a large foamy head on their root beer and some people don't. If you don't like all that froth, there's an easy way to get rid of it
You will need:

- milk or cream
- root beer

- two clear glasses
- a friend

An odd bit of science trivia makes a mystifying magic trick. To set it up, place a drop of milk or cream on the bottom of one of the glasses. No  one is likely to notice a single drop. Open a bottle of root beer and pour half of it into the other glass. Pour the soda from a height so a big head is formed. Hand the glass to a friend while saying, "I prefer mine without a head." Pour the rest of the bottle into the doctored glass. Yours won't foam.

INSIDER INFORMATION

Foam is a mass of bubbles. Plain water and most sodas do not foam. In order to foam, a liquid must contain a dissolved substance that allows bubble walls to form. Unlike most sodas, root beer contains protein that reinforces the bubble walls. When you open a bottle of root beer, releasing the pressure, carbon dioxide gas rushes to the  surface where tiny bubbles form and create a fairly long-lasting foam.

Milk contains fat molecules that interact with protein and prevent the bubbles from forming a stable foam.

A SQUARE EGG

Make a hard-boiled egg with corners.

THE SETUP

Another word for *oval* is *egg-shaped*. There are definitely no square eggs in nature. So imagine how surprised your family and friends will be when you serve an egg shaped like an ice cube.

Bacon and eggs, Dad?

You will need:

- an extra large egg
- a pot of water
- a stove
- cooking oil or spray
- a small plastic box
  about 1 1/2" wide x 1 1/2" long x 1 1/2" high
  (we used a small square box designed to hold
  paper clips)
- a spoon
- paper towels

CAUTION!
Because this activity involves using a stove, boiling-hot water, and handling a very hot hard-boiled egg, do this with an adult assistant.

To square an egg start by placing it in cool water and bringing the water to a boil. Let it continue to boil rapidly for ten minutes. While the egg is cooking, grease the inside of the box with oil or cooking spray. Turn off the heat, and have the adult assistant remove the egg with a spoon. Do not throw out the water. Place the hot egg on several paper towels. Wrap the towels around the egg and gently tap the egg to crack the shell all over. Unwrap the egg and bit by bit, carefully peel away the shell. Have your assistant occasionally dip the egg back into the hot water to wash off bits of shell and to keep the egg hot. When the shell has been removed, gently push the egg, pointed end first, into the plastic box. The egg should completely fit. Put the lid on the box if it has one, otherwise weigh it down with a plate. Place the boxed egg in the refrigerator for at least a half hour.

The cooled egg should slide out of the box easily. But it has now been permanently altered into a distinctly unnatural shape.

INSIDER INFORMATION

Egg white is made of water and protein molecules that are like tiny balls of yarn. Cooking unravels the protein molecules and causes them to bond to one another. Water is trapped in the spaces between the protein molecules. The liquidy egg white now has the consistency of a gel, or flexible solid. While the gel is still hot, the protein bonds can be manipulated. They are flexible enough to be molded into a square shape. Additional bonds continue to form between protein molecules until the egg is cold. Then the shape becomes permanent.

ANT-ACID

Make ants use a chemical weapon of destruction.

THE SETUP

You can become a chemical weapons inspector. Begin by monitoring the ant kingdom. Some of these insects are able to release a colorless, smelly, toxic acid that can blister human skin, corrode steel, and melt plastics. You can detect it without any danger to yourself with your trusty homemade acid-indicator paper.

You will need:

- baking soda
- measuring spoons
- water
- a liquid-measuring cup
- a shallow pan larger than a sheet of paper

- Astrobright Galaxy Gold paper (You can purchase this specific brand manufactured by Wausau Papers at many office supply stores such as Office Max and Kinko's. Note: Astrobright has two versions of this color. Only one works, so test it at the store with Windex. You can also get it online.)
- a few sheets of newspaper
- tweezers
- carpenter ants

First you have to make the paper. Dissolve one tablespoon of baking soda in a cup of water. Pour the solution into a shallow pan. Immerse a sheet of Astrobright Galaxy Gold paper in the solution. It will turn bright red. Carefully, lay the wet paper on the newspaper to dry. The red dye might stain, so handle it with caution.

When the paper is dry, you are ready to hunt for chemical weapons carriers. Take tweezers and the test paper outside. The most likely suspects are big, black carpenter ants that make their home in rotten wood. When you have found a colony, gently pick up one of the ants with your tweezers and hold it over the test paper. Your tweezer attack will make the ant defend itself with a spray of powerful *formic* acid. Wherever a drop of formic acid hits, the paper will turn bright gold.

When you're finished release the ant in the same place you found it.

INSIDER INFORMATION

Formic acid is the strongest acid produced by a living thing. One out of every ten ants in the world (that's a hundred trillion) is a small formic acid factory. They use it as a defense against predators. People use it too, in insecticides, food preservatives, textile and paper dyes, and disinfectants, among other things.

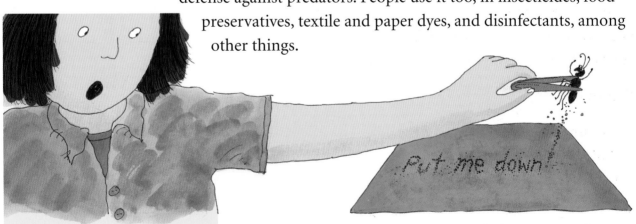

Ants make about twenty billion pounds of formic acid every year. However, we humans have not found a practical way to collect any quantity of it from ants. So industrial formic acid is produced synthetically, mainly from a waste product of paper mills.

BLOOD ON YOUR HANDS

Leave bloody fingerprints without actually bleeding.

THE SETUP

You can fool your friends by leaving blood red fingerprints on orangey-gold paper. They'll think you've got blood on your hands but they'll see that your uninjured hands are perfectly clean.

You will need:

- a sheet of Astrobright Galaxy Gold paper
- water
- baking soda

Prepare the blood bath by wetting a sheet of Astrobright Galaxy Gold paper. Dip your dry fingers into baking soda. Wherever you touch your fingers to the wet paper you will leave blood red fingerprints.

INSIDER INFORMATION

Galaxy Gold was not designed to be a chemical test paper. But it is. The yellow dye turns red in the presence of chemicals that are *alkalis* or *bases* (such as baking soda). It turns back to yellow when it comes in contact with chemicals that are *acids* (such as vinegar). The most famous acid-base test paper is *litmus paper*. Litmus is a natural dye that comes from lichens. The dye turns pink in acid and blue in bases.

If you're in a situation where you can't wet the paper, you can still leave a bloody mark. Dampen your fingers with a glass or household cleaner. Then touch your wet fingers to the paper. Clearly they contain alkalis.

CODE RED

Use Windex to read secret messages.

THE SETUP

You've probably tried writing secret messages on paper with lemon juice or milk and developing them with heat. Use this high-tech spy paper and get much more colorful messages.

You will need:

- white vinegar
- measuring spoons
- water
- liquid-measuring cup
- a paint brush or cotton swab
- a sheet of Astrobright Galaxy Gold paper
- microwave oven (optional)
- Windex
- a co-conspirator

Add a tablespoon of white vinegar to half a cup of water. Wet a paintbrush or cotton swab with the mixture and write your coded message on a sheet of Astrobright Galaxy Gold paper. Let your message dry naturally or speed up the drying process by nuking it for two minutes in a microwave oven. When the paper is dry, your message will be invisible. It is now ready to be delivered.

To be read, your message has to be "developed." Instruct your fellow spy to lay the paper flat on a surface that is easily cleaned. Have him or her spray the paper evenly with Windex. The message stays yellow while the rest of the paper turns red.

CAUTION!
This can be quite messy so be careful not to get the red liquid on clothing or surfaces that could be damaged.

INSIDER INFORMATION

In the previous experiment, Blood on Your Hands, you discovered how Galaxy Gold paper can detect acids and bases. In this experiment, you wrote on the paper with acid (vinegar). Since the paper is already acidic, there was no color change.

Acids and bases neutralize each other. Windex, which is alkali, neutralizes the acid in the yellow dye of the paper so that it changes to red. The writing contains extra acid from the vinegar. So extra Windex is needed to neutralize the message. If you want to erase your message completely, keep spraying with the Windex to neutralize the additional amount of acid—your "ink."

TWISTED THOUGHTS

Make a self-twisting rope.

THE SETUP

Twist a piece of string and let it go. The twist untwists. Always. Well, not always. Rope is permanently twisted string. It's not hard to make if you know the trick. Rope literally makes itself.

You will need:

- 3 24-inch lengths of string or yarn
- chair
- scissors

To make a rope, tie three pieces of string to a chair. Twist one strand in a clockwise direction until it is tightly wound. Don't let go—you know what will happen if you do! So, while holding on to your twisted string, twist the other strings in the same clockwise direction, one at a time. Then stretch out the three twisted lengths of string and let go of the ends. Ta da! A rope forms before your very eyes. Now cut it off the chair. Don't worry, the ends will not unravel.

INSIDER INFORMATION

When you let go and the string untwists, it wraps around the strands next to it. This keeps it from untwisting completely.

The main reason ropes are twisted is not to keep them from unraveling but to increase their strength: tiny fibers are twisted to make thread; threads are twisted to make stronger strings; strings are twisted to make even stronger rope.

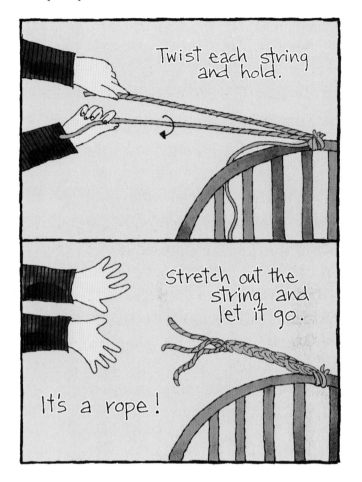

Twist each string and hold.

Stretch out the string and let it go.

It's a rope!

DROP SHOT

Pass a coin through a solid.

THE SETUP

Okay, you're not really going to pass a coin through a solid. However, people are going to believe you can.

You will need:

- a quarter
- a lipstick tube or other small cylinder with a diameter about the size of a quarter
- a thin latex glove (the kind used by doctors and dentists)

- a small clear jar
- a rubber band

Place the coin, heads up, on top of a small
cylinder standing on a tabletop. Rinse off
the inside of the rubber glove to get rid of its
coating of talcum powder. Stretch the palm part
of the glove over the coin by pulling down evenly in all
directions. Stretch the latex thin enough so that the image
on the coin is clearly visible. Now, ease off the pressure.
The latex will trap the coin and it will appear to be sitting on
the top surface of the latex. Warning: Don't pull too hard or the
latex will tear.

Stretch the glove gently over the mouth of a small jar being
careful not to dislodge the coin. Fasten the glove with a rubber
band. The coin, which is really on the underside of the
latex, looks as if it is sitting on top of it.

Once you're set up, invite an audience. Claim that
you can make the coin pass through the latex without
making a hole in it. Follow up by giving the coin a tap
from above. It will drop like a shot into the jar,
leaving the rubber undamaged.

INSIDER INFORMATION

Latex rubber is a material that has a
memory. You can bend it or stretch
it, but when the distorting force is
removed, the rubber returns to its
original shape. You're exploiting
this property twice in this
trick. The round shape of the
coin is a key element in trapping
it in the rubber. When the rubber is
stretched over the rim of the coin

then released, the latex underneath the coin pulls together to form a ring that holds the coin in place.

When you release the coin with your tap, the latex that was underneath the coin is then free to return to its original flat, unstretched state.

EXCITING SODA

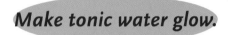

Make tonic water glow.

THE SETUP

Tonic water may not excite you—but you can excite it!

You will need:

- tonic water
- a glass
- an ultraviolet light (available at a party store or a lighting store)

Take some tonic and a glass into a dark room and shine an ultraviolet or "black" light on the tonic while you pour it into the glass.

Under ordinary light, tonic water is a clear, bubbly liquid. Under ultraviolet light it is transformed into an eerie, luminous fluid with a fluorescent blue glow.

INSIDER INFORMATION

Pure ultraviolet light is invisible to the human eye. It's just below our threshold of vision. You can see the glow of an ultraviolet light bulb because it isn't purely ultraviolet rays. Some longer, visible violet wavelengths are also emitted by the bulb.

Quinine, the bitter-tasting ingredient in tonic water, is

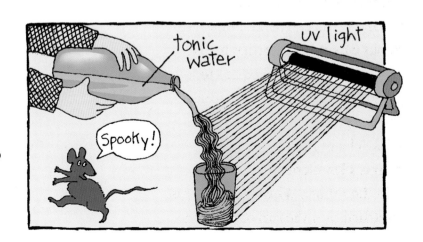

what makes the liquid glow. When ultraviolet light strikes quinine molecules they absorb its energy and become excited. This excited state isn't permanent, however. Almost immediately, the quinine molecules re-emit the extra energy—but as visible light. This process, where UV light is transformed into visible light, is called *fluorescence*. The glow of a fluorescent light bulb is caused by UV light striking a fluorescent coating on the inside of the bulb.

SOME OTHER REALLY COOL FLUORESCENT THINGS:

the Mylar strip on a new one-hundred dollar bill

a parakeet's feathers

urine

blood

certain kinds of flowers (Bees can see UV light. Some flowers have UV patterns to guide the insects to their pollen.)

laundry detergent with whiteners added

various white or day-glow papers

colored chalks (many are made with crushed fluorescent minerals)

CLEAN CUT

Make a saw from kitchen cleanser.

THE SETUP

Criminals in New York City once used an unusual saw to break out of jail. With only cotton string and powdered kitchen cleanser they cut right through the iron bars of their cell. You too can create this innovative tool.

You will need:

- powdered kitchen cleanser
- water
- a 2-foot length of cotton string

- a clamp
- a small piece of wood such as a pencil

string caked with cleanser

pencil

Sprinkle cleanser in the sink. Add a little water to make a thick paste. Rub the string in the paste until it is wet and caked with the cleanser. Straighten out the coated string and let it dry.

When the string is dry, clamp a pencil to a workbench. Hold a section of the string tightly between your hands. Rub the string saw back and forth across the pencil. Move to a new section of the string when the old one stops cutting.

INSIDER INFORMATION

Kitchen cleanser contains an abrasive substance. By embedding it in string, you give the string a cutting surface. Since the abrasive is fine, the cuts are tiny. It takes hundreds of them to sever a pencil. It also takes time. It took us about four minutes to cut through a pencil, so imagine how long it took to cut through iron bars!

EXCITING TV

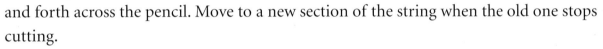

See an image on a TV that's turned off.

THE SETUP

Tonic water is not the only thing around the house that can get excited. TVs are very excitable, too.

You will need:

- a television set
- a strong flashlight

You must do this experiment in a dark room with the TV turned off. Hold the flashlight in one hand and place your other hand flat against the TV screen. Turn on the flashlight and shine the light all over the screen. Do this for at least two minutes making sure that all parts of the screen are illuminated.

Turn off the flashlight and take away your hand. You will see a dark image of your hand on a glowing screen and it will be visible for a few minutes.

You can also use your TV screen as a notepad. Put the lit flashlight against the screen and then write with the light. Extinguish the light and enjoy the luminous message you've left behind.

INSIDER INFORMATION

A TV picture is created by a beam of electrons that scans back and forth across the screen from top to bottom about sixty times a second. The back of the screen is coated with a material that becomes excited when struck by electrons. The light from a flashlight can also excite this screen-coating material. In each case, the material absorbs energy and re-emits it as a glowing light.

This phenomenon, called *phosphorescence*, is similar to the fluorescence you observed in Exciting Soda on page 245. There are, however, two big differences. First, phosphorescent material becomes excited when it is struck by *visible* light as opposed to ultraviolet light. And second, a phosphorescent glow continues for a few seconds after the light source has been turned off. This differs from a fluorescent glow, which disappears as soon as the UV light stops shining.

The black silhouette of your hand is visible because your hand kept the light from hitting the phosphorescent strips underneath it. Instead of a hole in the ozone, you've made a hole in the glow zone.

BOLT FROM THE BALLOON

Light a fluorescent light bulb with a balloon.

THE SETUP

How many balloons does it take to light a fluorescent light bulb? This isn't a joke! You *can* light a bulb with a balloon—and it only takes one.

You will need:

- safety glasses
- a fluorescent light bulb
- an inflated balloon
- a piece of wool or fur

CAUTION!
Be careful when handling fluorescent light bulbs. They might explode if broken. Do this with an adult assistant and wear protective glasses.

Bring your equipment and your assistant into a darkened room. Have the assistant hold the light bulb. Give the balloon a static electric charge by rubbing it repeatedly with a piece of wool or fur. (The length of time you need to rub will vary depending on how humid the air is.) A charged balloon will make the hair on your arms stand on end.

Touch the charged balloon to the prongs at the end of the bulb. Flashes of light will briefly pulse up and down the tube. This may not work if the humidity is high. If you're not successful, try again on a dry day.

INSIDER INFORMATION

Surprise! It doesn't take much energy to light a fluorescent bulb. That's why they're so cheap to run and are part of the green, energy-saving movement.

Rub the balloon on fur to give it a charge of static electricity.

A fluorescent light is a hollow glass tube painted on the inside with a fluorescent material. Some of the air has been pumped out of the tube and replaced with mercury vapor. When the light is turned on, electricity flows from one end of the tube to the other. The electrons strike the mercury atoms, which become briefly excited. When the mercury atoms return to their unexcited state, they release the extra energy as ultraviolet light. The UV light hits the fluorescent paint, where it is converted into visible light.

Touch the balloon to the end of the bulb.

When you rub a balloon, you give it a negative charge, which contains an excess of electrons. These electrons jump to the metal end of the bulb when you bring the balloon close. This

Excess electrons jump to the metal end of the bulb.

is enough energy to produce a brief flash of fluorescent light.

COUNTERFEIT MONEY DETECTOR

Identify bogus bills with iodine.

THE SETUP

The U.S. government tries to make money that is difficult to counterfeit beginning with the paper it is printed on. Perfect replicas of the design are easy to make with a high-tech color copier, but it's impossible for counterfeiters to duplicate the special paper.

You will need:

- a cotton swab
- iodine
- American paper currency
- assortment of other paper

Your medicine cabinet is the source of a test that quickly identifies most fake bills. Dip a cotton swab in the iodine. Touch it to paper money. The iodine will make a dull orange mark if the money is genuine. It will turn black on fake money and on other kinds of paper.

CAUTION!
Iodine is a poison. Use extreme care not to get it in your eyes or mouth. Have an adult present when you do this test. Also, be careful not to get iodine on your clothes or skin, as it leaves stains that cannot be removed easily.

INSIDER INFORMATION

Iodine turns black in the presence of a starch. Most paper contains starch, which adds bulk and holds the wood fibers together. The paper used for U.S. currency is mostly made of linen fibers, which cling together without any starch.

People who handle large amounts of cash are always on the lookout for counterfeits. To detect bogus bills, they mark them with a special pen that contains iodine ink. These pens can be purchased at office supply stores.

Money is being redesigned with many new safeguards to make a counterfeiter's life miserable. The paper used in ten-dollar bills and larger denominations is now manufactured with an embedded Mylar strip that has the value of the bill printed on it. In new one-hundred dollar bills, this strip is fluorescent and glows under ultraviolet light.

SHOWING YOUR TRUE COLORS

Wanna bet iodine is violet, not brown?

THE SETUP

Check with an adult before you do this trick because iodine is poisonous. If you ever put iodine on a cut, the first thing you felt was its sting. Then you probably noticed (as you were blowing on your wound) that it left a brown stain. It might surprise you to know that iodine is not really brown but violet. In fact, *iodine* comes from the Greek word for the color violet.

To make iodine show its true color, you'll need some greasy kid stuff—baby oil. You will also need a clear glass jar with a screw top. Half fill the jar with water. Add iodine until the solution is the color of tea. Pour an inch of baby oil on the surface of the water. Screw the lid on and shake. When the liquids separate, the oil will have a beautiful, violet color. Iodine is now showing its true color!

INSIDER INFORMATION

Pure iodine won't dissolve in either alcohol or water. To make the alcohol solution called tincture of iodine, which is what you find in your medicine chest, chemists have a trick. They use an iodine compound, sodium iodide, which does dissolve in water and alcohol. It can carry pure iodine along with it. A water-alcohol mixture of sodium iodide and iodine is brown. Pure iodine *is* soluble in oil, as the bright violet color proves.

Fluids don't all have the same properties. Scientists take advantage of the differences when separating materials that are mixtures. In this case, the pure iodine was extracted from the water solution with the oil. Since oil floats to the surface, it can be separated from the water.

7. FORCES OF DECEPTION

Karate experts use science to defend themselves. Long before reaching the black belt rank, they discover that mechanics, which is the branch of science dealing with forces and motion, is their most important defensive weapon.

Forces can be as invisible as gravity or air pressure. Or they can be as impossible to ignore as a karate chop! But regardless of whether it is in the form of push, pull, or collision, force can be made to work *for* you instead of *against* you.

In karate, force is never met head-on. Instead it is cleverly diverted or even turned back against an opponent. Some of the most spectacular and skillful moves often require little strength. They are tricky manipulations of force.

When forces meet head-on, if they are equal and in opposite directions, they cancel each other out and nothing happens. Two equal teams in a tug-of-war, for example, will often result in a stalemate. But unequal forces coming from *different* directions *can* affect an object. That's the secret of most martial arts. The angle of attack throws an opponent off balance when it comes from an unexpected direction.

When it comes to the direction of a force, gravity is the biggest downer of all time. But, surprise! Gravity can pull sideways or even up. The sun's pulling on the earth in a direction that is anything but down.

Gravity is the force of attraction between two masses, and when it's the only force operating, it draws the smaller mass to the larger one. The reason we think of gravity as a downer is because the most familiar example is the force of attraction between the giant earth and our body.

One way gravity exerts its force is very curious. All the weight of a body seems to be concentrated at a single center point. If a body has a supporting base, its "center of gravity" must be located directly over the base or the body will tip over. When an object has a regular shape, like the earth, it is easy to locate the center of gravity because it is at the geometric center. A seesaw is balanced at its geometric center, also its center of gravity.

But irregularly shaped objects, like the human body, do not have a center of gravity that necessarily coincides with the geometric center. In fact, the center of gravity can be moved around. Skiing, for example, is one sport where an athlete is constantly shifting his or her center of gravity to maintain balance. In this chapter, you may be moving your center of gravity around. That's where the fun comes in. The artful use of gravity can throw you totally off balance.

This chapter does not deal with self-defense, but a lot of the secrets that karate, judo, and jujitsu students learn are used here. Tricks based on mechanical principles will give you some surprise moves, too. We invite you to try mechanics. Don't make us resort to force!

FORCED ENTRY

Wanna bet you can use a hammer to slice an apple in midair?

THE SETUP

Here's one for the apple polishers. Start out as if you were going to slice an apple in half with a table knife. Press the knife far enough in to pick the apple up with it and it at arm's length. With a hammer, give the knife a sharp blow on the back of the blade. Strike as close to the apple as you can. The knife will cut through the rest of the apple, and the two halves will fall to the ground.

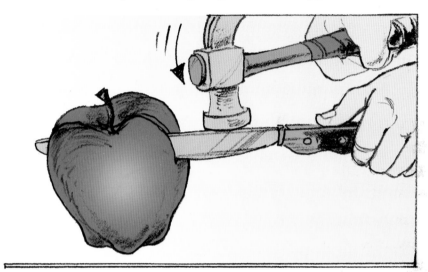

INSIDER INFORMATION

When you cut an apple, you overcome its resistance to being cut. There are two ways to do this: by applying a small force for as long as you need or by applying a large force for a shorter period of time.

When an apple rests on a table it is held steady and all the force goes into the apple. A small force for as long as it takes will get the job done. When the apple is in the air, a larger force is needed or the apple will travel downward with the knife. The blow of the hammer is so large that the resistance to the knife is overcome and the apple splits before it has a chance to travel with the knife.

UNCUTTABLE PAPER

Wanna bet you can slice an apple with a paper-wrapped knife without cutting the paper?

THE SETUP

Fold a piece of paper and place a knife blade in the fold. Cut an apple with the paper-wrapped knife. Use a steady downward pressure rather than a sawing motion. After the apple is split, look at the paper. It will not be damaged.

INSIDER INFORMATION

A knife can cut both paper and an apple. But it is easier to cut an apple because apple pulp offers less resistance than paper fibers do. The paper-wrapped knife doesn't cut the paper because you're not applying enough force. There's enough to cut the apple but not when the paper moves with the knife. If you hold the paper against the apple, the unwrapped knife will cut the paper. When you prevent the paper from moving with the knife, you can apply enough force to cut it.

NO HUMPTY DUMPTY HERE!

Wanna bet you can throw a raw egg across the room without breaking it?

THE SETUP

The most difficult part of this trick is to convince a parent to contribute a sheet. It helps if you offer to do the laundry. You won't have to. Trust us.

Have two friends hold up a sheet like a hammock with the back higher than the front. The upturn on the bottom is to prevent the egg from rolling out after the toss. They should pull against each other to give a fairly taut target. Choose a raw egg that is free of cracks and throw it as hard as you can at the sheet. Stand at any distance. Throw overhand or underhand, with any speed you want. As long as you don't miss the target, your egg will survive to become an omelet at another time.

INSIDER INFORMATION

According to Sir Isaac Newton (an "eggspert" in these matters), the force of a collision is determined by the mass of the object and the speed just before it hits.

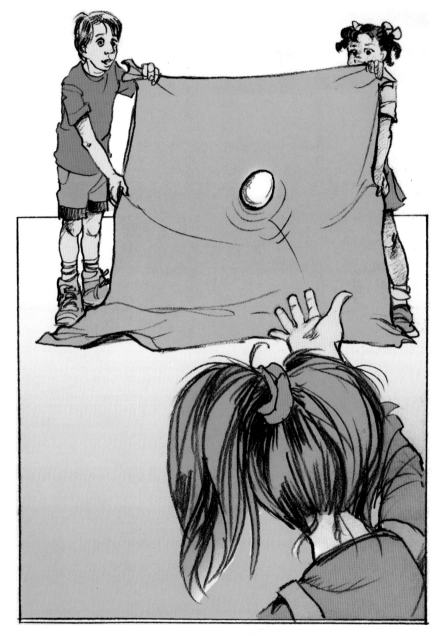

The sheet acts as a brake for your egg missile. It moves with the egg and stops it gradually. The sheet also protects the egg by spreading the force over a large surface area.

Eggs are stronger than you might think. After all, hens sit on them. The shape of the shell resists breaking when a force is evenly applied to the outside. However, a small force applied to the *inside* of the shell cracks it wide open. This design is good for baby chicks!

A LIGHT SNACK

Wanna bet you can make a puffed cheese snack rise through rice?

THE SETUP

Prove that a puffed cheese ball is really a light snack and defy gravity at the same time. All you need is some rice, a glass jar with a lid, and a snack ball. Add rice to the jar until it is about one-quarter full. Place the snack ball on the rice. Put the top on the jar and turn it upside down. Shake the jar from side to side. Do not shake it up and down. The ball will mysteriously rise through the rice.

INSIDER INFORMATION

When grains of rice are set in motion, they behave more like a liquid than a solid. An object floats in a liquid when its weight is less than an equal volume of the liquid. A snack ball weighs a lot less than an equal volume of rice. When you shake the rice, the motion gives it a buoyant force and the snack ball "floats" to the surface.

If you don't have cheese snacks handy, try popcorn, a Styrofoam ball, a cork, or a Ping-Pong ball.

Buoyancy isn't always an upper. Wanna bet you can shake down an object, such as a marble, that's heavier than an equal volume of rice?

FINANCIAL SUPPORT

Wanna bet you can support eight quarters on a dollar bill suspended between two glasses?

THE SETUP

If you think it's better to have folding money than coins, this trick's for you. The U.S. dollar has hidden strength that even bankers might find surprising. Fold a crisp, new dollar bill in half lengthwise. Then fold both lengthwise edges up to meet the center crease. The dollar will be folded like an accordion. Make a bridge between two glasses with the dollar bill. Arrange eight quarters along the length of your dollar bridge.

INSIDER INFORMATION

The "corrugated" dollar is amazingly strong. Ordinarily, a dollar bill supported only at its ends will not support the weight of even *one* quarter. The weight of the coin is greater than the structural strength of the dollar bridge. Pleating the bill redistributes the weight of the coins so that it is spread out. Now, the bill is able to support the coins. It's a secret strength that has lots of everyday applications.

Diverting the lines of force gives added strength to many materials. An I-shaped steel beam is as strong as a much thicker solid rod. This allows skyscrapers to be built with a lot less weight. Cartons are constructed with a corrugated sheet of cardboard sandwiched between two flat sheets of cardboard to make them sturdy. Wanna bet you can support yourself with a lot less money than you thought possible?

UP AGAINST THE WALL

Bet you can't pick up a dollar bill that's right in front of you!

THE SETUP

Stand with the backs of your heels against a wall and your feet together. Place a dollar bill on the floor about a foot in front of your feet. Now … try to pick up the dollar and stand up again without moving your feet or bending your knees.

INSIDER INFORMATION

That dollar is as safe as if it were in the bank. You can't pick it up. Here's why. When you stand straight against the wall, your center of gravity is directly over your feet (your base) as it should be. When you bend forward, you move your center of gravity forward. In order to keep your balance, you must move your feet forward too. This maintains the base under the center of gravity needed for stability. Since the rules of this trick don't allow you to move your feet, you're dollarless. And if you persist in trying to pick it up, you'll get a new base… your face!

While you are standing there with your back to the wall, here are some more wasted efforts.

Bet you can't jump!

THE SETUP

Keep your heels, hips, and shoulders against the wall. Without leaning forward, try to jump. What's the matter? Are your feet stuck to the floor?

Bet you can't lift your foot off the floor!

THE SETUP

Turn your right side to the wall. Put your right foot and cheek against the wall. Now try and lift your left foot off the floor.

INSIDER INFORMATION

Both of these stunts require you to shift your center of gravity away from the support base. The first can't be done without leaning forward and falling on your face, and the second can't be done without moving the wall. The body maintains balance with little adjustments so automatic that we never think about them.

SEX-LINKED BEHAVIOR

Bet you can't pick up a chair unless you are female!

THE SETUP

Here's something your mother can do but your father can't. Begin by having the subject back away from a wall to a distance of four foot-lengths. Place a chair or stool between the person and the wall. Instruct the person to lean over and rest his or her forehead against the wall. Now the subject must pick up the chair and try to straighten up without moving their feet or touching the chair to the wall.

INSIDER INFORMATION

The reason men can't do this trick is because they have big feet! Women have feet that are smaller in proportion to their height. So, when a man backs four foot-lengths away from the wall and leans forward, his center of gravity is father from his base than a woman's. He would have to rely on his leg muscles to compensate for this greater imbalance, and they just aren't up to the job.

POSSIBLE PITFALL

Before you do this stunt, take a careful look at the shoes of your potential subjects. Don't choose a girl who is wearing big, heavy boots. Your best bet is to select a male with big, heavy boots and a female with high heels.

TOE HOLD

Bet you can't jump forward on your toes!

THE SETUP

Hold your toes with your hands. Keep your knees slightly bent. Try to jump forward while hanging on to your toes.

INSIDER INFORMATION

You can jump right around the block backward, but you'll not get one single bound forward. A backward jump is possible because the support base moves first and you can keep your center of gravity over your feet without falling backwards. To jump forward, your center of gravity must move before your base. Holding on to your toes prevents you from making this shift without losing your balance. Without shifting your center of gravity, your leg muscles would have to be strong enough not only to lift your body off the ground but also to support the unbalanced position you would be in while jumping. We've heard that football players have such strength in their leg muscles, but we've yet to find someone who can do this stunt.

GLUED TO YOUR CHAIR?

Bet you can't get up from a chair! No gimmicks! No strings either!

THE SETUP

All you have to do to win is get up from a chair. Sit in a straight-backed armless chair. Keep your back against the back of the chair and put your feet flat on the floor. Fold your arms across your chest. Now, keeping your feet flat and your back straight, try to stand up.

INSIDER INFORMATION

We lied about the gimmick. The gimmick is gravity. In the sitting position the center of gravity is at the base of the spine. By trying to stand up with your back straight, you prevent the center of gravity from moving to a position above the feet, which are your support base. Human thigh muscles simply aren't strong enough to compensate for the balance problems during the getting-up period. So you remain glued to your chair.

NOSEDIVE

Bet you can't pick up a handkerchief with your teeth!

THE SETUP

Squat down. Place a broomstick under your bent knees and crook your elbow around it. You can rest your hands on the ground. Have someone put a handkerchief on the ground in front of you. Lean forward and try to pick up the handkerchief with your teeth without moving your hands forward or letting your knees touch the ground.

INSIDER INFORMATION

As you rotate forward toward the handkerchief, the center of gravity is shifting away from the stable position directly above your feet. Once it goes too far, you become unstable and you will fall on your nose.

ON YOUR TOES

Bet you can't stand on your tiptoes!

THE SETUP

Stand facing the edge of an open door. Your nose and stomach should just touch it. Place your feet on either side of the door slightly forward of the edge. Now try to rise onto your tiptoes.

INSIDER INFORMATION

You'll be caught flat-footed on this one. The reason you can't do this trick is because it moves your base of support out from under your center of gravity. In order to stand on your toes, you must transfer the center of gravity forward. To transfer the center forward, you must lean over. The door prevents you from doing this.

AN UNBEATABLE FASTBALL

Bet you can't beat me in a rolling contest!

THE SETUP

This rolling contest has three participants. Each person chooses an object to roll from one of these groups:

- spheres: marbles, golf balls, ball bearings (be sure they are solid balls, not hollow like a Ping-Pong ball)
- discs: checkers, plastic plates, coasters
- hoops: rings, tires, hula hoops

The contest must take place on an incline. Choose a slated board or a smooth sloping driveway depending on the size of the objects chosen. At a signal, let all three objects roll toward a finish line.

INSIDER INFORMATION

No one will beat you if you choose your objects from the groups of spheres. All spheres will beat all discs which will beat all hoops. We mean ALL. It doesn't matter how heavy or how big the objects are. Rolling speed is directly related to the distribution of weight around an object's center of gravity, known as its "moment of inertia." In all three kinds of objects, the center of gravity is the geometric center. But the weights are distributed differently.

In the case of the hoop, all the weight is located away from the center of gravity. Of the three types of objects, it has the largest moment of inertia. The solid ball has the smallest since its weight is most closely distributed around its center of gravity. The closer the mass or weight of an object is to its center of gravity, the smaller its moment of inertia and the faster it can rotate.

You've seen this principle at work as an ice skater goes into a spin. The spin begins with the arms extended. As the spin progresses, the arms are drawn toward the body, decreasing the moment of inertia by bringing the weight close to the center, and thus increasing the velocity of the spin.

STRONG WORDS

Bet you can't outpull a book!

THE SETUP

Open a big, heavy book and place it facedown in the center of a five-foot cord. Tie the cord in a knot along the spine. Grip one end of the cord in each hand at least a foot-and-a-half away from the book. Now pull and try to bring the cord into a perfectly horizontal position with the knot in the center.

INSIDER INFORMATION

The cord will come close to horizontal, but it will never straighten out. That's because your muscle power is not equal to the force of gravity pulling on the book. When the cord is in a vertical position over the book, the force you need to exert to prevent the book from falling is equal to the weight of the book. But as you move your hands apart, your muscle strength is delivered at an angle. Force delivered at an angle must be greater than the weight it is countering. The smaller the angle, the greater the force required. The closer you pull the cord to the horizontal position, the more strength you need to exert. The cord may snap before you level off.

This is really a tug-of-war between you and gravity. Gravity is a hands-down winner. But don't take our word for it. Try it yourself.

A PRESSING PROBLEM

Bet you can't keep your fists together!

THE SETUP

Here is the perfect trick to try on someone who is stronger than you. Have the strong person stand with arms extended, one fist on top of the other. To win, the strong person must keep the fists in this position as you try to separate them.

INSIDER INFORMATION

This is child's play. It is so easy to separate the fists that you only need to use your index fingers. With a quick strike, you push sideways on the back of each fist. They should move apart easily. (If the trick doesn't go as planned, check to see that the strong person isn't cheating by locking the lower thumb inside the upper fist.)

The strangest thing about this trick is that the harder the strong person tries to press the fists together, the easier it is for you to separate them. So urge your opponent to try harder!

In an effort to keep the fists together, the strong person concentrates all of his or her force in an up-and-down direction. Almost no strength is exerted sideways, which is where your attack comes from. Again, your independent force is in a different direction from your opponent's. That's why it is effective.

In addition, the fully extended arm cannot deliver nearly as much strength as a flexed arm. The force in a fully extended arm comes from the shoulder. In a flexed arm, the force to the fist comes from the elbow at a much shorter distance. This principle plays a larger role in the next trick.

A MATCH THAT'S NO CONTEST

Bet you can't break a match!

THE SETUP

Place a wooden match across the back of your middle finger and under the first and third fingers at the joints nearest the fingertips. Try to break the match by pressing up with the middle finger and down with the two others. Can't do it? Try pressing down with the middle finger and up with the other two. Still can't do it? Don't let the thumb and little finger help out. That's considered cheating.

INSIDER INFORMATION

This is an impossible situation because you are not using your fingers to gain a mechanical advantage. Your fingers can be used as levers, which are devices that can increase a force when used properly. The key to a lever is the location of the *fulcrum*, or point of attachment, and the force being delivered to it. When the force is close to the fulcrum, the force is increased. Thus, a crowbar can easily remove a nail from wood. But when the force is a distance from the fulcrum, it is weaker.

In this trick, the fulcrum is the set of knuckles where your fingers attach to your hand. When you try to deliver a force far from this point of attachment, your muscles are too weak to do the job. But move the match to the other side of the middle joints close to the knuckles and see how easily you can break it. Now your lever fingers can supply enough power.

LOWER THE BROOM

Bet you can't touch a broomstick to the floor!

THE SETUP

You will need four people, a big paper plate, and a broom. Put the paper plate on the floor. This is the target. Have three people hold a broom upside down about one-and-one-half feet above the target. They should hold the broomstick close to the bristle end. When they are in position, place your palm against the broom handle near the end. You may have to lie on the floor to do this. Now challenge the others to touch the broom to the target. As they try to push the broom down, you push sideways.

INSIDER INFORMATION

This is an example of forces working independently of each other. The sideways force you exert is independent of the downward force of the broom handle. Since you aren't opposing the downward force, you can easily deflect the broom handle away from the target with a smaller sideways force. So it doesn't matter how hard your three opponents push toward the ground, you can always prevent the broom from reaching the target.

NO PUSHOVER

Bet you can't push me backward!

THE SETUP

Hold a broomstick horizontally in front of you. Extend your arms with your hands gripping the stick about the same distance apart as your shoulders. Challenge someone to try to push you backward. He or she must grasp the middle of the stick and push using a steady, forward pressure (no sudden thrusts).

INSIDER INFORMATION

It's impossible to move you a single inch backward! The secret defense is force diversion, whereby you change the direction of your opponent's force. To do this, flex your elbows out like wings and push slightly upward to counter any pressure. The force that is supposed to knock you backward is diverted into your arms and upward.

POSSIBLE PITFALL

This trick depends on timing, so you may need to practice it to make your moves at just the right moment.

   While you have the broomstick and a friend, try this one, too.

Bet you can't throw me off balance!

THE SETUP

Hold the broomstick horizontally again, this time with your thumbs up, about six inches on either side of the center of the stick. Have your friend hold the ends of the stick and try to knock you off balance.

INSIDER INFORMATION

When your opponent pushes forward, you push the broomstick upward. The force of the push will be deflected away from any direction that could knock you off balance. Hands on the center of the stick, hands on the ends of the stick: it doesn't matter. You can win either way.

AN UNTEARABLE SITUATION

Bet you can't rip a tissue!

THE SETUP

You will need a paper tissue, a cardboard tube from a roll of paper towels, a rubber band, table salt or sand, and a broomstick. Stretch the tissue across the end of the paper towel tube. Fasten it in place with the rubber band. Pour four inches of salt or sand into the tube. Now hold the tube in one hand and press a broomstick into the salt. Try to push hard enough to rip the tissue.

INSIDER INFORMATION

The tissue is thin and the broomstick is strong, but you won't be able to rip that tissue! The force you put on the broomstick is not all going straight down the tube toward the tissue. There are many tiny spaces between the salt crystals. When you jam the broomstick into the salt, the crystals collide, sending the force in every direction. Salt absorbs some of the force and divides the rest so it is diverted to all the surfaces of the tube. Only a tiny fraction of the original force reaches the tissue. The human body is not a strong enough powerhouse to deliver the force needed to send the broomstick through the tissue.

For centuries, bags of sand have been used to stop speeding bullets in a dramatic adaptation of this marvel of nature.

A SURE RIP-OFF

Bet you can't tear a piece of paper into three pieces!

THE SETUP

Fold a piece of paper into thirds. Open it out again. Now cut or tear the paper equally along the folds so that only about an inch of paper keeps the strips together. Hold the tops of the two end strips. Now try to tear the paper so that the middle strip drops out and there are three separate pieces of paper.

INSIDER INFORMATION

Your strength here is a weakness. Paper, like all other materials, succumbs to force at its weakest point. The two tears you started in the paper are weak points, and they are not equal even if they appear to be. There is no way you can make the cuts perfectly equal. When you pull, the weaker tear gives way first. This makes that spot even weaker, so any more force will be delivered directly to that point, until it rips completely off. Then you are left without the opposing force needed to separate the other two strips of paper.

NOTHING TO GET TORN UP ABOUT

Bet you can't make two straight tears in a sheet of newspaper!

THE SETUP

The tears in this trick must be made at right angles to each other Take a single sheet of newspaper. Try to rip it in a straight line from top to bottom. If you succeed, then make the second tear from one side to the other.

INSIDER INFORMATION

You can't make perpendicular straight-line tears because newspaper is formed on a wire screen, which creates straight lines in one direction. This is called the grain. The other direction does not have these unbroken parallel lines.

A force always attacks the weakest point. The parallel lines of the grain are thinner than the rest of the paper. So when you tear with the grain, the rip runs down one of the lines made by the wire and you get a fairly straight edge. When you try to tear across the grain the force attacks whatever point is weakest and a jagged, irregular line is produced.

Not all paper has a grain. This is a good test. Tear into some experiments with paper toweling, computer paper, stationery, school writing paper, toilet paper, etc.

ELBOWED OUT

Bet you can't be lifted by the elbows!

THE SETUP

Stand upright with your elbows bent and held horizontally to your body. Rest your palms on your shoulders. Have two strong people hold your elbows (one apiece) and try to lift you off the ground.

INSIDER INFORMATION

Your elbow angle is the difference between success and failure in this trick. The positioning of the elbows forward of the center of gravity is what makes the elbow lift impossible. (Move your elbows back against your body, and you can be lifted easily.)

The elbows in front of your body move the applied lift force away from your center of gravity. The more you increase this distance, the more force is needed to overcome the resistance of your weight. It's truly amazing how such a small distance puts this trick outside the realm of human strength.

A PIERCING MOMENT

Bet you can't pop a balloon with a pin!

THE SETUP

Inflate and tie a balloon. Put a small piece of clear plastic tape on it. Now try to pop the balloon by sticking a pin through the tape.

INSIDER INFORMATION

The balloon is unpoppable! Air leaks out, but it won't deflate with a bang. Rubber and tape react differently to the stress created by the escaping air. The balloon skin is weak and rips when the air pushes against the edges of the hole. The tape is a stronger material and can resist the force of the compressed air.

An unpoppable balloon is a good party stunt, but can you see how this principle is used to make blowout-proof tires?

A RAW DEAL

Bet you can't fool me with a hard-boiled egg!

THE SETUP

You are the expert egg sorter in this trick. You will need a raw egg and a hard-boiled one. Without cracking either, you can identify the hard-boiled one just by spinning the eggs.

INSIDER INFORMATION

Hard-boiled eggs spin faster and longer than raw eggs. A hard-boiled egg is a solid. It spins easily. A raw egg contains a liquid. Liquid requires more force than a solid to set it in motion. Since you apply only one force to the egg when you spin it, the liquid inside the raw egg does not move as rapidly as the solid shell. This creates a drag between the inside of the shell and the surface of the liquid, which slows down and eventually stops the movement of the egg. While you're into spinning eggs, try the next trick.

RAW POWER

Wanna bet you can't stop a spinning egg?

THE SETUP

This trick requires raw power, so make sure you use an uncooked egg. Place it on its side on a tabletop and spin it vigorously. Stop the spinning egg but let go of it immediately. It will begin spinning again all by itself.

INSIDER INFORMATION

This is not a case of an egg with a memory! The spin on this trick is the liquid inside the egg. When you stopped the shell from moving, you didn't stop the liquid. As soon as you released the shell, the moving liquid set the whole egg in motion again.

A hard-boiled egg with its solid contents acts as if it is all shell. When you stop it, it stays stopped.

NO SHATTERING EXPERIENCE

Bet you can't break a light bulb on a concrete floor!

THE SETUP

Hold a burned out light bulb over a concrete floor. The metal end must be facing straight down. If you think you can break the bulb on the floor, drop it! Yes, drop it!

INSIDER INFORMATION

The bulb won't break. The reason is that the force of impact is absorbed by the metal part of the bulb, which is practically unbreakable. The glass, which *can* shatter when force is applied, is protected by the metal base. Although the bulb may bounce around on the floor, these little bounces will not be enough to break the glass.

CAUTION!

Do not throw the bulb at the floor. This may result in the bulb's hitting somewhere other than the metal end and the glass might shatter. For safety's sake, do not throw the bulb, just drop it.

LIGHTEN UP!

Wanna bet you can lose weight in one second?

THE SETUP

This is the quickest trick in the book. You can lose a lot of weight with our split-second weight-loss program. Here's how. Stand on a bathroom scale and note your weight. Quickly bend your knees while you watch the scale. As your body moves down, the pounds disappear. When we tried this, one of us, who will be nameless, lost 150 pounds—and then rocketed up to 250 pounds, which is as far as the scale registered. Fortunately, neither condition lasted too long.

INSIDER INFORMATION

When you bend your knees quickly, for a split second, the weight of your upper body is not supported by your feet. This "weight loss" shows up on the scale. Skiers use this technique and lift their body's weight off their skis so they can turn.

The downside of the split-second weight-loss program is the weight gain you experience at the moment you end your knee bend. Not only do you get back all your original weight, but the sudden stop of your upper body's motion shows up as additional weight on the scale. The amount of weight gained or lost depends on how fast you bend your knees. The faster you bend them, the more you lighten up—and fatten up!

BIONIC ARM

Wanna bet you can't lift my hand from the top of my head?

THE SETUP

Sit down and place your open hand on top of your head. Spread your fingers as wide apart as possible and hang on to your head. Here we go! Have a friend grip your forearm as close to your elbow as possible and try to lift your hand off your head. Use a straight upward pull with no sudden movements. Your "bionic" arm can't be moved.

INSIDER INFORMATION

Surprise, your arm is a machine! It's a simple machine, but nevertheless a machine: which is any device that increases your strength or your speed. In this case your arm is a lever. Here's how it works. The force required to lift your hand is greatest next to your elbow and the least next to your wrist. To lift your hand from this position, the lifter would have to be three or four times stronger than you are. Your mechanical advantage is considerably less when the lift is at your wrist.

NO STRINGS

Wanna bet a yo-yo will climb a string no one is holding?

THE SETUP

This is the world's greatest yo-yo trick. No kidding. You can make a yo-yo defy gravity and climb up the string after you let go. It takes a little practice to master, but it's worth it.

Make a yo-yo "sleep" (if you don't know how, consult a local yo-yo pro). Then take the string off your finger and hold it between your thumb and forefinger. Now slap your hand while you watch the yo-yo. As soon as it starts to come up the string, let go. The yo-yo will charge up the string. Catch it in your hand. Some professionals use this trick to end their act, catching the wound-up yo-yo in their pocket.

INSIDER INFORMATION

When a yo-yo sleeps there is almost no friction between the string and the spinning axle of the yo-yo. A jerk on the string increases the contact between the string and the axle, creating enough friction to rewind the string. A slap is a stronger, quicker force than you normally give with wrist action, and the rewind is quick enough to be completed before the string has a chance to fall.

STACKED ODDS

Bet you can remove only the bottom checker of a stack without touching it!

THE SETUP

Stack eight checkers on a smooth surface. Strike the bottom checker briskly with the edge of a table knife.

INSIDER INFORMATION

The bottom checker snaps out and the stack remains stacked, just one checker shorter.

There is a law of physics that explains this trick: the law of inertia. An object at rest will remain at rest unless acted upon by an outside force. In this case the knife exerts the outside force *but only to the bottom checker.* The only force acting on the rest of the stack is friction. If the bottom checker moves off fast enough, the friction is so small that it has no noticeable effect on the rest of the stack.

The same principle is in effect here as in the trick where you pull a tablecloth out from under a fully set table. If you are really good with the checker gimmick, then you might set your sights on the tablecloth.

STRONG-ARM TACTICS

Bet you can hold off ten people!

THE SETUP

Your secret ally, science, will enable you to keep ten strong people from pushing you against a wall.

Place your palms against the wall, fingers pointing up, arms outstretched. Brace yourself. Have your ten people line up behind you, each one with hands on the shoulders of the

person before him or her. At a signal, everyone pushes with all their strength to press you to the wall.

INSIDER INFORMATION

You won't fold. You will withstand them all. The reason is that each person absorbs the force of the one directly behind him or her so there is no cumulative force. As long as you can withstand the force of the person directly behind you, you can beat the whole lineup. As a sneaky precaution, choose the weakest one to stand directly behind you.

GETTING DOWN

Bet you can keep a friend in a chair with one finger!

THE SETUP

Have a friend sit in a chair chin up, head back. Put your index finger against the forehead and press. Tell your friend to try to get up.

INSIDER INFORMATION

Your friend is now a prisoner at your fingertip. In a resting position the center of gravity of the body (the point at which all weight seems to be centered) is located over the place where it rests (the base). In a seated position the center of gravity is in the seat. In order to stand, the center of gravity must shift to over the feet. The head *must* move forward to make this shift. The slight pressure against the forehead is just enough to keep your friend sitting tight.

FRIENDLY GET-TOGETHER

Bet you can out-tug a tug-of-war!

THE SETUP

You can out-pull four big people with this stunt. No kidding. You will need two broomsticks and about twenty feet of strong rope. This trick can be done with two or four other people. Our directions are for two people. Have both people hold a broomstick in front of them. They should stand about three feet apart. Tie the end of the rope securely to one broomstick about a foot from the end. Wind it around both broomsticks about five times. Be sure the rope does not cross itself at any time. You hold the end of the rope next to one of the

broomstick holders. When you give the signal, the holders try to keep the two broomsticks from coming together while you pull on the rope. Much to everyone's amazement, they will not be able to resist your force. You will pull the tug-of-war together single-handedly. This trick is even more impressive with four people, two on each broomstick.

INSIDER INFORMATION

Mother Nature is giving you a mechanical advantage here. You are setting up a pulley system. Pulleys are simple machines that change the direction of force. A single change of direction doesn't make a job easier, but when you change directions more than once, you have gained a mechanical advantage. When you wrap the rope around the broomsticks you have four changes of direction, so you can multiply your pulling power by four.

Let's say that everyone exerts a force of fifty pounds. The tug-of-war is at a stalemate, with equal amounts pulling against each other. You give one team (the one pulling in the same direction you are) an advantage with your force. It tips the balance and you win. Yay!

FAKIR FAKE OUT

Bet you can lift a jar of rice with a knife!

THE SETUP

You will need a jar with a narrow mouth (we used a mayonnaise jar), uncooked rice, and a table knife. Fill the jar to the brim with rice. Stab it quickly a number of times with the knife. The level of rice goes down because the stabbing causes the grains to pack together tightly. Add rice to the jar to keep it filled. After twenty or thirty stabs, give a quick, long thrust into the rice with the knife. The knife will stick into the rice so you can lift the entire jar with the knife handle.

INSIDER INFORMATION

The preliminary knife stabs rearrange the rice grains so they become packed tightly enough to press against the knife blade with a force that will allow you to lift the jar into the air.

We called this trick "Fakir Fake Out" because it is a common stunt performed at Indian fairs.

TOUGH SHAPE

Bet you can squeeze a raw egg without breaking it!

THE SETUP

This squeeze play is simple. Be certain that when you squeeze, your hand completely surrounds the egg and you put pressure evenly on all sides. That's all the gimmick there is. Just make sure you're not wearing a ring and there are no cracks in the eggshell.

INSIDER INFORMATION

Believe it or not, an egg is cleverly designed to withstand force. The oval shape of an egg is extremely strong when forces are applied evenly to it. Uneven forces crack it, so do this over a sink just to be on the safe side.

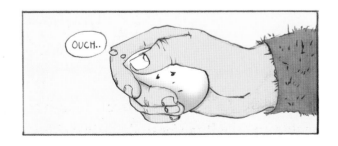

For a fun variation, try supporting some heavy books on eggshell halves. Crack two raw eggs in half (eat the contents as scrambled eggs). Wash out the shells and trim them with scissors to remove any jagged edges. Set the four shells, dome side up, on a table under the four corners of a very heavy book. See how many other books you can add to the eggshell tower before it collapses. Bet you'll be surprised at the results.

BURNING A CANDLE AT BOTH ENDS

Bet you can make a candle seesaw by itself!

THE SETUP

Peel the wax off the bottom end of a birthday candle to expose the wick. Stick a long sewing needle through the candle so it is centered on the needle. Set two glasses on some aluminum foil and rest the ends of the needle on the rims of the glasses. The foil is there to catch the drips. Make sure the candle is close to horizontal before you proceed.

Ask the okay of an adult before you light both ends of the candle. Watch it seesaw back and forth as if it had a life of its own. Truly an amazing stunt!

WHAT A DRIP!

INSIDER INFORMATION

There is almost no chance that the candle will burn evenly at both ends. As the burning progresses one end gets lower, wax drops from it, and it rises in reaction to the sudden weight loss. This begins the seesaw motion, which continues as the lower side drops wax, and the pattern begins again. This simple back-and-forth exchange is called harmonic motion. A common example is a pendulum swinging back and forth.

Now you know the ups and downs of burning a candle at both ends.

IN ORBIT

Bet you can make a ball defy gravity!

THE SETUP

We can tell you how to keep a ball in an upside-down jar even when there is no lid. You will need a Ping-Pong ball and a large jar with a narrow mouth. A mayonnaise jar or a pickle

jar is great. Place the ball on a table and put the mouth of the upside-down jar over the ball. Hold the jar by the bottom and rotate it rapidly with a wrist motion. The ball will move around and around the inside of the jar. As the motion speeds up, the ball will climb the sides of the jar. Lift the rotating jar off the table. The ball will stay in the jar until you stop the motion.

INSIDER INFORMATION

With a flick of your wrist you set the ball in orbit. Circular motion creates centrifugal force. This force draws objects away from the center of the motion. In this case the centrifugal force is pushing the ball against the walls of the jar with a strength that defies gravity.

THE DROPLESS DROP

Bet you can stop a leak with gravity!

THE SETUP

Most leaks are caused by gravity, but did you know you can use gravity to stop a leak? Make two quarter-inch holes on opposite sides of a paper cup. Fill the paper cup with water. It leaks, right? You can stop the leak if you hold the cup so that your fingers block the holes. Find some place outside where you can drop the cup a distance. (We dropped it off a deck onto a patio.) Watch it as it falls. Not a drop comes from the holes!

INSIDER INFORMATION

Water leaks out of the cup when it is not falling because the weight of the water above the holes presses down on the water near the holes and pushes it out. But when gravity is acting on the entire cup and its contents as it is falling freely, there is no water pressure to push the water out the holes and it stays in the cup. Free fall has a price! Water pays!

STOP THE DROP

Use paper clips to prevent keys from hitting the floor.

THE SETUP

A ring of keys is clearly heavier than three paper clips. But the three clips can counterbalance the keys and stop their fall.

You will need:

- keys on a key ring
- a piece of string about one yard long
- 3 paper clips
- a pen or pencil

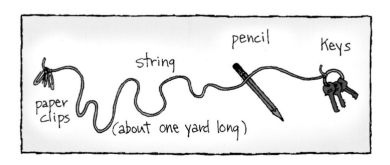

Tie the keys to one end of a piece of string and the paper clips to the other end. Hold a pencil horizontally in front of you with one hand. Grasp the paper clips in the other. Drape the string over the pencil so the keys are hanging down. Make the string between the pencil and the clips horizontal. Two-thirds of the string should be between the clips and the pencil.

Now, let go of the paper clips. Naturally, the keys drop. But amazingly, they don't reach the ground. The paper clips spin around the pencil and wind up the string. Six wraps are enough to break the fall of the keys.

⅔ of the string is held horizontally.

And ⅓ of the string hangs down.

INSIDER INFORMATION

The second you release the paper clips, gravity acts on the keys and the clips, and both start to fall. Because the keys are heavier, they are falling with a greater force than the clips, winning the tug-of-war with the string. As a result, the length of string between the clips and the pencil gets shorter and shorter. The combined force of the falling clips and the shortening string causes the clips to rotate around the pencil. The shorter the string gets, the faster the clips rotate. After a series of wraps, the keys stop falling. This is because of the friction between the string and the pencil. Friction is a force between two surfaces that resists motion. Six wraps usually provide enough friction to stop the fall of several keys.

AN ALARM CUP

Use a paper cup to make a VERY loud roar.

THE SETUP

Believe it or not, a paper cup and dental floss can blast everyone out of bed.

You will need:

- a paper cup
- a wooden toothpick
- a 24-inch length of waxed dental floss, preferably the ribbon kind

With the toothpick, punch a small hole in the center of the bottom of a paper cup.

Thread the dental floss through the hole. Tie this end of the dental floss around a broken-off piece of the toothpick to keep the floss from slipping back through the hole.

Hold the cup in one hand and grasp the dental floss between your thumb and index finger. Gently pull your fingers along the string. The sound speaks volumes!

INSIDER INFORMATION

Your roaring cup creates sound the same way a violin does. As your fingers move along the dental floss the sticky wax turns the stroke into a lot of tiny stops and starts. This causes the string to vibrate. Rosin on a bow does the same thing to a violin's string. The cup amplifies the vibrations.

Your paper cup is not a one-note instrument. Tie the loose end of the floss to a stationary object. Pull the cup so the thread is tight and then run your fingers down the string; the tighter the string the higher the sound. Now try plucking a tight string.

Dental floss music has never really become popular. Aside from the fact that this instrument makes a terrible sound, there's another drawback. The string has to be replaced when the wax becomes smooth.

THE FIFTY-FIVE CENT FIX

Do a coin-flip trick you can't lose.

THE SETUP

When you drop a coin you have a fifty-fifty chance of getting heads. When you drop a pair of coins, you can stack them in a way that also stacks the odds. You can't lose! The coin that starts out on top ends up on the bottom one-hundred percent of the time.

You will need:

- 2 quarters
- 1 nickel

Make a sandwich of the coins with the nickel in the middle. Hold the stack of coins between your thumb and index finger so the coins are horizontal.

Cup your other hand about ten inches below the coins. Spread your fingertips apart so you release the bottom quarter yet still hold on to the top one. The quarter starts its downward trip with the nickel

riding on top. Surprisingly, when the two coins land in your hand, the quarter is on top.

INSIDER INFORMATION

Why does the nickel always end up below the quarter? The coins flip. Holding on to the top quarter makes it

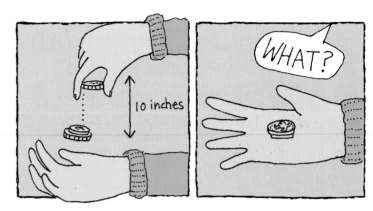

nearly impossible to release both sides of the bottom quarter at the same instant, so one side drops sooner, causing both coins to rotate. It takes a fall of about ten inches for the nickel and the quarter to flip over (turn 180 degrees).

If the coins flip 180 degrees in a ten-inch drop, how far would they have to drop to make a 360-degree rotation so the nickel is back on top? You might think twenty inches. But gravity is working here, causing the coins to accelerate as they fall. It would take a forty-inch drop to accomplish this feat. When they landed from this height they'd probably bounce apart anyhow.

A CANDLE TAKES A BATH

Burn a candle under water.

THE SETUP

Light a candle in a bowl of water and it will continue to burn even when the wick is below the surface of the water, creating the oddest shaped candle you've ever seen.

You will need:

- a six-inch candle
- a short candleholder with a spike or waterproof tape (adhesive or duct tape)
- matches
- a glass bowl
- scissors
- cold water

CAUTION!
This trick involves fire so get an adult assistant.

The hardest part of the setup is attaching the candle to the bottom of the bowl so that the candle doesn't float when you add water. If you can't find a short candleholder with a spike, light the candle and drip melted wax into the center of the bowl before adding water. Make a puddle of wax that is wider than the

candle. Quickly stick the candle into it. Let the wax cool and harden. Tape the wax to the bowl with waterproof tape for extra holding power.

Fill a bowl with cold water up to the rim of the candle. Straighten the wick of the candle Light it and wait.

INSIDER INFORMATION

A very thin wall of wax remains standing as the candle burns, preventing the water from extinguishing the flame. The water draws so much heat from the wax that the outer layer never gets hot enough to burn. If you wait long enough, your submarine candle will become a thin, hollow tube. Bet your friends won't be able to figure out how you made it.

DOUBLE RINGER

Make a bell ring with two different sounds.

THE SETUP

You might think a bell can ring with only one sound. Not true! You can get it to make two different sounds at the same time. One sound is the familiar ring produced by a clapper

hitting the side of the bell. You can add a
second sound, an uninterrupted penetrating
tone, with a piece of wood.

You will need:

- a large handheld, bell-shaped metal bell
- a smooth wooden stick, such as the handle
  of a tool or a wooden spoon

With your less-favored hand, grasp the bell
by the handle, making sure that you are
not touching the bell itself. The bell should
be facing down. Hold a piece of wood in
your other hand. Press the wood against the
lower rim of the bell and move it repeatedly
around the circumference of the bell with
a smooth, circular motion. The bell should
start to hum softly and get louder and
louder. If it doesn't, check to make sure that
you are keeping the wood in contact with
the bell and that your hands aren't.

   Once you've built up a vibrating hum, move the stick away and gently ring the bell
normally. Listen for the two distinct sounds coming from the bell.

INSIDER INFORMATION

A bell rings because metal vibrates a long time after it is struck. (You can eliminate the ring
by holding the bell rather than the handle. If your hand prevents the metal from vibrating,
the bell makes only a short clunky sound as the clapper hits the side.) The vibrations in
your double-sounding bell are created in two ways: by a single sharp hit and by many
small ones. The bang of the clapper is obviously a sharp hit. What you might not realize is
that wood stroked along the rim creates many small hits. The wood appears to be moving
smoothly around the lip of the bell, but it's not. It is slipping and stopping many times per
second. Another demonstration of this kind of sound generation is a ringing crystal glass
caused by running a wet finger around the rim.

The double-ringer has two tones because the clapper makes an impact sound that is different from the ringing tone.

WHERE'S THE RUB?

Feel invisible ridges on a refrigerator magnet.

THE SETUP

Common flexible magnets (the kind with advertising on them) have a secret. They look and feel smooth. However, they have a hidden roughness. You can't see it but you can feel it.

You will need:

- a flat rubber or plastic refrigerator magnet
- scissors
- a piece of white paper (optional)
- iron filings (optional)

Cut a flat rubber magnet in half. Press the unprinted sides together. Depending on which way you put them together one of three things can happen: they don't stick together, they stick weakly, or they stick strongly.

You won't be able to detect the hidden roughness of the magnet if the pieces don't stick together. So rotate one piece ninety degrees. It will either stick strongly or weakly to the other piece. In each case, though, when you rub the pieces back and forth against each other, they will feel as if they have ridges.

INSIDER INFORMATION

A magnet is made from a material that can attract pieces of iron and other magnetic materials. If a bar-shaped magnet is suspended so that it can swing freely, it will line up with one end pointing north and the other pointing south. The end pointing north is its north pole; the end pointing south, its south pole.

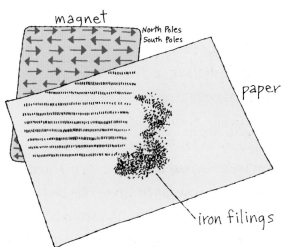

Flexible magnets are not a solid magnet. They are made of many rows of tiny bar magnets embedded in a rubber sheet. A row of north poles alternates with a row of south poles. The rows are about an eighth of an inch apart. You can see where the magnetic rows are if you place a piece of paper over the magnet and sprinkle it with iron filings. The filings will form a pattern over the magnetic rows of the magnet beneath the paper.

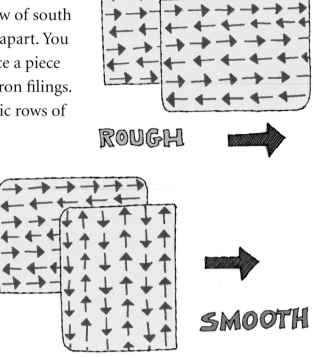

When the two pieces of the magnet are aligned so that the magnetic rows are parallel, you feel the corrugation as you pull them across each other. The jerky motion is caused when like poles repel each other and unlike poles attract each other. Your senses of touch and hearing interpret this as a rough surface.

When the rows are at right angles they don't line up and so the attraction is too weak to form a bond. That's why the magnets' surfaces move smoothly past each other.

REPULSIVE WRITING

Use your TV to see how a copier works.

THE SETUP

Xerox and other copying machines use static electricity to write. You can, too. See the inspiration behind the dry copier with your TV set and some talcum powder

You will need:

- a television set
- talcum powder and a powder puff
- dust cloth and glass cleaner or a used sheet of fabric softener

Begin with a clean, dry TV screen. Turn on the TV for at least five minutes. Then, turn it off. Write a simple message on the screen with your finger. Dip a powder puff into talcum powder and shake it in front of the screen so that the dust drifts toward the TV.

A thin layer of talcum powder will coat the screen except where you wrote your message.

When you are finished, erase your message by cleaning the screen with glass cleaner or a used sheet of fabric softener from the dryer.

INSIDER INFORMATION

Modern copying machines use a process called *xerography*, which means "dry writing." It is based on the principle that an electric charge will attract dust. A television screen gets a static charge when the TV is on and holds the charge for a short time after the set is turned off. Wherever you touch the screen, you get rid of the charge. The tiny particles of powder are attracted to the charged areas and cling there. They are repulsed wherever there is writing.

In a copying machine, dark areas of the image become electrically charged and attract particles of powdered ink. Through a complicated process, the ink is transferred to white copy paper where it is fused to the paper with heat.

We Dare You!

SOUND BYTES

Listen to your computer on the radio.

THE SETUP

Your computer gives off radio waves that you can hear. It's not exactly music to your ears, but it's interesting listening.

You will need:

- a computer
- a small AM/FM radio

There are three possible sources of computer radio waves: the monitor, the hard drive, and the microprocessor.

To listen to your monitor, turn it on. Set the radio to receive AM and tune it to an area where there is no station. Turn the volume to max. Bring the radio close to the monitor. Move it away. You should hear a difference when the radio comes close to the monitor. Click the monitor on and off. The noise you hear is radio waves broadcast by your monitor.

To listen to your hard drive, place the radio close to it. Set it as you did above. Activate the drive by opening or copying a file. You should hear a change in sounds.

To listen to your processor, you'll need to switch the radio to FM. You'll also need to know the speed of your processor because it broadcasts radio waves on that frequency. Tune to whatever frequency most closely matches your computer's speed. For example, if your processor operates at 100 MHz (megahertz) tune your dial to 100 FM. To get the most interesting broadcast, play a video game with the sound effects turned off. What you hear is computer radio at its best.

INSIDER INFORMATION

Computer broadcasting is no surprise to the government. The Federal Communications Commission (FCC) regulates all devices that emit or receive

radio waves. Look at the back of your computer and you will see its FCC identification code. There are a limited number of radio wave frequencies. The FCC assigns different frequencies to radio and television stations, short wave radios, and cellular phone companies. This is done to ensure that you receive a signal without interference from other sources. The FCC's regulations make sure that the radio waves given off by your computer are weak and will not interfere with other incoming signals.

8. MATHEMATICAL DUPLICITY

And now for a word from the math department. WAIT! Don't close the book. We know most people hate numbers and think arithmetic is boring, so we didn't put any addition, subtraction, multiplication, or division games here. What's left? Lots. Math isn't always about counting or adding or multiplying or any of those boring things that your calculator does. We promise you won't have to do any adding, subtracting, multiplying, or dividing. And except for one trick, you won't even have to count.

Here's what you are going to do: cut, slice, twist, and bend. Doesn't sound much like math, does it? But these are the kinds of things you do in geometry, the part of mathematics that deals with shapes and surfaces. Take topology, the mathematics of form and shape. It's fascinating. We are going to fool you with topological oddities, like a strip of paper that has only one side and a dollar bill that mysteriously transfers its curves to other objects. Topologists are concerned with the things that remain the same about a surface of a shape no matter how much you squeeze or twist it. To topologists a human being has a shape equal to that of a doughnut. They also claim that you can't get all the hairs on a furry ball to lie flat. There will always be two spots where the hairs point away from each other. And topologists gave mapmakers a hand when they discovered you only need four colors to make any map, no matter how complicated the map. Actually, you are probably familiar with topology and don't know it. If you've done mazes or solved jigsaw puzzles, you are into topological games.

Betting on tricks is math. The calculation of odds is called probability and it belongs to a branch of mathematics called statistics. Even fixed bets, like the ones in this book, can be expressed mathematically. They are "beyond chance." In fact, the whole theme of this book—winning bets—is a branch of mathematics called *probability*. We're betting you will probably want to continue your winning streak. Let us count the ways!

CLIP JOINT

Bet you can't keep two paper clips from hooking together!

THE SETUP

You will need a dollar bill and two paper clips for this trick. Fold a dollar bill into a flattened "S" shape. Hold it so that you are looking down on the "S." Take a paper clip and hook the short, single wire over two thicknesses of the bill. Hook the short, single wire of a second paper clip over two thicknesses of paper on the other side of the dollar curve as shown in the picture. Now straighten the bill by grasping the ends and pulling sharply. The two paper clips will fly into the air and hook together.

INSIDER INFORMATION

Although the two paper clips are not touching on the bill, they miraculously hook together when you snap the dollar. This stunt is based on a topological phenomenon called transference of curves. The "S"-shaped curve made by the folds in the dollar bill is transferred to the paper clips when the dollar is straightened.

   If the exact mechanism of this oddity interests you, pull slowly on the ends of the bill. You may be able to see what is happening. The trick doesn't always work when the bill is pulled slowly, but sometimes it does. So don't make any bets on the slow move. If you're interested in this transfer of curves, try the next trick.

GRIPPING ACTION

Bet you can knot a string without letting go of the ends!

THE SETUP

Set a piece of string about a foot long on the table in front of you. Fold your arms across your chest. With your arms still folded, grasp the left end of the string with your right hand, and the other end with your free hand. Hang on to the ends of the string and unfold your arms. Surprise! The string is knotted.

INSIDER INFORMATION

This is a math trick, believe it or not. The gimmick that makes it possible is called "transfer of curves." Your arms had the knot in them before you picked up the string. What you did was transfer the knot from your arms to the string.

OUT OF ORDER

Bet you can't flip and turn a book and have it end up in the same position as when you turn and flip it!

THE SETUP

Hold a book in your hands as if you are going to read the front cover. Flip it over from bottom to top. Then turn it ninety degrees in a counterclockwise direction. You will end up with the spine facing you and the back cover on top.

Now hold the book as if you are going to read it again. The same two operations are going to be performed, but in reverse order. Turn the book ninety degrees in a counterclockwise direction. Flip it over, bottom to top. The back cover will be on top, but the spine now faces away from you.

INSIDER INFORMATION

Sequence is the key word in understanding why this trick doesn't work. In a sequence involving two different kinds of operations (and flips and turns are two different kinds of operations), the sequence of the operations will affect the outcome. Wonder why we put this in the math chapter? It belongs here, all right, for direction of motion and position are mathematical properties.

CURSES, COILED AGAIN

THE SETUP

This is an old carnival trick that has fooled people for hundreds of years. It's based on topology, a part of mathematics. You can still find candidates for the bet. It involves nothing more difficult than trapping a belt around a pencil.

You will need a belt that has distinctly different surfaces on the inside and the outside. Fold the belt in half with the inside surfaces together. Coil the belt, beginning with the fold end, to form a flat circle. The center of the coil has an "S" shape. One loop of this "S" is formed by the belt's inside and the other by the belt's outside. Put a pencil in the half of the "S" curve formed by the inside surfaces. Grasp both ends of the belt and pull. The belt will unwind but it will be held by the pencil. You are now ready to do the old garter con. Say:

> ### Bet you can't catch the belt with the pencil like I showed you!

INSIDER INFORMATION

In spite of what you've demonstrated, no matter where your friend places the pencil, you can pull the belt free. Here's how the trick is rigged.

1. If the pencil is placed in the half of the "S" that is the outside of the belt, just hold the ends and pull the belt free.

2. If the pencil is placed on the inside curve take one end of the belt and unwind it a turn. Now grasp both ends and pull. The belt slips free. (You'll give away the secret of this trick if you make the unwinding too obvious. Pretend you are straightening up the coils.) By unwrapping one end, you are folding the belt the other way. The inside is now the outside. The manipulation is so far away from the original fold that it isn't obvious what you have done.

ON PAPER THE ODDS LOOK GOOD... BUT

Bet you can't fold a sheet of paper in half more than twelve times!

THE SETUP

This challenge has no restrictions. All you have to do is fold a piece of paper in half more than twelve times. Use any kind of paper, any size, and any thickness—as long as it can be folded in half. Divide the paper in half evenly on each fold. The folds may be in any direction: lengthwise, crosswise, or even on a diagonal. Try it. We dare you. This is such a sure thing we even double dare you.

INSIDER INFORMATION

When we first wrote this book people thought that the limit to the number of folds was nine. If you take an ordinary sheet of paper the thickness doubles with each fold as a geometric progression. On the first fold you have a thickness of two pieces of paper, on the second, four. The third fold creates eight layers. By the time you make the seventh fold you are trying to crease a wad of 128 separate sheets. That's like trying to fold a book. But when Britney Gallivan was in high school a few years ago she solved the problem and found that the limit was 12.

Britney bought a jumbo roll of toilet paper that was three-fourths of a mile long. It took her and her parents seven hours to fold it in half, end upon end, twelve times. She also worked out the mathematical formula that predicts this limit. For this, she is forever famous. Great project for extra credit!

AN INSIDE JOB

Bet you can slice a banana without peeling it—and without using a knife!

THE SETUP

For this slippery operation you will need a ripe banana, a needle, and a thread. Stick the threaded needle into a spot on one ridge of the banana and bring it out at the next ridge. Pull the thread taut but leave a three- or four-inch tail sticking out of the original hole. Push the needle back into the second hole and bring it out the next ridge. Repeat until you have gone completely around the banana. Then hold both ends of the thread in your hand and pull the thread completely free of the banana. For a really special surprise, make more "secret slices." Peel … and eat your experiment.

INSIDER INFORMATION

This trick looks much more difficult than it really is. The principle behind the slicing is simple. All the fancy sewing has merely run a circle of thread around the outside of the fruit inside the skin. The thread is strong enough to act as a knife and to cut through the soft flesh of the banana. This is a math maneuver called "sectioning."

TIME'S UP

Bet you can't figure out a simple arithmetic problem!

THE SETUP

We promised no number games, but this is an exception to the rule that arithmetic is dull. It's too good to pass up because it's wonderfully simple and a perfect sure-win bet. Try it! Here is the problem to be solved:

You are to travel from Point A to Point B and return. On the trip from A to B, you travel at thirty miles per hour. How fast would you have to travel from B to A in order to average sixty miles per hour for the round trip?

INSIDER INFORMATION

The answer everyone quickly gives is ninety miles an hour. Wrong! This is an impossible journey. Think of it this way: Imagine that the distance from A to B is one mile. Sixty miles per hour is a mile a minute. So it would take two minutes at the average speed of sixty miles per hour to make the round trip of two miles. Now, the first half of the trip—one mile—is to be made at thirty miles per hour. This would take two minutes. You can see there is no time left for the return trip.

LOOSE CHANGE

Bet you can pass a quarter through a hole the size of a dime!

THE SETUP

Cut a hole the size of a dime in the center of a piece of paper. Try to slip a quarter through the hole without tearing the paper. Won't fit? It will if you fold the paper in half, place the quarter in the fold, and bend the paper upward as you grip it at the outer edges of the crease. With a little manipulation the quarter will slip right through the dime-size hole.

INSIDER INFORMATION

It's topology again. This numberless math deals with surfaces. Folding the paper enables you to distort the circle to an ellipse. An ellipse is a shape that is like a circle. Topologically it is the same. It has a short diameter and a

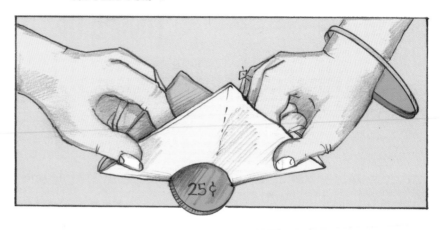

long diameter. The quarter slips through the long diameter in a stunt that is baffling because we convert a two-dimensional shape into a 3-D one.

THE GREAT ESCAPE

Bet you can make a rubber band jump from one finger to another!

THE SETUP

Hang a rubber band over the index finger of your left hand. Take the free end in your other hand and turn the loop so that one strand is forward. Pull the band down and

around the middle finger. It is important that the strand that is forward on the index finger also be forward on the middle finger (see the diagram). Now loop the band over the top of the middle finger and place it on the end of the index finger.

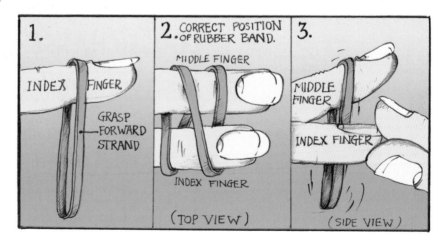

Grasp the end of your index finger with your right hand and bend your middle finger. The band will snap free of the index finger and hang on your middle finger. Mysterious.

Topology tricks you here, too. It appears that your index finger is completely tied up. It is not. The rubber band is looped so that the middle finger opens the circle. The loops on the index finger appear to be the ends of the circle but they actually are the middle.

PICKING UP LOOSE CHANGE

Bet you can't pick up the last cent in this game!

THE SETUP

This fooler is a two-person game played with twenty pennies. Each player takes turns picking up one, two, or three pennies. The one who picks up the last penny is the winner.

INSIDER INFORMATION

The con is set into action by insisting that your opponent go first. Now, if you can count to four, you are the winner. The fix is based on a simple mathematical calculation—multiples of four. The number of pennies you take each time depends upon how many pennies your opponent takes. The total for the combined moves must be four. (If your opponent takes three pennies, you take one. If two are removed, you take two.) By going second you keep the number of remaining pennies divisible by four. On your opponent's fifth turn, there will be four pennies remaining. Since three is the maximum number that can be picked up on a single move, you win! Yay!

DOUBLE CROSS

Wanna bet you can draw parallel lines that intersect?

THE SETUP

Hold two pencils or pens side by side against each other. Place the parallel points on a piece of paper. Move the paper under the pens so that a figure eight is created. Don't tilt the pens. Keep them at right angles to the paper at all times. The parallel lines will intersect each other at the center of the figure eight.

INSIDER INFORMATION

By definition parallel lines are lines that are always the same distance from each other. This is the one and only requirement of parallel lines.

When most people think of parallel lines, they think of *straight lines*. They are the only parallel lines that can never cross. Curved parallel lines, on the other hand, can double-cross you.

A STACKED DECK

Wanna bet shuffling doesn't make a difference when the cards are stacked right?

THE SETUP

Arrange a deck of cards so that the black and red cards alternate. Cut the deck. Make sure the bottom cards are opposite colors. Shuffle the cards once. Deal cards from the top of the deck in pairs. In spite of your shuffle, they will always be red/black pairs.

INSIDER INFORMATION

You can be a card shark if you use a little mathemagic. What appears to be miraculous is really the result of a math law. It is called the *Gilbreath Principle* after the mathematician/magician who formulated it in 1958.

If you don't see the math behind the magic, do the trick with the cards face-side up. Stack your deck and cut it so one red and one black card face up. Imagine you are shuffling the deck. Put one card down to represent the first card to hit the table in your shuffle. If it is black, both halves of the deck will now have a red card up. It doesn't matter which half of the deck supplies the next card. If you put a red on a red, then the next two cards will be black and your red/black pair combination will be continued.

THE WILL THAT WOULDN'T

Bet you can't divide by five!

THE SETUP

This challenge is really a map puzzle. To win, you must draw a map that solves this story puzzle:

A farmer had five sons. When he died, his will had these instructions for the division of his land among the sons:

1. Each son had to be a neighbor to all the others.
2. The land of any two brothers had to have at least one edge in common, not just a point.
3. Each brother's land had to be in one piece.

INSIDER INFORMATION

It seems that five figures, no matter what their size or shape, cannot share common sides. Ferdinand Möbius, the topologist who devised the Möbius strip, thought up this puzzle more than a hundred years ago. Only in recent years have mathematicians proved why this is so but it took a computer to show it!

This topographical oddity has been put to practical use, though. Mapmakers can show any number of separate regions with only four colors because of the fact that only four regions can share a common side. Check it out on a colored map.

FOLDING MONEY

Wanna bet you can flip George Washington on his head without turning a dollar bill upside down?

THE SETUP

Hold a dollar bill so that the picture of George Washington is facing right side up. To flip him, you must fold the bill in half three times. The sequence of folds is all-important.

Fold 1: the top edge folds forward to meet the bottom edge.
Fold 2: the right edge folds back to meet the left edge.
Fold 3: the right edge folds forward to meet the left edge.

The folding is complete. Now comes the all-important unfolding sequence.

Unfold 1: the back of the left side unfolds toward you.
Unfold 2: the top of the right side opens like a book.
Unfold 3: the bottom edge is lifted up to reveal George standing on his head.

INSIDER INFORMATION

This trick won't work if you reverse your steps and unfold the bill in the same sequence as you folded it. George flips only if you use a different pattern to unfold. This shows how important proper sequence of operations is in mathematics.

In other words, follow orders.

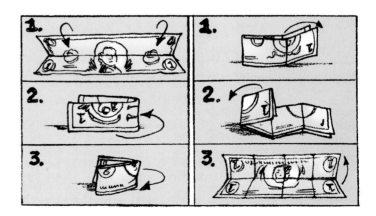

NO END IN SIGHT

Wanna bet you can get trapped in a math game? Start with any number you like, you'll always wind up with the number 4.

THE SETUP

Don't try this trick unless you can spell and count. Think of any number in the universe. Write it in numerals. Then write it in words and count the letters. Write this number in numerals. Then in words. Keep going until you are caught in the loop. No matter what number you started with, you will end up with four. Every time. Promise.

INSIDER INFORMATION

The word four is the only numeral in the English language with the same number of letters as its value. Count on it.

IT'S ALL RIGHT

Wanna bet you can draw a triangle with three right angles?

THE SETUP

A triangle is a three-sided figure with angles that add up to 180 degrees. A right angle is 90°. Three right angles total 270°. So a triangle with three right angles sounds impossible. And it is, if you draw it on a flat surface. The trick is to draw your "impossible" triangle on a sphere. We suggest marking an inflated balloon with a felt-tip pen.

There are two ways you can make your triangle: (1) Draw the three right angles first. The corners should be set up so that straight lines will connect them to make a triangle with sides about the same length. (2) Draw a right angle and extend one line around about one-third of the ball. Make another right angle and extend that line around one-third of the ball. Now draw the third right angle and extend the line until you reach your starting point.

INSIDER INFORMATION

Your triangle enters the third dimension in this trick. The rules of 3-D math are not the same as they are for two dimensional surfaces like a piece of paper. Topologists are concerned with the mathematics of form and shape. They are interested in what happens to the 3-D triangle when it is reshaped into two dimensions. Deflate the balloon and you will see that your figure is closer to being a normal triangle. If you could make the rubber perfectly flat, the triangle would have three 60° angles and would be a normal triangle.

CROSS REFERENCE INDEX

INDEX

Become a part of our *We Dare You!* video project.

We're creating a video version of this book—and we want YOU to be the stars!

Go to www.vickicobb.com to watch the videos that have already been done, and then do your own. Just pick your favorite trick in *We Dare You!*, get a digital video camera and some friends, and start filming.

The website has all the information you need, like where to send the videos once you're finished.

Have fun!

—Vicki Cobb and Kathy Darling